Mobile Game Design Essentials

A useful and detailed resource for designing games for mobile devices

Dr. Claudio Scolastici

David Nolte

BIRMINGHAM - MUMBAI

Mobile Game Design Essentials

First published: November 2013

Production Reference: 1141113

Published by Packt Publishing Ltd.

Livery Place
35 Livery Street
Birmingham B3 2PB, UK.

ISBN 978-1-84969-298-4

www.packtpub.com

Cover Image by Jarek Blaminsky (milak6@wp.pl)

Credits

Authors
Dr. Claudio Scolastici
David Nolte

Reviewers
Diane Harding
Kahl Sada
Mehul Shukla
Francis Styck
Sergio Viudes Carbonell

Acquisition Editor
Rubal Kaur

Lead Technical Editor
Neeshma Ramakrishnan

Technical Editors
Shashank Desai
Iram Malik
Manal Pednekar

Project Coordinator
Shiksha Chaturvedi

Proofreader
Lucy Rowland

Indexer
Mariammal Chettiyar

Graphics
Yuvraj Mannari

Production Coordinator
Adonia Jones

Cover Work
Adonia Jones

About the Authors

Dr. Claudio Scolastici is a former researcher at the Department of Cognitive Sciences of the National Research Council of Rome.

In 2002, he started working in the video game industry as a tester for Electronic Arts. After he graduated in General and Experimental Psychology with a specialization in Artificial Intelligence, he worked as a consultant game designer for Italian game developers such as SpinVector and Palzoun Game First.

In 2012, he joined the No.One indie team to develop XX La Breccia, the first quality first person shooter ever made in Italy using the Unreal Engine.

Today he authors tutorials on game development for Digital Tutors and Game Programming Italia, and acts as a game design consultant for indie developers and start-ups in Rome, where he currently resides.

David Nolte graduated with a Bachelor of Fine Arts degree from the University of Hawaii, Manoa.

He spent 15 years in the advertising industry in Honolulu, working his way from paste-up artist to print production manager. He then worked 23 years in the video game industry as a game designer and production manager. Most of that was time spent working on Tetris and its variants for a variety of platforms.

He was the producer of Faceball 2000, the only real-time first person shooter released on the original Gameboy. It won best Gameboy Game of the Year award at the Consumer Electronics Show, 1991. He has over 20 published games to his credit on a variety of platforms.

About the Reviewers

Diane Harding has been a software developer for over 35 years, and has extensive expertise in the design and development of large-scale software packages that integrate data from a wide variety of sources, for interactive screen editing and display, as well as database archival. She has developed web-based applications with access via web browser (portal) or graphical user interface, and has been a fluent programmer in Fortran, C, C++, SQL, Perl, XML, Java, and JSP. Her background also includes extensive technical and numerical analysis experience in Ocean Sciences including side-scan sonar, bathymetry, and multi-static acoustics. She was born and raised in Hawaii and went on to attend the Massachusetts Institute of Technology, where she received a degree in Applied Mathematics. She currently resides in Kailua, Hawaii.

Over her career, Diane Harding has been a senior software engineer for the Smithsonian Astrophysical Observatory, Cambridge Massachusetts, for the University of Hawaii Institute of Geophysics, Honolulu, for Fugro Seafloor Surveys, Inc. based in Seattle, Washington, and for Applied Marine Solutions, a DOD contractor based in Hawaii.

Diane Harding has co-authored and contributed to articles and abstracts published in *EOS, Transactions of the American Geophysical Union* and other journals, as well as worked as a technical editor and a contributor on numerous work-related proposals submitted to various government funding agencies. She has also generated user and technical manuals for the software packages developed, for distribution to the end users and installation of the applications.

Kahl Sada fell in love with video games thanks to Alley Cat, but only with Metal Gear Solid did he realize that being a game designer was his lifetime dream. He started creating games with RPG Maker then moved to Unity 3D to create more interesting and deep gameplay. Specializing in Guerrilla Prototyping and in Gameplay Balancing, he is now a full-time employee of Lunar Walkers LTD.

Mehul Shukla is one of the PlayStation® Mobile specialists in the SCEE R&D Developer Services Team. The Developer Services Team provides front-line engineering support for all game developers, large or small, on all PlayStation platforms. He provides technical support and performance advice to developers all over the globe on the PSM community forums on a daily basis.

He has also given technical talks about PlayStation® Mobile development at a number of games industry conferences and academic events.

Mehul joined SCEE R&D right after his University education. He has a Master's degree in Games Programming and a Bachelor's degree in Computer Systems Engineering.

He has also worked as a technical reviewer for *PlayStation® Mobile Development Cookbook, Packt Publishing*.

> I would like to thank the authors, David Nolte and Claudio Scolastici, for the hard work they have put in and for sharing their invaluable experience of the games industry. There is a lot I have learned during the reviewing of this book and I hope others too can benefit from it. I wish the authors all the best for the future.

Francis Styck has been developing games since his college days at UNLV, while pursuing an Engineering degree in the 1980s, when games were written in Assembly language on the Atari 800 and Commodore 64. He continued with his education at UNLV and graduated with an MBA in 2001. Today, he is still writing games but now uses the power of C++, Marmalade, and Cocos2d-x to support many platforms and devices. You can stay in touch with Francis using LinkedIn at `http://www.linkedin.com/in/styck`.

Sergio Viudes Carbonell is a 31-year-old software developer from Elche, Spain. He works developing apps and video games for the Web and Android.

He has played video games since his childhood. He started playing with his brother's Spectrum when he was just 5 years old. When he bought his first PC (well, his parents did), he was 14 years old, and started learning computer programming, computer drawing, and music composition (using the famous Fast Tracker 2). When he finished high school, he studied Computer Science at the University of Alicante.

His interest in mobile devices started with his first smart phone, eleven years ago in 2002, when he bought the first Symbian device from Nokia, the Nokia 7650. He really liked the idea that he could develop software that could run everywhere. So, along with his studies and his job, Sergio started creating simple mobile apps for his phone. About three years ago he decided to create his first video game for mobile devices. He really enjoys developing for mobile devices, he likes to compose music, to draw, and of course, he likes to play video games.

So, he decided to put all his hobbies together and develop his first video game for his favorite mobile platform—Android.

So far Sergio has released three games, several apps, and he continues developing apps and games for Android.

He has worked as the technical reviewer of the book, *AndEngine for Android Game Development Cookbook, Packt Publishing*.

www.PacktPub.com

Support files, eBooks, discount offers and more

You might want to visit www.PacktPub.com for support files and downloads related to your book.

Did you know that Packt offers eBook versions of every book published, with PDF and ePub files available? You can upgrade to the eBook version at www.PacktPub.com and as a print book customer, you are entitled to a discount on the eBook copy. Get in touch with us at service@packtpub.com for more details.

At www.PacktPub.com, you can also read a collection of free technical articles, sign up for a range of free newsletters and receive exclusive discounts and offers on Packt books and eBooks.

http://PacktLib.PacktPub.com

Do you need instant solutions to your IT questions? PacktLib is Packt's online digital book library. Here, you can access, read and search across Packt's entire library of books.

Why Subscribe?

- Fully searchable across every book published by Packt
- Copy and paste, print and bookmark content
- On demand and accessible via web browser

Free Access for Packt account holders

If you have an account with Packt at www.PacktPub.com, you can use this to access PacktLib today and view nine entirely free books. Simply use your login credentials for immediate access.

Table of Contents

Preface **1**

Chapter 1: Operating Systems – Mobile and Otherwise **9**

Operating systems **10**

Mobile operating systems **11**

Android 12

Google Play and Amazon Appstore 13

App development 14

Games for Android 15

Eclipse versus Intellij 17

iOS 18

The App Store 19

Development on iOS 19

Xcode 20

Using Xcode 21

Windows Phone 23

Windows Phone Store 24

Developing apps with Windows Phone 24

Developing a game for Windows Phone with XNA 25

Java ME 27

Developing games with Java ME 29

NetBeans 30

BlackBerry 32

The BlackBerry App World 33

Developing games for BlackBerry 33

Summary **34**

Chapter 2: The Mobile Indie Team **35**

A matter of size **36**

Key roles in a successful team **36**

What it takes **37**

Commitment 37

Cohesion 37

Software development methodologies 38
Discipline 38
Professional training 38
Passion for games 39
The roles in an indie mobile team 39
The game designer 40
Designer at work 40
Designer tools 41
The practices of game design 41
Academic formation and personality 43
No game is ever done! 44
The game artist 44
Brushes and canvas 44
Forms of art 45
2D graphic assets 45
3D graphic assets 46
Art schools and creative types 47
The programmer 48
The programmer's kit 48
Coding departments 49
Learning to be a programmer 50
The game tester 51
The tools of deconstruction 52
Aspects of game testing 53
Skills of a professional player 54
University of Gamestop 55
The game producer 56
Keeping things organized 57
Key questions of a producer 57
Skills for all! 58
Who is the producer? 59
The sound designer 60
Creating music and sound fx 61
Audio skills and tasks 62
Schools of sound production 63
Audio personality 63
Summary 64
Chapter 3: Graphics for Mobile 65
Pixels and vectors 68
Pixels 68
Vectors 69

The graphic file formats **70**
Raster graphics 70
Vector graphics 71
Videos in videogames 72
Software to create game graphics **73**
Resolution issues with mobile games **75**
2D graphic assets **76**
Sprites 76
Backgrounds 77
Tiles 78
The parallax motion 78
Masking 78
3D graphic assets **80**
3D models 80
Texturing 81
Materials 82
UV Mapping 84
More on textures 85
Baking 85
Animations 86
Designing a character for mobile **87**
The character design process 87
Silhouettes 88
Colors for mobile **89**
The user interface and HUD **90**
Summary **91**
Chapter 4: Audio for Mobile **93**
Digital sound technology **94**
Analog versus digital 94
Recording and playback 94
Recording 94
Playback 95
Types of game sounds **96**
Dynamic audio 96
Adaptive audio 96
Interactive audio 96
Non-Dynamic linear sounds and music 96
Diegetic sounds 96
Adaptive 96
Interactive 97
Non-Dynamic 97

Non-Diegetic sounds 97
Adaptive 97
Interactive 97
Kinetic gestural interaction 97
The audio editing software 98
Avid Pro Tools 98
Sound Forge/Sonic Foundry 99
Audacity 100
Ableton Live 100
Designing audio for mobile games 101
Planning the audio in advance 101
Hardware limitations for mobile games audio 102
The role of audio in mobile games 102
Listening conditions for mobile games 103
Best practices for mobile games audio design 103
Scripting skills for a mobile audio designer 104
File compression 104
Looping background music 104
To learn more 105
Final advice 105
Summary 106
Chapter 5: Coding Games 107
Main features of programming languages 107
Libraries 109
Abstraction 109
Implementation 109
Usage 110
Game programming 110
C++ 111
Memory management 112
Objects 113
Complaints about C++ 113
Java 114
Memory management 114
Syntax 115
Java for mobile – Java ME 115
Objective-C 116
Cocoa 116
Cocoa Touch 116
Xcode 116
Working with objects 116
Extending classes with categories 117

Protocols define messaging contracts 117
Values and collections 117
Blocks 118
Objective-C conventions 118
Getting started 118
HTML5 119
Canvas 119
HTML5 and Flash 120
Issues with HTML5 120
HTML5 games 121
Conclusions 122
Scripting languages 122
Structure of a game program 123
Initialization 123
The game loop 123
Termination 124
Conclusion 124
Summary 125
Chapter 6: Mobile Game Controls 127
Input technology 128
Touchscreens 128
Keypads 129
Touchscreen gestures 130
Single–tap 130
Double–tap 130
Long press 131
Scroll 131
Spread and pinch 131
Pan 132
Flick 132
Multifinger tap 132
Multifinger scroll 133
Rotate 133
Input interfaces for mobile games 133
Built-in devices 134
GPS 134
Accelerometer 135
Camera 136
Microphone 138
External controllers 139
Gamepads 139
Analog sticks 141
Touch-enabled cases 141

Grip 142
Cabinets 143
Headphones 143
Future technologies 144
Eye tracking 145
Brainwave readers 145
Summary 146
Chapter 7: Interface Design for Mobile Games 147
The role of the user interface 147
Approaching user interface design 148
UI in videogames 149
Designing the UI 155
Aesthetics 156
More on vectors and rasters 156
Designing icons 158
Best practices in UI design 159
Search for references 160
The screen flow 161
Functionality 162
Wireframes 162
The button size 163
The main screen 164
Test and iterate 164
Evergreen options 165
Multiple save slots 165
Screen rotation 166
Calibrations and reconfigurations 166
Challenges 166
Experiment 167
Summary 167
Chapter 8: Mobile Game Engines 169
What engines can do 170
What engines can't do 172
Game engines 172
2D game engines 172
Torque 2D 173
Cocos2D 173
Corona SDK 174
3D game engines 175
Shiva 3D 175
Unity 3D 177
Top-quality engines 179
Unreal/UDK 179

Educational engines 181
GameMaker 182
GameSalad 183
Unity3D Tutorial – part 1 **184**
Tutorial part 1A – importing 3D models 186
Tutorial part 1B – setting up the scene 192
Summary **195**
Chapter 9: Prototyping **197**
Steps in the prototyping process **197**
Defining the prototype 197
Building the prototype 198
Testing the prototype 198
Fixing the prototype 198
Prototyping styles **198**
Horizontal prototype 198
Vertical prototype 199
Types of prototyping **199**
Disposable code 199
Your imagination 200
Pencil and paper 200
Visual prototypes 201
Interactive prototypes 201
Reusable code 201
Why prototype? **202**
What to avoid **202**
Tools **203**
Tools for rapid prototyping 204
Unity3D tutorial – part 2 **204**
The player's ship 205
The aliens 211
Firing 220
Summary **227**
Chapter 10: Balancing, Tuning, and Polishing Mobile Games **229**
Balancing **230**
Symmetry 230
Randomization 231
Feedback loops 231
Game director 231
Statistics 231
Tuning **232**
Tuning strategies 233

Difficulty settings **234**
Global difficulty 235
Unity 3D tutorial – part 3 **235**
The barriers 235
The player's ship reprise 239
Refining the details 240
Adding a GUI 249
Adding audio effects 261
Particle system effects 266
Unity 3D tutorial summary 268
Summary **269**
Chapter 11: Mobile Game Design **271**
The basic game design process **272**
The dos and don'ts of game design **275**
Dos 275
Don'ts 275
Designing mobile games **276**
Hardware limitations 276
Screen size 277
Game controls 277
Audio output 278
File size 279
Processing power 279
Mobile design constraints 279
Play time 279
Game depth 280
Mobile environment 280
Smartphones 280
Single player versus multiplayer 281
The mobile market **281**
Mobile gamers **282**
Business models **283**
Premium 283
Freemium 284
Ad supported 284
Hybrid 285
Choosing the right business model 285
What makes games fun **287**
The four keys to fun – the game mechanics that drive play 287
Hard fun – emotions from meaningful challenges, strategies, and puzzles 287
Easy fun – grab attention with ambiguity, incompleteness, and detail 288
The people factor – create opportunities for player competition, cooperation, performance, and spectacle 289

Raph Koster and Roger Caillois 290
Summary 291
Chapter 12: Pitching a Mobile Game 293
The pitch document 294
Importance of pitching 294
Game concept 295
References 296
Prototypes 296
Stuck? 296
Genre 296
Target audience 297
Key features 297
Target platform and competitors 297
Game mechanics 298
Control scheme and interface 298
Scoring system and achievements 299
A gameplay example 299
Screen flow and screens relationship 299
Game flow 300
Tech 300
Screenshot 301
Team/Designer resume 301
Lilypads pitch document 302
Concept 302
Genre 303
References 303
Target 305
Platform 305
Competitors 305
Key features 305
Character design 306
Game mechanics 306
Score 309
Virtual currency 310
IAP (In-App Purchase) 310
Achievements and leaderboards 311
Additional game elements 311
Screen flow 312
Game flow 313

Tech 313
Game features 314
Platform 314
The iPhone 4 314
Game screen study 315
A list of assets 318
Graphics 318
Audio 319
Software 319
Schedule and budget 320
Summary 321
Index 323

Preface

The mobile segment of the video game industry has quickly become the best opportunity for a development team wishing to enter the video game market. Since the appearance of the Snake game for the Nokia cell phones in 1997, the number and quality of video games developed for mobile has constantly increased, while mobile phone hardware has improved dramatically.

The main factor that makes the mobile video game segment a very interesting opportunity these days is that, although not everybody has a console or a PC at home, in most parts of the world everybody has a cell phone.

Another factor is that the hardware capabilities of mobile phones have improved quickly. In about ten years, we have moved from devices with monochromatic small screens with limited input opportunities that could only run the simplest games, to devices with true color displays and gyroscopes with almost the same potential of consoles such as the PS2, if not better.

Also, for a team of people who want to jump into this industry, it is a good opportunity because, generally, it takes less resources to develop a game for mobile than for console or PC games.

In fact, the scope of a mobile game tends to be narrower than a traditional game, which means that to make a mobile game it requires fewer people for development, less time to get to shipping, lower investments to buy the tools, and in the end, less money in general.

Should the game go well and sell, the potential revenue can be very high!

On the other hand, the mobile segment is not necessarily a gold mine where everybody can easily find nuggets. The design of a mobile game requires several factors to be taken into consideration, as we will show you throughout this manual.

First, the device itself puts some limitations on what can be achieved. Though screens are getting larger and allow better resolutions, still they are not TV screens and monitors. The audio capabilities of mobile phones are several steps below their console or PC counterparts.

Game controls have to rely on the touchscreen or make use of sensors available on smartphones, which is an opportunity but also a constraint if we consider the flexibility of a common gamepad, or the combination of mouse and keyboard in PC games.

The experience of playing a mobile game on the bus is totally different from that of a console game played on the couch in the living room.

If we exclude the iPhone platform, there are literally thousands of different handset types on the market. Developing for a market this diverse can be daunting. Compared to this variety, the traditional segmentation of the video game market among the three consoles made by Sony, Microsoft, and Nintendo, is almost nothing.

Finally, and this is a consequence of all that we stated before, there have never been so many games available at the same time as there are now for mobile phones. This means that any new game for mobile phones has to face a hard struggle against other games which compete for a share of players.

The aim of this book is to offer a guide to those who are willing to test their skills in this potentially very profitable segment. It will provide useful information about the tools you need to develop, well-done games for mobile, how to take advantage of the limits of a mobile phone to design perfect gameplay, and which are the best business models to adopt in order to make money out of your games.

Examples of mobile games such as Doodle Jump, Fruit Ninja, and Angry Birds show us that the right decisions and the proper tools make success possible. We'll help you with that by offering you hands-on examples, extensive background information, useful insights, and a wealth of knowledge on the subject!

What this book covers

Chapter 1, Operating Systems – Mobile and Otherwise, describes the differences between the most important mobile platforms (iOS, Android, and Windows Phone) and the most popular software which are used to develop games and apps for each one of them.

Chapter 2, The Mobile Indie Team, offers a description of the main roles to be covered in an indie team of mobile game developers, the suggested formation background, and the tasks each one of them is accountable for.

Chapter 3, Graphics for Mobile, offers an explanation of the relevant 2D and 3D graphic formats used for mobile games, the techniques used to create such assets, and the most popular software to create 2D and 3D graphics for mobile games.

Chapter 4, Audio for Mobile, discusses the creation of audio for mobile games, the different audio types used in games, and the most popular software the professionals make use of to create audio for games.

Chapter 5, Coding Games, offers a description of the most popular coding and scripting languages used in game development, their strengths and weaknesses, and the description of the basic structure of a game program.

Chapter 6, Mobile Game Controls, focuses on the characteristics of the touch interface of today's smartphones and the use of built-in sensors and other external devices as input devices to control mobile games.

Chapter 7, Interface Design for Mobile Games, delves into the theory of user interface design and offers a description of popular models and techniques to create user interfaces for games in general and mobile games in particular.

Chapter 8, Mobile Game Engines, is about the most popular game engines used to develop games for mobile, detailing the strengths and weaknesses of each one of them. With this chapter we also begin our tutorial to create a game with Unity 3D from scratch.

Chapter 9, Prototyping, is focused on the techniques and tools used to prototype games, providing a list of useful software to achieve the task. The chapter also contains the second part of the Unity 3D tutorial.

Chapter 10, Balancing, Tuning, and Polishing Mobile Games, offers a description of the actions required to smooth the angles of a game's gameplay and the techniques used to achieve a perfectly balanced gameplay. In this chapter, we also get to the conclusion of the tutorial with Unity 3D.

Chapter 11, Mobile Game Design, explains the design process of a mobile game and delves into the specific difficulties related to designing games for today's smartphones, based on their hardware, the specific fruition models of mobile games, and the characteristics of the mobile market.

Chapter 12, Pitching a Mobile Game, is a practical guide to the creation of the presentation document of an actual mobile game. The document, which contains a description of the most relevant aspects of a mobile game, is essential to explain your projects to potential investors.

What you need for this book

As the book will provide you with all the basic knowledge you need to develop mobile games, there is no prior knowledge or skills that are required to understand its contents.

On the other hand, we tried our best to make this book a practical guide to mobile game development and therefore a basic knowledge of any 2D and 3D modeling software, as well as some familiarity with the interface of Unity 3D is welcome.

As they are industry standard, we mainly used Photoshop for 2D assets, 3D Studio Max for modeling, and Unity 3D as the game engine to create the practical contents of this book. What follows here are the links to download the trial version of each one of them:

- `https://creative.adobe.com/products/photoshop`
- `http://www.autodesk.com/products/autodesk-3ds-max/free-trial`
- `http://unity3d.com/unity/download`

Who this book is for

This book is for anyone who ever happened to have an idea for a mobile game but didn't know how to approach its actual development.

If you ever thought about creating an indie team of mobile game developers, this book will help you build it. We will also guide you in choosing the software required for mobile game development. We will help you understand the strengths and weaknesses of each mobile platform, defining optimal gameplay based on the specific characteristics of today's smartphones. Finally, we will assist you in choosing the right business model for your games and finally helping you to create pitch documents to present your mobile game ideas to potential investors.

If mobile games development is your passion, this book is the right starting point to trigger your career in the gaming industry!

Conventions

In this book, you will find a number of styles of text that distinguish between different kinds of information. Here are some examples of these styles, and an explanation of their meaning.

Code words in text, database table names, folder names, filenames, file extensions, pathnames, dummy URLs, user input, and Twitter handles are shown as follows: All noncode files are held in a directory called `Supporting Files`, where you'll want to put images, text files, and other stuff.

A block of code is set as follows:

```
while(!gameEnded)
{
  HandleInput();  //Reads keyboard, mouse or any other
                  //kind of input used by the player

  Update();       //Updates game logic and, based on info
                  //gathered with the previous step

  Draw();         //Draws graphics on screen,
                  //a process called Render.
}
```

New terms and **important words** are shown in bold. Words that you see on the screen, in menus or dialog boxes for example, appear in the text like this: "Once **Windows Phone Game (4.0)** is selected, type a name for the project in the text box and click on **OK**."

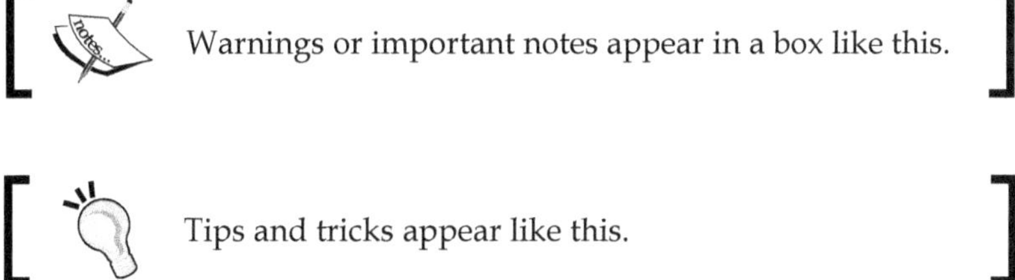

Warnings or important notes appear in a box like this.

Tips and tricks appear like this.

Reader feedback

Feedback from our readers is always welcome. Let us know what you think about this book—what you liked or may have disliked. Reader feedback is important for us to develop titles that you really get the most out of.

To send us general feedback, simply send an e-mail to feedback@packtpub.com, and mention the book title via the subject of your message.

If there is a topic that you have expertise in and you are interested in either writing or contributing to a book, see our author guide on www.packtpub.com/authors.

Customer support

Now that you are the proud owner of a Packt book, we have a number of things to help you to get the most from your purchase.

Downloading the color images of this book

We also provide you with a PDF file that has color images of the screenshots used in this book. You can download this file from https://www.packtpub.com/sites/default/files/downloads/2984OT_Images.pdf.

Errata

Although we have taken every care to ensure the accuracy of our content, mistakes do happen. If you find a mistake in one of our books—maybe a mistake in the text or the code—we would be grateful if you would report this to us. By doing so, you can save other readers from frustration and help us improve subsequent versions of this book. If you find any errata, please report them by visiting http://www.packtpub.com/submit-errata, selecting your book, clicking on the **errata submission form** link, and entering the details of your errata. Once your errata are verified, your submission will be accepted and the errata will be uploaded on our website, or added to any list of existing errata, under the Errata section of that title. Any existing errata can be viewed by selecting your title from http://www.packtpub.com/support.

Piracy

Piracy of copyright material on the Internet is an ongoing problem across all media. At Packt, we take the protection of our copyright and licenses very seriously. If you come across any illegal copies of our works, in any form, on the Internet, please provide us with the location address or website name immediately so that we can pursue a remedy.

Please contact us at `copyright@packtpub.com` with a link to the suspected pirated material.

We appreciate your help in protecting our authors, and our ability to bring you valuable content.

Questions

You can contact us at `questions@packtpub.com` if you are having a problem with any aspect of the book, and we will do our best to address it.

1
Operating Systems – Mobile and Otherwise

Developing games for mobile requires many decisions to be taken. Two very important ones concern the platform to develop your game for and the tools you are going to use.

Will your game be developed for a single platform or many? Which are the most popular operating systems of today's mobile phones? Which are the best tools to work with each of them?

In this chapter, we will describe what an operating system is and we will provide an introduction to the most important mobile operating systems (OS).

We will also introduce the reference tools and software to develop games for each mobile platform mentioned.

In this chapter, we will cover the following topics:

- A general discussion on operating systems
- Mobile operating systems
- Android development
- iOS development
- Windows Phone development
- Java ME development
- BlackBerry development

Operating systems

An operating system (OS) is a collection of software that manages device hardware and provides common services, which allow programs to run on a device, be it a mobile phone or a personal computer.

The operating system acts as an intermediary between programs and the computer hardware, and thus, operating systems can be found on almost any device that contains a computer—from cellular phones and video game consoles to supercomputers and web servers.

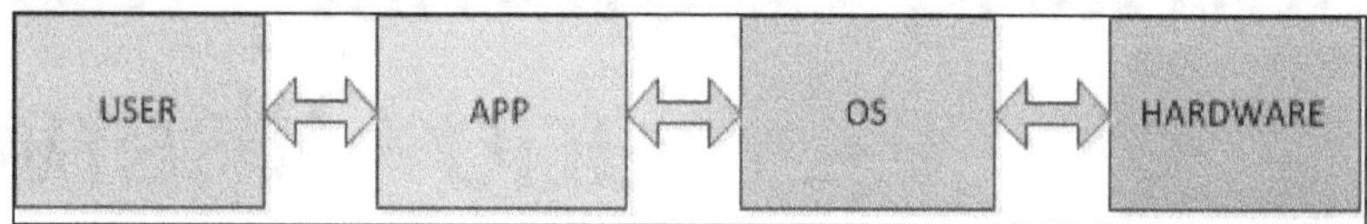

The revolution of personal computers (PC) began with the introduction of BASIC and DOS Operating Systems. These operating systems ran on terminals composed of a case containing the main hardware, a monochromatic screen, and a keyboard. All these fit on a common desk, allowing computers to enter people's houses.

At that time, software used to run on magnetic tapes or on a number of 5'1/4" disks. The following image shows an old school PC of the early '80s:

The PC became an object of common use with the introduction of visual environments made of icons that could be processed with the use of a device called mouse. This solution turned operations into metaphors of real world actions: select and drag an icon to move a file, single-clicks to select contents, and double-clicks to open them.

The main advantage of this new approach to computing was that it didn't need an expert to use a computer for basic operations. Anyone could use a PC!

The evolution of visual interfaces led to touch interfaces, made possible with the introduction of screens that could process touch actions directly on the screens of the devices. This system allows users to use their fingers instead of the mouse of desktop PCs, thus triggering a revolution in user interfaces and user experience, as well as offering the possibility of developing devices, such as tablets and smartphones, that could handle the same basic operations available on a desktop PC on a smaller mobile device.

At present, the computing environment is dominated by a few operating systems. For mobile devices, there are iOS, Android, Windows Phone, Java ME, and BlackBerry. BREW and Bada, which used to be quite popular, are now out of the race.

Each OS has distinctive characteristics and a development story of its own. So before we start talking about mobile development, we will provide you with an overview on each one of them.

Mobile operating systems

- **Android**: Android is the open source mobile OS (developed by Google and Open Handset Alliance and released in 2007) that powers smartphones of the last generation. The main manufacturers of such phones are Samsung, HTC, Sony, LG, and Motorola. Android-equipped devices were developed to be the competitors of the Apple iPhone; they share a similar touch interface and the same orientation towards the development of applications made by third party developers to meet any user's need. Apps can be downloaded from an online store called Google Play.

- **iOS**: iOS is Apple's mobile OS used on the iPhone, iPod Touch, iPad, and AppleTV. Released in 2007, iOS is based on OSX, the operating system running on Mac PCs. Like OSX, it is closed source and proprietary to Apple devices. It uses the Cocoa Touch interface for use solely with touch screen technology. It shares the benefits of OSX's stability and rapid development, as well as the capability of easy porting between iOS and OSX.
- **Windows Phone**: This is a proprietary OS developed by Microsoft. It replaced its predecessor Windows Mobile in 2010. The latest version (Windows Phone 8) has many common features and components with Windows 8 which facilitates moving apps between the two. It is possible to port Windows Phone games to iOS and Android using tools, libraries, and resources made available by Microsoft.
- **Java ME**: Java ME is an open source, free-to-use OS, developed by Sun Microsystems. It is a trimmed-down version of Java so it can run on any Java-enabled device. It is very popular among developers due to its ease of use and that its games don't need porting to run on various devices. There is a vast community that supports Java with tools, code libraries, and instruction. Though not as popular in the US as it once was, it is still in use in Eurasia and South America.
- **BlackBerry**: This is a proprietary OS developed by RIM for its line of smartphones that mainly aim at the enterprise market. Thanks to its peculiar instant messaging and push e-mail features, and to high level security protocols as well, BlackBerry smartphones are the devices of choice for people who need a reliable handset to support their business needs.

Android

Android is a Linux-based operating system designed to run on touch-screen mobile devices, mainly smartphones and tablets.

Released around 2007, Android was initially developed by the Android Corporation. It was then acquired by Google, who founded a consortium of hardware, software, and telecommunication companies, named the Open Handset, to further support and develop this open source project.

Today, Android powers hundreds of millions of mobile devices all over the world. Numbers say that new Android phones are activated at the rate of one million per day!

The main factor that made Android a favorite for consumers is its open source approach. It can count on an enthusiastic community of passionate developers and hundreds of hardware, software, and carrier partners whose support make Android the fastest growing mobile operating system to date.

With such partners, Android is capable of continuously pushing the boundaries of mobile hardware and software forward, allowing developers to build any kind of applications that can take advantage of the latest mobile technologies, and to support users with many differentiated and powerful applications to expand the capabilities of their mobile devices.

The main drawback with Android is that, due to the high variety in the hardware it runs on, updates tend to be quite slow in reaching devices when compared to iOS. Porting Android to specific hardware is a time and resource consuming activity for manufacturers, with the result that newest devices are prioritized, leaving older ones behind.

On the other hand, the large community of Android enthusiasts can balance this bias, building and distributing their own modified versions of the OS with new features and updates, faster than the official manufacturers.

Android gives its developers a wide range of tools to take full advantage of the hardware capabilities of each device, both smartphones and tablets. For example, it allows having a user interface that automatically adapts to look its best on each device regardless of the screen size, by defining a common set of instructions for all shared form factors and a separate set which contains optimizations for each specific device.

Android UI is based on direct manipulation through touch inputs that resemble real world actions, such as swiping, tapping, and pinching. It also takes full advantage of internal hardware, such as accelerometers, gyroscopes, and proximity sensors, to further improve the experience.

Google Play and Amazon Appstore

Google Play is the premier marketplace to sell and distribute Android apps, and has been used to download more than 25 billion apps at the rate of 1.5 billion per month.

It gives complete freedom to its users to define when and what to publish, letting developers maintain full control with regard to the devices to develop for, the technology to use, and the target audience to address.

Users also have complete freedom to adopt any business model for their apps: priced, free, with in-app products or subscriptions, as well as defining pricing and supported currencies for transactions.

Google Play also helps its users to get visibility for their products, with weekly sales charts and rankings, thus allowing even more visibility.

The premier language to develop Android apps is Java, using the Android software development kit. Other tools are available as well, such as the Native Development Kit that allows applications to be built in C and C++. Cross platform mobile frameworks are available too, such as Phonegap, Titanium, or Rhomobile.

App development

When developing apps for Android, especially if you are new to Android development, it is recommended that you use the Eclipse Integrated Development Environment (IDE). It is the fastest way to get started and it offers several guide projects as well as tools integration to make the the developer's life as easy as possible.

The Eclipse IDE is an open source project that basically consists of a collection of plugins that integrate with the platform, to provide a wide range of features. Most of these plugins are written in Java.

Android Development Tools (**ADT**) is a plugin for the Eclipse IDE that is designed to provide a powerful, integrated environment in which to build Android applications.

The ADT plugin for Eclipse is provided with the Android SDK. The SDK is a collection of tools that allow developing, testing, and debugging applications developed for Android.

Though the premier code language for Eclipse is Java, Eclipse is a multi-language environment that allows other languages to be used as well.

If you are an eager C\C++ programmer and prefer to develop your games in native code language, then the NDK is a very helpful tool set that allows, for example, reusing already existing code libraries and possibly increasing performance. But such options have their costs. Generally speaking, native code on Android doesn't always produce a performance improvement, while it increases the app complexity. So, the decision whether to use the NDK or not should never be dictated by the assumption that "I simply prefer programming with C\C++".

Games for Android

When pondering the decision whether to develop a mobile game on Android, there are two types of device to take into consideration as reference models, based on their processor (CPU) and Graphic Processing Unit (GPU), the piece of hardware that specifically takes care of graphics on the display. As we write, there is the HTC Dream (or G1), the first Android powered phone, which is equipped with **Half Video Graphics Array** (**HVGA**) screens and average 500 MHz CPUs (low-end). The other model is the Nexus One, which is equipped with a **Wide Video Graphics Array** (**WVGA**) screen, a faster CPU, and a GPU that support OpenGL ES 2.0 hardware acceleration (high-end).

Since performance changes very much between the two groups, it is very important to carefully choose the target device for your game, because games that can scale between high and low end devices get, obviously, a broader audience.

What follows is a description about how a new Android project is started with Eclipse:

1. First you need to create an **Android Virtual Device** (**AVD**).
2. Navigate to **Window** | **Android SDK** | **AVD Manger** | **New**.
3. You can leave all parameters with the current default settings, but if you plan to use multi-touch features, you need to work with Version 2.2 or higher.

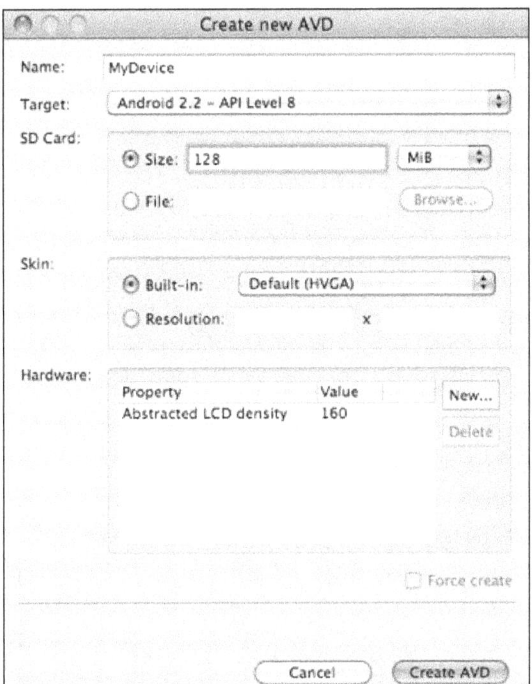

4. Click on **Create AVD** to create your virtual Android Virtual Device to work with.

Then you need to create a project.

1. From the menu, navigate to **New | Project** and choose **Android Project**.
2. The name of your game is set in the **Application name:** space, while classes are grouped in the **Package name:**.
3. Again, set **Android 2.2** as **Build Target**.

   It is then very important to flag the **Create Activity:** check. The activity is the class that is instantiated when starting application. It handles input (actions on touch screen), creates the window that displays the game, and other necessary activities.

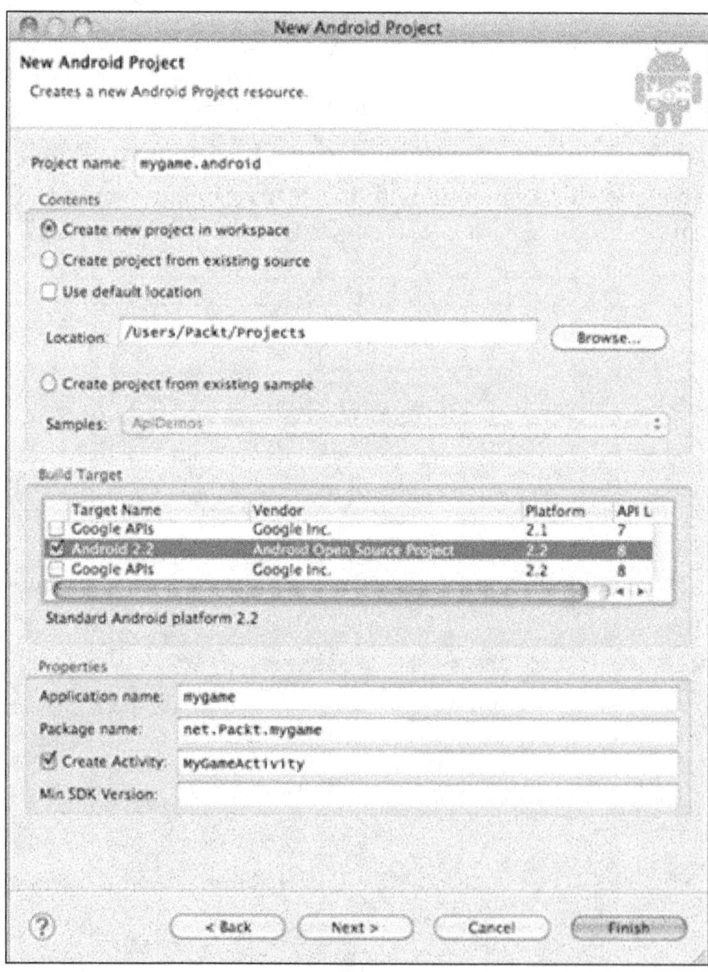

4. Click on **Finish** to create your application. Now you can run your newly created application.
5. Right-click on the project and navigate to **Run As** | **Android Application**.
6. Choose the Virtual Device you configured before and remember that you don't need to close its window once it has started—Eclipse launches the application you are working on inside the current running device, so it will save you some time having the Virtual Device already running!

These are the basic steps to create a new project and launch an application on a Virtual Device with Eclipse. The creation of a working app is beyond the scope of this preparatory chapter on the Android platform, but we will come back with more details in the later chapters of the book.

Eclipse versus Intellij

Eclipse is not the only possible choice to develop games for Android. Among the others, Intellij can be considered the main competitor of Eclipse, which mainly works with Java.

Eclipse offers a larger number of plugins and supports multiple coding languages, because it is easier to extend, compared to Intellij. When working on specific new technologies, it is very likely that if a plugin exists, it will be an Eclipse plugin.

On the other hand, when dealing with completion of code and assistance, Intellij is definitely better (and faster) than Eclipse. Especially for rookie developers, Intellij can give you a hand improving your code and offers a friendlier user interface. The learning curve is smoother and developing with Intellij generally feels easier and more natural.

From a performance point of view, Eclipse works better than Intellij. Projects open faster and they are handled more efficiently, especially very large ones.

To make a general statement, Intellij is easier to use, thanks to a more user friendly user interface, while Eclipse is more versatile, thanks to a larger number of available plugins and a stronger community behind it.

A last thing to consider: Intellij provides a full functional 30 day trial version, and then a license is required for commercial purposes, while Eclipse is an open source project and thus, its license is totally cost free.

iOS

iOS is a mobile operating system developed by Apple. It was released in 2007 for the iPhone and the iPod Touch, and then was extended to support the iPad. It is Apple's specific policy that the iOS cannot be installed on non-Apple devices.

With around 25 million devices sold in the last quarter of 2012 (falling from 35 million in Q2) and more than 250 million of total units sold, the iOS that powers the iPhone (the iPad and iPod as well) is, together with Android, the best target platform for those who intend to develop mobile games.

The Apple Store, the distribution platform where iPhone apps can be downloaded, hosts more than 700,000 applications and downloads have been counted in the order of more than 30 billion.

The direct manipulation of icons using multi-touch gestures is the basic concept behind the iOS user interface and a trademark of mobile devices developed by Apple. Regardless of many attempts to imitate its distinctive user experience by other manufacturers, the iPhone must be acknowledged as the device that offers the best UI\UX in the entire smartphone market.

The interface elements are sliders, switches, and buttons. The interaction is via actions, such as swiping, tapping, and pinching, with each of these actions having a meaning in the Apple iOS environment.

Applications also make use of the sensors and other features, such as the accelerometer, to obtain effects, such as shaking the device to undo the last action or rotating it to switch between portrait and landscape modes.

iOS is Apple's mobile version of the OS X operating system used on Apple computers, but not many people know that the OS X operating system is Unix based.

Apple tends to be a company with a strong bottom-up control policy on their devices. A positive consequence is that updates of the iOS platform are released methodically and developers are informed when updates will be coming, in order to plan accordingly and be sure that their newly developed apps will keep working and will be stable on the new platform.

Together with the fact that all iOS devices are built by the same manufacturer, there is no need for multiple tests on many different devices for newly developed apps, as can be the case for example, when developing software for Android or Java ME.

The App Store

When a new application is developed for the iOS, it can be distributed through the Apple Store. Developers are free to set any price above a minimum for their apps or games, of which, Apple takes 30 percent of the revenue, while the developers take 70 percent. In case the app is distributed for free, the only cost to the developer is the necessary membership fee needed to install newly created apps on physical devices.

To submit your game to the Apple Store, you first set its selling price, then you need a descriptive text for the game that will be found in the App Store, three icons (29x29, 57x57, and 512x512), a launch image that appears while the game is loading, one-four screenshots of your game, and the contract information. If the game is not rejected for some reason by Apple's full time reviewers, in around 10 to 15 days it will be available in the store (depending on the shipping date you provided for your game). Reasons that games are rejected can be, among others, that it contains pornography, it is considered malicious software, or it is not stable.

Development on iOS

Most consumers agree that iOS devices offer a better UI experience and its development tools are generally considered more user friendly.

This is a result of the importance Apple always gives to design and its distinctive focus on innovation and user experience. The down side of this approach is that Apple wields quite lot of control on what people can or cannot do with its devices.

The iOS is not an open environment in the first place. It puts excellent tools in the hands of developers, tools that generally allow making hard things as easy as possible, but the cost is that when working with iOS it can be frustrating being limited to Apple's features. When compared to Android or Java ME platforms, which are open source and thus, put total control in the hands of the developer, working with iOS may seem limited in some ways, as its approach is based on the assumption that "the platform developer knows better than you". In other words, if you need to achieve something that was not provided by the manufacturer, you need to struggle to bypass several constraints.

The iOS SDK is the software development kit used to make native applications for the iPhone and iPod touch, released in 2008 by Apple.

Though developers can make use of the SDK to build their own applications for the iPhone, loading an application onto the devices is only possible after paying an iPhone Developer Program fee, which costs $99 per year.

The no-cost alternative is to run apps in the iPhone simulator, which is provided with the SDK and runs your application in pretty much the same way as an actual iOS device. The simulator is quick to launch and debug, and is a very efficient tool to test both logic and interface of your apps or games. Touch gestures and sensor events can be simulated as well with the mouse. For testing multi-touch interactions well, you need to pay the fee.

All the necessary tools for the SDK are contained in a single installer package that is easy to download, though not very light (it is a single 4.5 GB file). Moreover, if a new update is available, you need to download and reinstall everything. It seems like the iOS SDK team doesn't believe in patches!

There are other barriers which may come into play when developing for the iOS. Unless you use specific cross platform tools, iOS apps require a Mac to be developed, which means that if you don't already have one, you may be forced to buy a Mac to develop with iOS. This can be a high entry cost since Macs generally are much more expensive than their PC equivalents. Naturally, a developer needs a computer to develop apps anyway, but for example, Android apps can be developed on Mac, PC, and Linux machines equally and without much effort.

Another crucial element when deciding whether to develop apps and games for the iOS, is the lack of a feature called garbage collection. Garbage collection means that the developer is not asked to learn the rules to manually manage the memory of the device when developing apps. With such a feature, a programmer is not required to specify which objects to de-allocate in order to free memory resources for other computing.

Garbage collection is a way to enhance the performance of an application and to drastically accelerate the development process. For this reason alone, most programmers would agree that the absence of such a feature in the iOS environment makes it preferable for beginners to develop apps for Android.

Xcode

The development environment for iOS SDK is called Xcode (now distributed in its Version 4) and like iOS and OS X, it is written in objective-C.

Xcode contains all the necessary development tools made by Apple to build applications for OS X and iOS: a source code editor and a user interface editor.

Together with the Cocoa framework, it provides a very productive and easy-to-use development environment, powerful enough to develop the same kind of tools used by Apple to produce iOS.

For example, as you write code, Xcode finds mistakes in syntax and logic, highlights them, and also suggests fixes.

Workflow in the IDE is performed in a single window, so that all relevant info is available at once.

The UI editor, called the Interface Builder, permits specifying the details of the user interface and its connections to the logic and data of the app in a very intuitive graphical environment, and to work very closely with the source code editor to get from design to implementation as quickly as possible.

Using Xcode

To create a new project with Xcode, follow the given steps:

1. Navigate to **File | New Project**. A dialog will appear, as shown in the following screenshot:

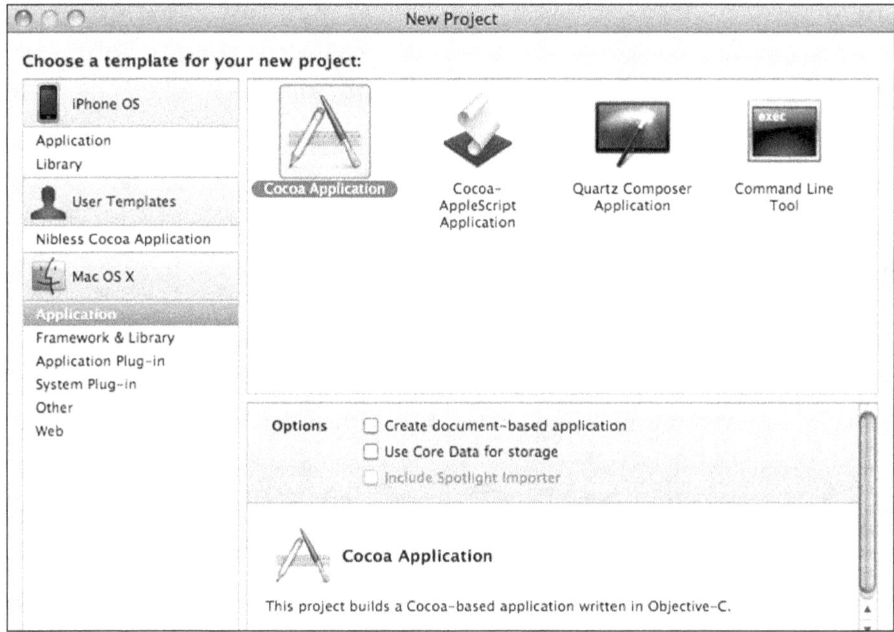

2. Once a new project has been started, you need to name it and choose the device type for it to be built (generally iPhone).

3. In the **Company Identifier** field, use a unique string. It will be used to generate a **Bundle Identifier** for your game.

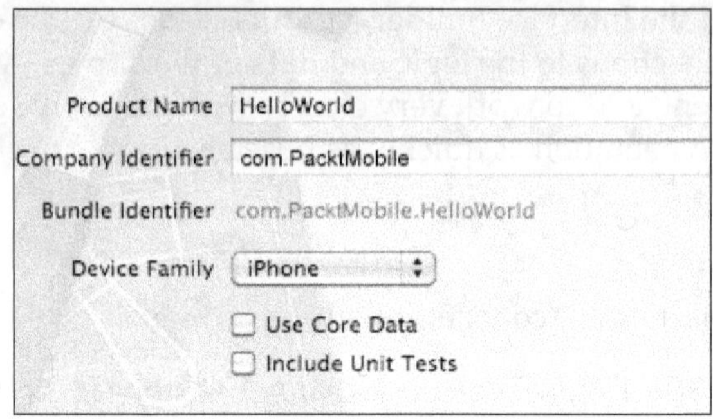

Now a quick glimpse at the structure of the app, which, as we said, is written in Objective-C language.

There will be a `main.m` file that instantiates the App Controller, while objects are declared in header files (`*.h`).

All non-code files are held in a directory called `Supporting Files`, where you'll want to put images, text files, and other stuff.

The directory structure of your newly created project could look like this:

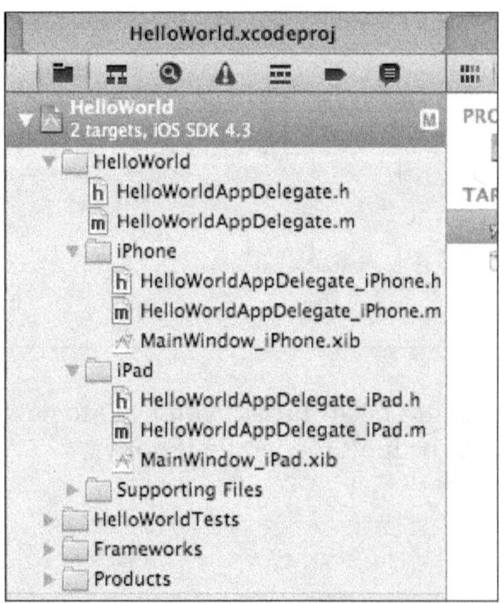

More on game developing for iOS will be seen in the later chapters about mobile engines. For now, this ends our trip in the iOS world.

Windows Phone

Windows Phone is the operating system developed by Microsoft for mobile devices and is the successor to its former Windows Mobile platform.

While Windows Mobile OS was mainly aimed at enterprises, with Windows Phone, Microsoft turned its attention to the consumer market, allowing easier access to third party services and development, and thus to indie mobile games development as well.

To further improve the usability of Windows Phone, Microsoft developed a new design language, called Modern Style UI, to create a new user interface and set minimum requirements for the hardware the new services run on.

To get to the widest audience and target the emerging Asian markets (China in primis), in 2012, Microsoft released an update to its OS, known as Tango, which lowered the requirements for devices to run Windows Phone, allowing the new OS to effectively run on lower-end hardware.

On February 2011, at a press event in London, Microsoft and Nokia CEOs announced a partnership between the two colossi for Windows Phone to become the primary operating system for Nokia smartphones, thus declaring Windows Phone as the third competitor in the smartphones OS market against Android and iOS.

The first Nokia phone models to run Windows Phone are the Lumia 800 and the Lumia 710.

By the end of 2012, Microsoft released the latest edition of its mobile platform, Windows Phone 8, that replaces the previous CE-based architecture with one based on the Windows NT kernel and several shared components with the new Windows 8 (developed for PCs and tablets), allowing applications to be easily ported between these two platforms.

As we said, Windows Phone features a new user interface named Modern Style UI. The main innovation of the new UI consists in Live Tiles that are displayed on the so-called Start Screen. Tiles are links to apps (contacts, web pages, and media items) that dynamically update their icons in real time, for example, showing the number of unread messages for an e-mail account or live updates for a weather app.

Another innovation is the organization of features into Hubs that allow content integration with popular social networks, such as Facebook, Windows Live, and Twitter, so that, for example, the Pictures hub shows photos made with the camera equipped on the phone. From the Hub, users can directly comment and like updates on their favorite social networks.

The main Hub for the interests of this book is, obviously, the Widows Phone Store!

Windows Phone Store

The **Windows Phone Store** (formerly, Windows Phone Marketplace) is the service provided by Microsoft to allow users to browse and download applications developed by third parties for their Windows Phone powered phones. The Modern Style UI presents a panoramic view, where users can browse items by categories, see featured items, and get details, such as ratings, reviews, screenshots, and pricing information.

The Windows Phone Store was launched in 2010 along with Windows Phone 7 and by 2012, it already offered more than 100,000 available apps.

To submit apps to the Windows Phone Store, an annual subscription fee of $99 is required, which offers an unlimited number of submissions on the **Apps+Games** section of the store.

Apps must be approved by Microsoft: a strict control is wielded on the contents in order to forbid pornography, promotion of violence, discrimination, hate, usage of drugs, and the like to be included in the applications available on the Windows Phone Store.

For apps that are sold on the store, Microsoft takes 30 percent of the revenue (70 percent goes to the developer). Developers are paid only if they reach a set sales figure, but above a revenue of $25k, the shares become 20 percent to Microsoft and 80 percent to the developer.

Developing apps with Windows Phone

Apps and games for Windows Phone can be designed with Visual Studio 2010, Standard and Express editions.

Windows Phone 8 offers full support for native C\C++ libraries, thus allowing easy porting of Windows programs to Windows Phone 8. This also allows developers to port iOS and Android applications, since much of their code can be maintained, thus widening the range of available apps for Windows Phone.

Desktop games designed for Windows 8 can also be easily ported, thanks to the full support Windows Phone offers to Direct X architectures, and HTML 5 can be used to develop apps as well, depending on the features needed by games and apps.

To specifically develop high performance games, XNA is the optimal IDE Microsoft offers to developers to include the best graphics and audio for your mobile games for Windows Phone.

There is also the Windows Phone SDK 8.0, which offers all the tools needed to develop games for Windows Phone: editors, software templates, and the Windows Phone Emulator 8 for testing your apps. The Windows Phone SDK provides a stand alone Visual Studio Express 2012 edition for Windows Phone or works as an add-on to Visual Studio 2012 Professional, Premium, or Ultimate editions.

Testing apps on Windows phone devices requires a developer's account and a registered testing device.

Remember that the development of Windows Phone 8 apps is supported only on 64-bit Windows 8 Pro or higher: Windows Phone apps cannot be developed on Windows 7, Windows Server 2008, and 2012.

Developing a game for Windows Phone with XNA

To create a new Windows Phone project, follow the steps shown:

1. Navigate to **File | New Project**.

   A dialog window that lists several project templates appears as shown in the following screenshot:

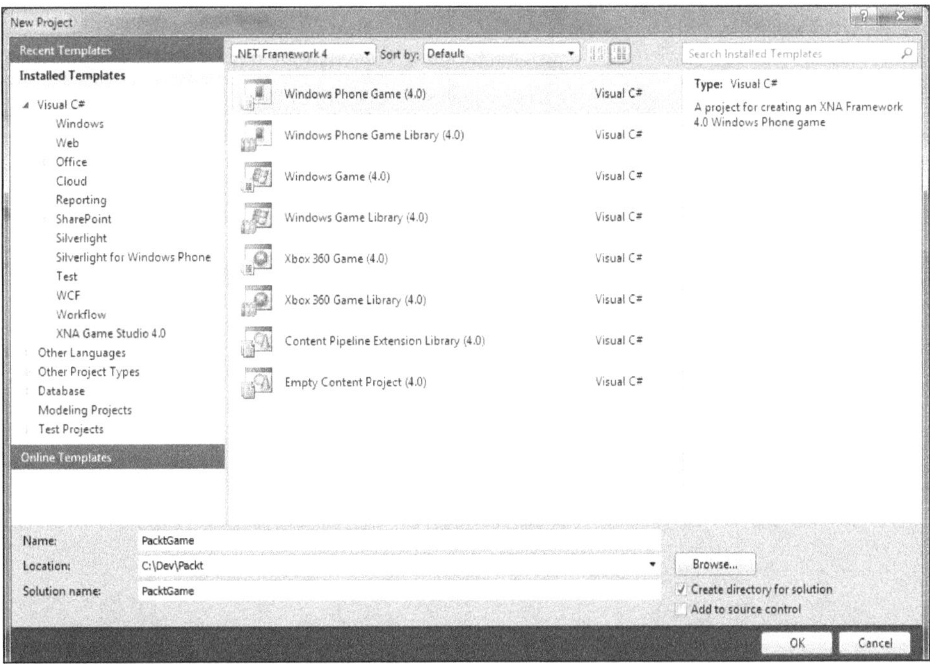

The dialog window contains the following project templates:

- **Windows Phone Game (4.0)**: This is a project for creating an XNA Framework 4.0 game application for Windows Phone.
- **Windows Phone Game Library (4.0)**: A project for creating an XNA Framework 4.0 game library for Windows Phone.
- **Windows Phone Silverlight and XNA Application**: A project for creating a Windows Phone Silverlight Application capable of rendering graphics using the XNA Framework.
- **Content Pipeline Extension Library (4.0)**: A project for creating an XNA Framework 4.0 Content Pipeline Extension Library.

2. Once **Windows Phone Game (4.0)** is selected, type a name for the project in the text box and click on **OK**.

   A new dialog appears which requires us to select the version of Windows Phone to target, as shown in the following screenshot:

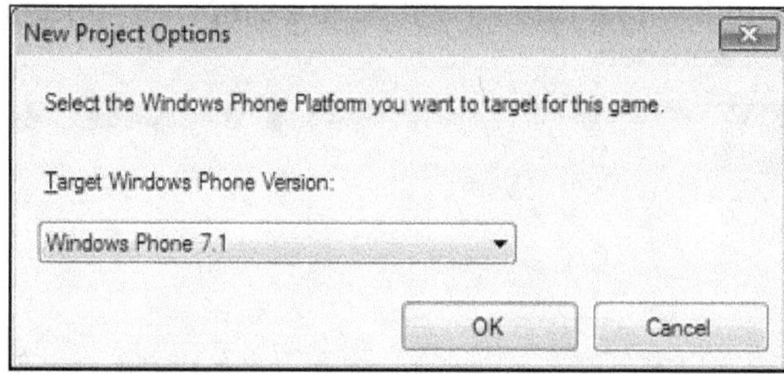

3. Select the Windows Phone OS version and click on **OK**.

The following screenshot shows the features contained in the new Windows Phone project:

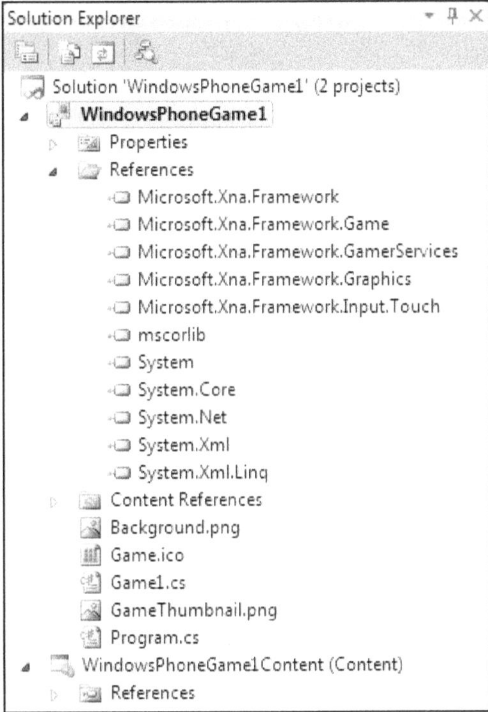

The properties control several aspects of your current project. They include general application settings, debug settings, and additional project resources. The Project Designer can be used to modify the values of these properties.

Many tutorials on how to develop apps for Windows Phone can be found on the Internet. You can start your searches from `http://dev.windowsphone.com/en-us`.

Java ME

Java ME is a platform designed for mobile devices and PDAs by Sun Microsystems.

Although it is not used on today's newest mobile platforms, such as iPhones and Android-powered smartphones, it is still very popular on low-end devices, such as the Nokia's Series 40, and in general, on several million devices worldwide that are Java enabled.

For the first decade of the 21st century, Java has been the most popular choice for game development, as it was identified as the most convenient and versatile platform to develop mobile games. It has been considered as a standard and was backed by all major mobile phones makers, and still most of the present day mobile phones are Java-enabled.

The reason why Java ME is so popular is that it is a free and open platform that keeps the development costs low and provides all the necessary flexibility, while support for developers is freely available.

Its highly portable nature, expressed by the sentence "write once, run anywhere", ensures that a game written having a specific handset in mind will work with all other handsets which are Java enabled as well.

Applications and games written with Java ME are stable and robust, allowing developers to create the best performing mobile apps.

Its programming environment is especially suitable for developing games, considering that Java ME apps can run both online and offline. And, in any case, Java ME is supported by most of today's smartphones.

The usual problems with mobile games development, that relate to screen size, memory availability, and app download size, can be effectively approached with Java ME, thanks to specific development frameworks that detect the device characteristics and provide enough flexibility so that the app itself can adjust.

Java ME is an industry-wide technology, with most manufacturers offering a range of devices that support it. Your Java ME game will not only have the opportunity to run on over one billion Nokia cell phones in use today, but it can also reach over three billion devices which are still in use all over the world!

Though Java ME is losing a significant share of the mobile phone market due to the proliferation of the iPhone, Android, and BlackBerry platforms, there are still several reasons to consider this technology, the most important being that development with Java ME is cheaper and easier, compared to the other platforms.

Even if it can be said that it is a dying platform for mobile apps, and games in particular, Java ME is still the prevalent supported platform in many parts of the world, especially India, Middle East, and Southeast Asia, which are, as we know, emerging and promising markets, as well as North Africa and South America, the latter being a very profitable market for mobile games, too.

Developing games with Java ME

Mobile devices powered by the Java ME platform implement a profile called **Mobile Information Device Profile** (**MIPD**). Profiles contain a configuration of a restricted number of Java libraries, a minimum amount of classes needed for the Java virtual machine to work.

The profile which is implemented on Java ME powered mobile phones is called **Connected Limited Device Configuration** (**CLDC**), and it provides the most basic libraries and virtual machine features to run a Java ME environment.

The CLDC, coupled with the MIPD, allows us to develop downloadable apps and games that run on a very large number of cell phones and PDAs.

The MIPD basically contains a GUI, a data storage API, and a basic gaming API that allow developers to build their own applications, called MIDlets.

The latest available MIPD version, the 3.0 specification approved on December 2009, includes several new features that enable Java ME developers to create sophisticated and compelling mobile applications.

The MIPD 3.0 extends the capabilities of Version 2.1 with the following features:

- Enables multiple concurrent MIDlets
- Enables MIDlets to run in background
- Enables auto-launched MIDlets and screensavers
- Enables inter MIDlet communication
- Tightens specs to improve cross device interoperability
- Improves the UI for applications
- Better support for devices with larger displays
- Enables richer and higher performance games

There are several different ways and tools to create MIDP applications: code can be written in a plain text editor, or one can use a more advanced IDE, such as NetBeans, IntelliJ (with bundled Java ME plugin), or Eclipse (with plugins, such as Eclipse ME).

NetBeans

NetBeans is an open source IDE to develop apps and games for Java ME-powered devices. Applications can be developed from a set of modular software components called modules and can be extended by third party developers. Among its features, it includes the Update Center module that allows users to download upgrades and new features into the running application, so that reinstalling an upgrade or a new release does not force the users to download the entire application again.

The latest released version of NetBeans is 7.2.

To create a new project with NetBeans, follow the given steps:

1. Start the NetBeans IDE.
2. Navigate to **File | New Project**.

   The New Project Wizard will open. Expand the Java category and select Java Application as shown in the following screenshot:

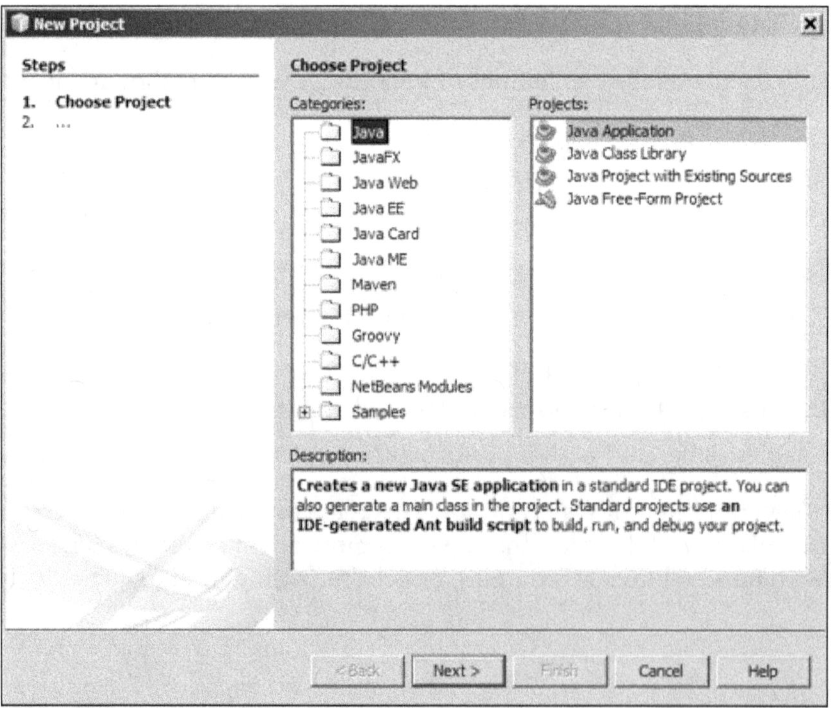

3. Click on **Next**.

In the **Name and Location** page do the following (refer to the following screenshot):

1. Name your project in the **Project Name:** field, such as `HelloWorldApp`.
2. Leave the **Use Dedicated Folder for Storing Libraries** unchecked.
3. In the **Create Main Class** field, type something like `helloworldapp.HelloWorldApp`.

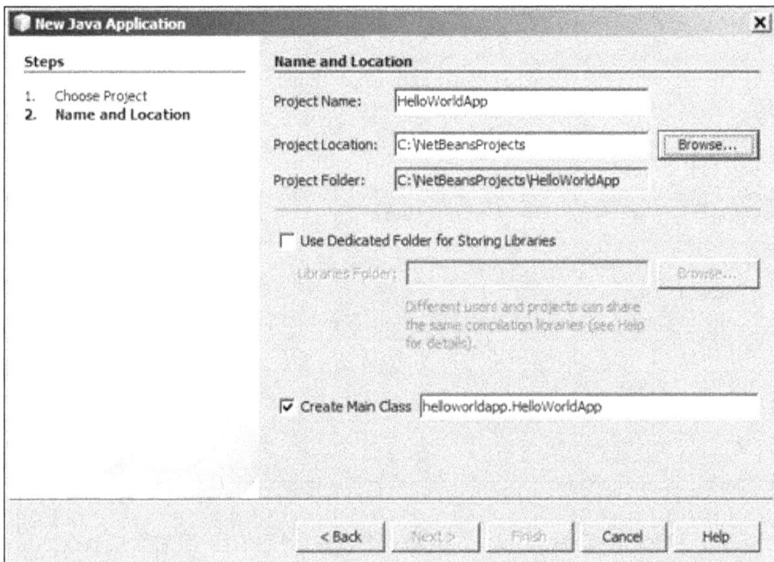

4. Click on **Finish**.

Your project is now ready to go.

The Project window contains a tree view of the components of the actual project, in particular, the source files and the libraries.

The Source Editor window contains a file called `HelloWorldApp` with code.

Use the Navigator window to navigate between elements related to the selected class.

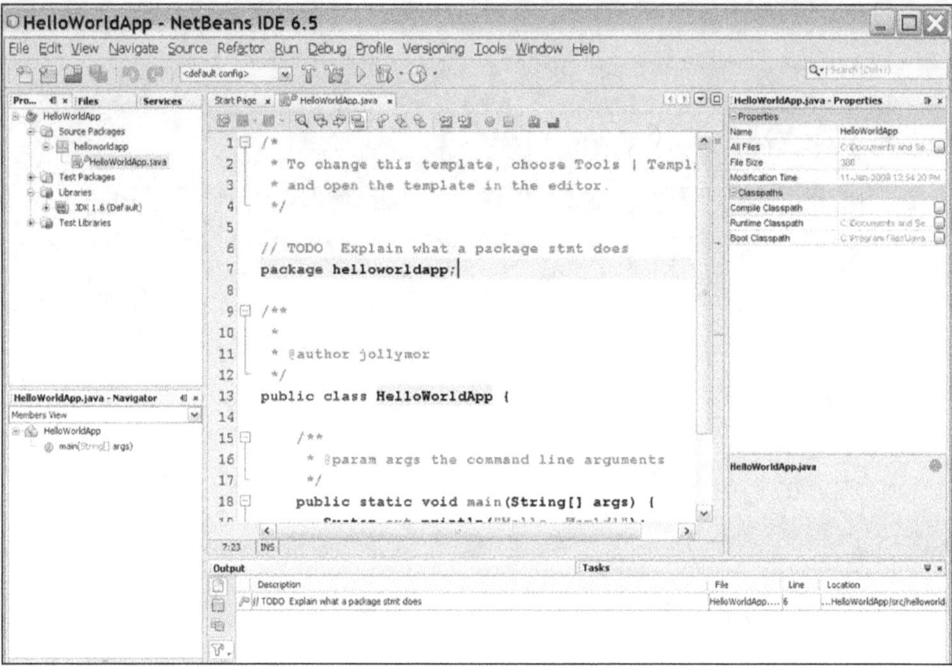

No need to delve into further details here. The Web is full of good tutorials, if you are interested in improving your knowledge of the Java ME platform, starting with:

`https://netbeans.org/kb/docs/javame/gamebuilder-screencast.html`

BlackBerry

For the sake of completeness, we mention here the characteristics of the BlackBerry operating system. Though it doesn't offer the same commercial opportunities as iOS or Android-based phones, with about eight million devices worldwide, BlackBerry can be an interesting market niche, less competitive but not necessarily less remunerative than the iOS or Android markets. Studies state that the average revenue for a BlackBerry app is about $4000 per month, much higher than average revenues for the apps developed for iOS and Android.

Moreover, Reasearch In Motion (RIM) (the company behind BlackBerry devices) offers a guarantee that if a quality certified app doesn't make $10,000 in the first year, they will pay up the difference to the developers. No other platform owner company offers such a guarantee!

BlackBerry is a brand of smartphones and handheld devices developed by RIM. The main features of these devices are the ability to send and receive push e-mails and instant messages, while maintaining a high level security. That's what made BlackBerry an optimal choice for companies that provide their employees with smartphones for business use. They also share many features of other smartphones, including media players, Internet browsers, cameras, and obviously, gaming capabilities.

The OS used by BlackBerry devices is a proprietary environment developed by RIM and designed to take advantage of their distinctive input devices: the track wheel, the track ball, the track pad, and the QWERTY keyboard. The BlackBerry OS also provides support for Java MIPD 1.0 and 2.0 (refer to the *Java ME* section), thus allowing third party developers to create apps for this platform.

A developer must have an account with RIM and be digitally signed in order to guarantee his/her authorship.

There are several tools that can be used to develop games for BlackBerry, such as the open source project GamePlay, that don't require developers to learn entirely new skills to build apps for the platform.

With the BlackBerry 10 platform released in 2013, one can find many reasons to consider this option, having the BlackBerry Play Book tablets in mind!

The BlackBerry App World

The BlackBerry App World is the service provided by RIM to BlackBerry owners to browse and download apps for their devices. Launched in April 2009 and with fewer apps than the Apple Store or Google Play, the BlackBerry App World offers all fundamental services provided by its direct competitors: intuitive user interface to browse applications by category, the possibility of reinstalling already purchased apps, several flexible payment options, and a rating and review system for apps available for shopping.

Apps submitted to the App World must be approved by RIM and a fee of $200 is involved in the submission process, which covers 10 submissions. Note that the fee is refunded if the developer's account is not approved.

Developing games for BlackBerry

When getting to the game development for BlackBerry, there are two options available.

The first is to build native apps using the BlackBerry SDK and its C++ framework. The BlackBerry SDK is aimed at the newest devices equipped with OS 10 and to the BlackBerry tablet, known as the PlayBook. Being a framework for native apps, it guarantees better performances, thanks to the full integration with the specific APIs of the BlackBerry platform.

The other possibility is to use the Java SDK, or even better, the Java Plugin for Eclipse which extends the Eclipse development framework. The main advantage, for a developer, of using Java to create games for BlackBerry is that MIDlets (Java applications) can equally run on any device powered by OS 7 and on, thus widening the potential audience for their games.

Everyone interested in delving into the game development for BlackBerry can research on the Internet, starting from:

- For native apps:

  `https://developer.blackberry.com/develop/platform_choice/ndk.html`

- For Java MIDlets with Eclipse

  `https://developer.blackberry.com/java/documentation/overview_2006571_11.html`

Summary

We have discussed what an operating system is and how it acts as the interface between the hardware and software of a computer or a handheld device.

We mentioned the general characteristics and evolution of the operating systems running on Personal Computers and examined in detail today's most popular mobile OS (Android, iOS, Windows Phone, Java ME, and BlackBerry).

We also provided the basic references to approach the development and distribution of apps and games for mobile platforms and gave a general description of the best tools to develop for each of them.

In the next chapter, we will discuss the working pipeline of a typical indie mobile team and provide a description of the main roles. We will also describe the tasks each role is accountable for, the most popular tools to accomplish these tasks, and provide information on the academic background expected for each role.

2

The Mobile Indie Team

Assembling a good team with the right people is the first step towards the production of a well-done title. The process of videogame development is a pretty tough one and it requires talent, skill, patience, and an iron will.

This is especially true for an indie team, because as a team of people who usually don't work under the constraints of a solid company, they can easily break up during the development process for the most unexpected reasons!

When choosing the members of your mobile team, you'd better look for people who have both talent and the ability to effectively cooperate with other people to create the perfect title, in order to trigger your career in the gaming industry.

The following chapter provides a detailed description of the key roles to cover in a mobile indie team, the tasks they are responsible for, the skills they need, and the academic courses that can help them get those skills.

In this chapter, we will cover:

- A presentation of the mobile team and the key roles to cover
- What it takes to develop mobile games
- The game designer
- The game artist
- The programmer
- The game tester
- The game producer
- The sound designer

A matter of size

One of the most interesting aspects of mobile game development is that it offers opportunities to small teams to effectively get into the competition. From a certain perspective, mobile game development recalls the age of early computer games, when a team of few members shipped games that could gain worldwide popularity. Electronic Arts got their start by publishing indie developers' products.

Generally speaking, mobile games tend to have a limited scope when compared to common high budget/high quality (AAA) console or PC titles. Mobile games are designed to be played in small chunks and rely on simple game mechanics that require fewer assets, less programming, and shorter testing and debug time. This means that mobile games require less people for development and can be developed by teams of one or few individuals for every key role.

A good reason to keep the mobile dev team small has very much to do with the progress. Working progress can slow down either if the team is too small or too big. With a limited amount of work and too many people on each role, the responsibility is shared among too many members and the progress slows down because nobody feels really responsible for what needs to be done. The more people on the team, the greater the chance of miscommunication and wasted effort.

Another important reason to keep the team small is that the larger the group, the higher it costs! Though mobile gaming can become a very profitable niche, the low price of such products means that you usually don't make millions out of a single mobile game and it is imperative to keep the development costs as low as possible.

Key roles in a successful team

Though it is very important that each member has a well-defined role, when dealing with small teams it is likely that one member will have multiple roles and that those roles are shared between more than one member.

This is one reason why small teams usually offer better career opportunities to those who can cover several roles. Working in a small team, where people are required to work on different aspects of the game at the same time, they have the opportunity to show their different talents and thus to advance their careers. It is also a good opportunity to learn new skills and expand their overall expertise.

Generally speaking, the key roles that need to be covered in a mobile dev team are: Design, Art\Modeling, Programming, Sound, QA\Testing, and Production. These are all key aspects of a game development and each of these roles will be explored in the following sections of this chapter.

The following figure represents the average subdivision of total cost for the production of a game among the different departments (source: `gamecareerguide.com/`).

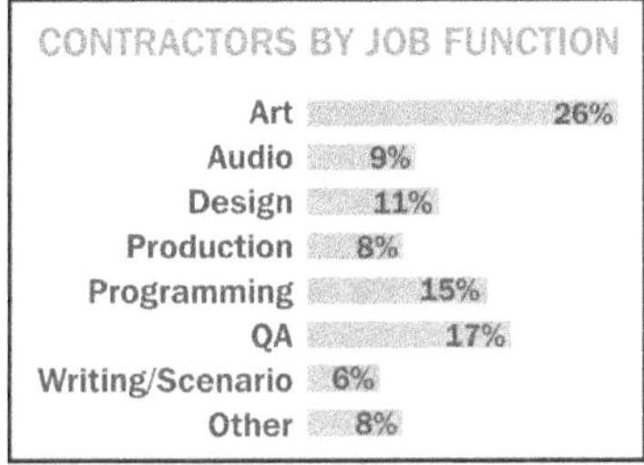

What it takes

Game development is a lot of work! There is a huge amount of things to do even to make simple games. Before we delve into the details of each role in a team, it is worth saying something about the cross competencies that each individual should have for that team to be effective and reach its goals.

Commitment

In videogame development, (almost) any element of the game needs to be created from scratch. Every pixel requires someone to draw it, any action performed by a character needs someone to animate it, any event needs to be coded, any sound effect must be composed, and the list is long. It is not by chance that the inclusion of digital contents in movies led to a large increase in cost.

Cohesion

Any activity that is shared among different people requires the group to hold together on the common goal, especially in a small group where each person is responsible for a key element of the project.

To develop a game requires weeks, or months, more reasonably. During this period, any sort of problem that arises can hinder the course of the project: the code doesn't work as expected, graphics mess up when imported in the engine, design questions with no clear answers, for example.

If all the team members don't support each other and cooperate in such tight spots, the project can easily turn into a failure, with the consequent loss of time, money, and more important, team morale. When things go bad, you simply need the right people around you, who can provide constructive criticism and help team mates to make the best use of their talents.

The first experience of one of the authors with an indie team risked to turn into a complete failure, with the consequent loss of time and money, when the professional we were supposed to work with decided to quit. When that happened, we all felt very bad and our morale was as low as it could be. If it wasn't for our friendship as a group, we couldn't have reached the goal to make that game anyway!

Software development methodologies

Videogames are software, of course, and software has proven processes and methodologies that increase the chance of reaching one's goal while minimizing waste.

There are several methodologies to develop a software, each one with its own pros and cons. Agile software development is a very popular software development methodology among today's game developers, based on an iterative and incremental approach, where teams periodically examine the short term progresses of their work and set new short term milestones according to their results. You can find resources on Agile development at `http://agilemanifesto.org/`.

Discipline

When developing a game, there is never enough time. The iterative nature of the creative process implies that it is very likely that the project's initial schedule suffers delays and missed milestones.

It is thus very important that each team member is well organized with his work and is able to advance his work day by day. This is especially important when dev teams work remotely, which is often the case with indie projects.

People who have freedom to work on their projects as they please tend to postpone work for other activities, with the consequence that project deadlines may be delayed leading into a disaster.

Be sure that the people in the team are reliable and will take their responsibilities seriously.

Professional training

Whenever possible, look for people who have degrees in their field. There are many skilled people who are self-taught, and experience is what counts more in the end. Still, a good formal training helps people learn fast and overcome their limits due to lack of experience.

A general rule is that, when building up the team, people covering the key roles should have previous experience working on a project in the same or a similar position. They should at least have already worked on a true project, working in a team. The reason for having experienced people in key roles is that they can provide reliable previsions when drafting the schedule of the project. They know what they can do and the time it takes to do it. Inexperienced people, on the other hand, could underestimate their assigned task, with the result that the project deadlines fail and a new schedule needs to be made.

It is also true, however, that once the key roles are assigned to experienced people, hiring talents, even with few or none experience, can provide an invaluable resource for the team on the long run.

Passion for games

Well, it is very easy to understand that to develop games for a living, it is important that those who are part of the team love videogames. We have spoken about the high level of commitment required to achieve important goals and the need to make a lot of personal sacrifices. Out of our personal experience, it is very likely that a brand new dev team interested in developing videogames will be asked to do other things in order to be able to develop games, such as working on web sites or other kinds of non-gaming apps to support their business.

If these people are passionate about developing games, it will be easier to commit themselves to things which they don't really like doing, having their main goal in mind. Otherwise, they could simply give up, for working takes away the most important resource from people: their time. Indie game development is an opportunity to turn a passion into a profession, but only if you can give the time it takes!

The roles in an indie mobile team

What follows here is a review of the main roles required for an ideal mobile indie team. For each role, we provide a description of duties, skills, personal traits, and the academic formation.

We don't mean that this list of roles is a requirement for any team; it is possible for people getting into the game industry to have different backgrounds.

Also, we don't mean that each role represents a person. There can be people covering more than one role, as it is likely that more people will share one role.

The game designer

The game designer defines what happens in a game and what the player does to progress through it. He is responsible for turning a game play idea into a detailed design document, which is constantly updated and used by all other team members as a reference guide to develop their part of the project.

During the pre-production phase of a game, the designer is responsible for defining what the game is about, its story and the game world, what the game mechanics are, which features the game will implement, what its Unique Selling Points are, and its main competitors.

This information flows into the pitch document of the game, a sort of presentation document of a game-to-come, usually presented to potential investors to get the approval on the project, as for example, with the videos on Kickstarter. We will address the pitch document again by the end of the book, when we will create one for a mobile game.

During the production phase, the work of a game designer consists of checking that all the team members work towards the realization of the vision he has in mind. With the producer, the game designer acts as the coordinator of the project and a living wiki. Whenever a team member has a question on how a specific piece of game should work or look like, he will look to the game designer to provide the answer. Be ready for that and know your game!

Designer at work

Game design starts with a good idea. It can be a nice game mechanic, the idea of a cool character or a piece of a story: anything can provide the inspiration for a good game. A popular indie game called **Braid** finds its premises in the consequences of a bad love delusion.

The next step is to convey this idea to the rest of the team in a way that ensures everyone understands what the idea is. This sounds simple, but is far from it. A game designer needs a wide variety of skills as well as good ideas. Good ideas are plentiful, everyone has a few. The trick is getting something built that somewhat resembles that good idea. The main tool the designer uses to convey his/her idea to the other members of the team is, as we have already said, the design document.

The designer should have a working knowledge of the team's skills, such as art, sound, programming as well as a background in playing games. A designer needs the ability to analyze game play and to articulate what works and what doesn't work in a game.

Since mobile game development is involved here, the designer should also have a thorough knowledge, from both commercial and technical perspectives, of the mobile platform: trends, technical advancements and solutions, successful genre and control schemes, profitable business models, strengths, and weaknesses. We expect to provide you with such fundamentals within this book!

Designer tools

There are several tools the designer is expected to be able to use to accomplish his/her tasks.

- **Pencils and paper**: Any game mechanic description should begin with a sketch of some sort to explain how it works. If you can't sketch the idea for a game mechanic, it probably isn't a good mechanic.
- **Text editors and software**: To create mind maps and schemes, text editors and software are a strongly recommended requirement, as they are necessary to create documents and presentations that can be shown and shared with the other team members to better communicate the ideas behind a game and throughout all its development process. Spreadsheets with data and formulas are included.
- **Image editors**: These are necessary as well to create schemes, fake screenshots, basic level sketches, and any other reference image that can be helpful to convey the idea the designer has in mind. A design document with no images is not a good one.

It is also very likely that the game designer is required to create the so-called white boxes for the game levels, at least the main ones. In such cases, the ability to use 3D modeling software to create geometries becomes very important, as well as an advanced knowledge of the most popular game engines to create basic terrains and the relevant geometry of a game level.

The practices of game design

In a small team, the designer can be accounted for practically implementing the specific aspects of a game. Depending on his/her background, he can help the programmer with additional coding and scripting, he can be in charge of level design or help the artists with graphic assets, he can take care of updating a developer's blog for the project for communication purposes, and he is responsible for designing and managing testing sessions of the game during its development.

Being in charge of so many different tasks, a game designer needs many other skills to accomplish all of them. Some of these skills are acquired during high school studies, while others require academic studies or experience coming from confronting specific working situations, so it takes time to develop them.

- **Communication**: The number one most important skill for a game designer is communication. Being able to talk to a programmer, artist, writer, tester, sound designer, producer, marketer, and financier in a way they each understand is crucial to the success of your project.
- **Technical writing**: Formal technical writing skills are also very important for the game designer. Grammar, punctuation, and spelling are essential for creating a clear design document. The design document is the source your team will go to when they have questions. Keeping it easy to read and up to date is crucial for the success of your project.
- **Drawing**: A designer should be able to draw at least a bit. Mocking up screens is essential for the design document. Knowing how to use Photoshop and/or Visio will aid the designer greatly. A picture is worth a thousand words, especially in game design.
- **Programming\Scripting**: A designer should have an understanding of the principles of programming. You don't need to be able to actually write code, but it wouldn't hurt. Knowing the basics of programming will allow you to format the information in your design document to best serve the programmer.
- **Scripting languages**: Familiarity with scripting languages, such as Java or LUA, will allow you to directly interact with the game engine your programmer has built, saving time and money. You can also test your own ideas without using up the programmer's work cycles.
- **Math**: A designer should know math, at least to algebra level. When boiled down to the basics, games are a set of math problems. This sounds boring, but go back and look at the paper and pencil version of Dungeons & Dragons. It's all statistics!
- **Finance**: The game designer must understand the costs of the decisions they make. Changing direction mid-project can cost a lot of money/time. Prototype early and often to make sure the design works.
- **Psychology**: Yes, games punch some very basic human feedback buttons, such as reward behavior, aversion feedback loops, and the like. Understanding what these are will allow you to build a truly addictive experience. Yeah, that sounds bad, but it's what we do!

Academic formation and personality

How does one learn how to design games? A good place to start is by using pencil and paper, a deck of cards, a chess board, poker chips, whatever is at hand. Take an existing game and modify it. ForAC example, tick tack toe is an interesting game to start with. Fundamentally, it's a broken game, since the player who moves first will always win unless they make a mistake. Try to think of ways to fix that: a bigger board, different types of moves or pieces, add dice and/or cards, and so on. A game designer is a person who asks himself how things work and how their behavior can be described by rules.

As Raph Koster (a brilliant game designer) once wrote:

> "*Games are not their graphics or their frame rate, they are their rules.*"

A good rule of design is to take the action the player will do most often and prototype it. If your testers enjoy it, perfect it and set it aside. Then define the second most frequent action the player will do, find how it will complement action #1, implement and test it. Continue on to action #3, repeat the process. For a first time project, it's probably best to lock down the design at action 3-5. Every action added will significantly increase the complexity of testing and debugging.

A designer must be open to criticism coming from other team members and testers. Ideas come and go and it is very important for a designer to never feel too attached to any of them.

Finally, if you want to be a designer, you need to have a life. Go out and get a liberal arts degree, take up a sport, make lots of friends, and have adventures. All of these things will enrich your life and give you the material to make great games.

Most videogame designers have a Bachelor's Degree in Computer Science, Arts, Computer Engineering, or Experimental Psychology.

Though not strictly required, a strong University background can help you develop those skills that can get your first step into the gaming industry.

More important, a University background can help you develop that specific forma mentis that makes you willing to keep learning as you progress in your career. That is really important when your line of work has to do with technologies and habits that change so fast, as in the world of game development.

In the last few years, several universities and private schools worldwide have started offering various courses in game design that teach the basics of this extraordinary discipline.

No game is ever done!

You will always find things you want to change. It is the nature of the beast. Usually you just run out of resources and say, "it's good enough". If you have ideas on how to improve the game, file them away and save them for the sequel.

More about the role of game designer and his/her tasks can be found at the following links:

`http://penny-arcade.com/patv/episode/so-you-want-to-be-a-game-designer`

`http://www.raphkoster.com/2012/09/26/mailbag-i-want-to-become-a-designer/#more-4280`

The game artist

The game artist is responsible for creating in-game art: characters, animations, game objects, backgrounds, environments, and game interface.

No need to say, artwork is very important in a videogame! Graphics are the most prominent characteristic of a videogame and they are also important from a marketing point of view. Most of the time, customers are attracted to a title by its visual characteristics. When judging a game from its preview, if gameplay is unavailable, the game is judged solely on its visual appeal.

In the early days of computer videogames, a single artist could cover all the graphic needs of a game. As time passed, it required more people to be involved in the creation of the graphics for a title, and this lead to the creation of groups of artists as part of the development team.

In a mobile team it is very likely that graphics will be made by two to three people with a separation of duties, such as one artist on 2D graphics (concept, sprites, game interface, and textures) and one or two on the production of 3D assets (models, animations, 3D environments, and lighting).

Brushes and canvas

Game artists need several tools. First and foremost, an artist must be able to draw and sketch, using pencil and paper. Once the sketches are approved, there comes the time to create real assets for the game using dedicated software. The most important tools for a game artist are image editors, such as Photoshop, Paintshop, Illustrator and modeling software, such as 3D Studio Max, Maya, Blender, and Zbrush. We will talk about them in the chapter on game graphics.

Forms of art

The production of graphic assets for games involves many different activities. We will delve into the details of the operations related to the production of graphic assets for mobile games in the next chapter of the book. For now, let's just have a look at the main duties of the game artist.

2D graphic assets

The 2D graphics are the foundation of any game. Videogames were born 2D and 2D graphics are always required, even for 3D games. The following list describes the main fields of 2D graphics for games:

- **Concept art**: This consists of sketches, storyboards, and free hand drawings that reproduce key aspects of a game, such as the main character, the villain, relevant game environments, and crucial game mechanics. Concept art is mainly used to convey the look and feel of a game: the ability to convey maximum content with minimal complexity is a key factor for creating optimal concept art.
- **Sprites**: These are 2D representations of any game object of a title. The ability to draw convincing characters and objects using few pixels is a talent that is fundamental to those who want to be proficient with 2D assets creation.
- **Backgrounds, terrains, and tilesets**: These are the construction blocks for any bidimensional game. Tilesets, in particular, are very important, because they save system memory for your game.
- **Interface**: Any game, whether it is 2D or 3D, needs an interface to provide the player with relevant information during gameplay (score, lives and energy, ammo), as well as menus and presentation screens for the game. The artist takes care of creating the assets for the game interface.
- **Textures and materials**: 3D objects and characters need to be improved with 2D graphic assets that add details to a model and make its surface interact with the lighting environment of the game engine. The artist is accounted for creating these assets.

The following figure represents a concept design sketch for a space ship, taken from the material for a space shooter made by one of the authors:

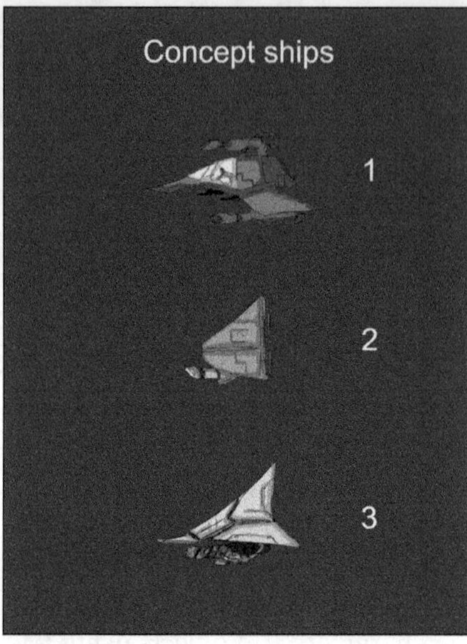

3D graphic assets

The advent of 3D and the improvement of mobile devices hardware offer the opportunity to mobile developers to create beautiful 3D titles for the mobile market.

The following list describes the main fields of 3D graphics in games.

- **Models**: 3D characters and game objects must be modeled with dedicated software. Actual games and mobile games too tend to make extensive use of 3D graphics, so it is very important for a game artist to be proficient with 3D modeling and for a team who wants to develop mobile games to have at least one guy good at that.
- **Animations**: Animations for game characters are usually made with the same software used to model them. Characters' animation is crucial for a game's appeal, because everyone is good at evaluating if an animation is good, especially for humanoid characters, thanks to their experience of the real world. An inferior animated character immediately stands out from the rest of the game to ruin the player's experience.
- **3D environments**: These are crucial elements of a polished game; it is very important for a game artist to be capable of depicting believable worlds that make the player feel immersed in the game action.

- **Lighting**: Though mobile games don't usually rely very much on player's immersion, the use of light and colors is very important to produce nice game levels. It is thus important for a game artist to have at least some basic understanding on how to use light to convey emotions.

A typical mobile game development team can rely on just two or three artists. Consider the previous list as a reference to evaluate candidates for the position of an artist, based on their proven skills.

Art schools and creative types

The artists should study the basics of fine art: art theory and history, composition, color and form, and space and light.

Art schools and academies are the institutions of choice for those interested in becoming artists. These are schools that provide their students with the necessary courses on life drawing, graphic design, color theory, photography, animation and technical drawing, anatomy and the dynamics of movement, among others.

Naturally, a good art school is only the first step. Then it is necessary for these people to practice as much as they can and get proficient with their tools to develop real assets for games.

As for the artist's character, there is no need to explain that an artist has a creative nature and as such, creative types may not be comfortable with discipline. On the other hand, artists who want to work in the videogame industry need to balance this aspect of their personality to complete their daily tasks.

They must be analytical as much as they are creative, and fight their innate tendency to chaos to allow the other team members to work effectively with them and keep up with the project schedule.

Finally, artists must be capable of putting their creativity at the game's target audience service, sacrificing their personal taste, and possess a thick skin to deal with the daily criticism that their creativity will undergo during the development of the game.

More about the game artist and the creation of graphics for games can be found at `http://www.gamecareerguide.com/features/413/game_art_and_animation_an_introduction.php`.

The programmer

Programming, and videogame programming in particular, can be pretty similar to performing magic, in some ways.

It has to do with crafting formulas learned from books, a knowledge hard to grasp and to understand, that allows those who are initiated to make anything they wish happen on a computer or other device screen!

Out of the fantasy metaphor, the programmer is the guy who takes care of coding things that happen in a videogame, the one who turns the math and logic behind it into commands and functions and he is probably the most important professional in a videogame team. You can have the most appealing design in the world, the best graphics and sounds, but without someone coding this stuff, your game simply won't exist!

In the early days of videogames, when games were nothing more than geometry performing on the screen, the programmer was the team, as he took care of design and artwork too.

As the complexity of games increased, programmers began to focus on just coding. Over time, different kinds of programmers became necessary and now we have specialized roles, such as lead programmers, engine\physics programmers, AI programmers, and gameplay programmers.

A mobile team, on the other hand, will hardly have more than two people taking care of coding. The team's game designer is more likely to help the programmer, if not with hard coding stuff, at least with scripting game events.

The programmer's kit

The basic tools of a programmer falls into three main categories: coding languages, Integrated Development software, and Version Control Systems.

Coding languages are a topic that could cover entire books by itself. Packt already offers several books on the different coding languages and their characteristics; we suggest referring to these books for an in-depth analysis on the subject.

Generally speaking, C++ is the language of choice for game developers. Any ideal candidate for the programmer position in a mobile game dev team must be at ease with such a language and have developed some kind of project with it, even as an indie game or some school project. He must be proficient with concepts like destructors, classes, inheritance, constructors, and constants.

Integrated Development Environment is software that allows you to develop code for projects and games. The development environment of choice for C++ is Microsoft Visual Studio, a professional tool that offers everything you need to produce high quality coding, including a code editor, debugger, several development tools to design GUIs, web apps, classes, data schemes, content exploring tools, and much more useful stuff.

Game engines may have their own built-in coding IDE, for example, Unity 3D now comes with a tool named MonoDevelop.

A true IDE is not even always necessary. Many coders, especially when dealing with scripting languages, such as UScript, are happy enough with text editors, such as ConText, which offers some basic functions of auto indent and text aligning according to a given set of available coding languages, recognized by the software.

Version Control Systems are software used to manage the changes in documents and computer programs. These software cover a strategic role when more than one person work on the same part of a project; as it is usually the case for programmers on a game.

GIT is one of popular, free, and open source Version Control software which you can use for your projects. You can find it at `http://git-scm.com/`.

Coding departments

The mobile team game programmer has several duties to attend to, mainly because he basically is in charge of everything involving coding. The list includes, among others:

- **Game engine\Physics programming**: The game engine consists of developing a framework of some sort that can effectively manage everything that makes a game what it is: graphics, audio, input and controls system, data saving, networking, and anything else that is necessary. Since there are already excellent game engines today, such as Unity 3D, Corona, or the Unreal Engine, the mobile programmer very rarely needs to create a game engine from scratch.
- **Physics**: Physics simulation is a very common feature of today's 3D videogames. Game engines include a plugin to manage physics and so-called rigid bodies (game objects subjected to physics). A coder is hardly requested to develop a brand new physic engine, except when he's requested to develop the game engine itself.

- **Artificial Intelligence**: As a general statement, mobile games generally aim to be not too challenging , so as not to frustrate the player, thus they rarely rely on sophisticated AI algorithms. The smaller scope of mobile games implies that AI programming for such games may be considered less problematic than that of popular AAA titles, in many ways.
- **User Interface**: The User Interface of your game will strongly affect its appeal to players. Touch controls must work as expected, they must be responsive, and the information displayed on screen must be clear and well displayed. By ensuring this is so, you improve the chances of selling your game.
- **Network**: With the outbreak of social networks and the demand for sharing, no mobile game should lack a feature that allows people to upload their scores on public online leaderboards or share their results with friends. Moreover, the free-to-play business model that is so popular among today's developers requires a reliable data exchange dynamic between the game and the servers accounted for the service. Most of all, the game-server communication must be hack-proof and trustworthy. Network programming is so important that it is considered one of the hardest and most challenging aspects of game programming in general.

Learning to be a programmer

Exceptionally talented people apart, programmers will typically have a degree in Computer Science or Engineering. They need a very robust knowledge in linear algebra and mathematics, both in 2D and 3D space. Vectors, rotations, distances, curves, and matrices must be their daily bread.

They need to know several coding and scripting languages, such as C\C++, Java, and LUA, because the more experience they have with game engines and their scripting languages, the easier it will be to get hired by a team. Programmers also need to know about efficient programming, because efficient code optimizes performances. Code that provides consistent performances on both high end and low end devices can be a key factor for the success of your game!

They must excel at problem solving. Whenever a game designer depicts a game mechanic, he is actually defining a problem for the coder to solve. The best problems are those which don't have a single solution, so it is very important that a game programmer is solid with analysis and is able to define a set of potential solutions before choosing the one which seems better.

As for their personal characteristics, the times of the weird, introvert guy who codes alone in a dark room are long gone. Efficient software development and teamwork relies on communication, it is mandatory for a good programmer to be able to meet with the other team members to correctly address problems and define an optimal job schedule. As a fact, the most popular game development practices, such as Agile development, require team members to continuously interact with each other.

A programmer should also be in constant thirst for knowledge. The coders with 30 years experience will tell you that they are still learning, for game programming never reaches its end point: new technologies arise, new methodologies become popular, and new languages become available. Most of all, when something is new, it is very likely that no one can help you to understand it. You need to become a disciplined self-learner if you want to be a cutting edge programmer!

More about videogame programming and the role of game programmer can be found at the following link:

`http://www.gamecareerguide.com/features/412/game_programming_an_introduction.php`.

The game tester

The game tester is the member of the team who takes care of checking that the game works as expected and doesn't crash, that controls are clear, intuitive, and effective, that game mechanics are consistent, that the game logic works properly, and that gameplay is fun.

Game testing can be called into play at different moments during the development. As a general rule, a game should enter its testing phase as soon as a prototype is available. There is no better way to understand if a game mechanic is a good one than by asking someone to try it and provide feedback.

It is mandatory that the tester is not a person who's developing the game, because the objectivity of the tester's opinion is a crucial element in any stage of its development, and in the early stages in particular. Generally speaking, the cost of correcting a mechanic is proportional to the time that has passed since its implementation.

The thing that should be immediately clear, especially to our younger readers, is that testing a game doesn't mean that people are paid to merely play it! Sure, they need to play the game to test it, but finding and reporting bugs has little to do with playing games. A good tester must be able to describe the bug in detail and explain how it can be reproduced to help the development team to identify its causes and correct them.

That the testing is a low entry level job in the game industry, is just half the truth. As we will see during the course of this section, a good tester requires competency, and exceptional communication skills. But it is also true that if you cannot prove your talent in art, programming, or business administration with a strong portfolio or work experience, then starting out as a full time tester for a big game developer or a team is a very good way to kick-start your career in the game industry!

The tools of deconstruction

The main tools for a mobile game tester are mobile phones and their interfaces, mostly touch interfaces and gyroscopes. The tester thus needs to be at ease with mobile devices and their features to test mobile games.

During the early stages of development, it is very likely that testing will be accomplished on emulators, software that approximates the functionality of a mobile device on a PC for testing purposes. There are several reasons to use emulators in the early stages of development. One is that sometimes application development involves the use of scripts that can be dangerous to run on actual devices, because they could destroy some phone functionality or lead to a break of terms of agreement with an operator. Another is merely that the actual devices may not be available.

On the other hand, the fact that a game works on the emulator doesn't mean that it won't have problems when running on the actual phone, due to the fact that, as we said, the emulator only approximates the functionality of a phone, it's not the phone itself.

Another problem with emulators is that, since they run on PCs, they don't allow testing the touch interface of the phone. Most of the times, touch commands are replicated via the mouse, which means, for example, that multitouch functionality cannot be tested at all. At some point, a game needs to be tested on the real devices it is meant to run on! More on the practices of game testing will be seen in *Chapter 9, Prototyping*.

The following screenshot represents a screenshot from a standard software debug report:

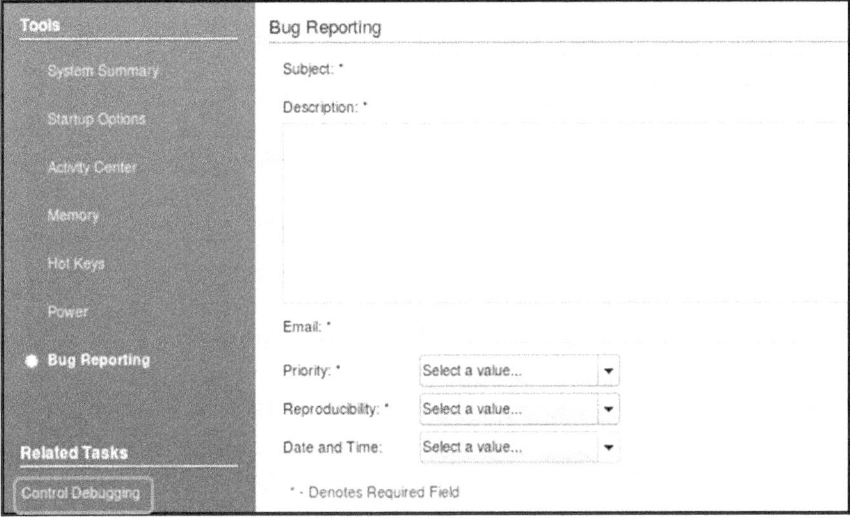

Aspects of game testing

There are several aspects of a game that need to be tested and different game genres require different testing methodologies. A mobile game tester must accomplish specific tasks that depend on the distinctive characteristics of mobile phones and handheld devices. Among them are the following:

- **Functionality testing**: This aims to look for general problems with the game or its User Interface, in order to check for issues regarding stability, game mechanics, and glitches (game asset failures).
- **Compatibility testing**: This is meant to check that the game works with different hardware and software configurations. It is a very important practice for PC games and for mobile titles in particular. It is crucial to test the game performances on low end and high end devices to check them.
- **Localization testing**: This checks that all in-game text and speech are correct in titles that are shipped in different languages. There is no need to say that, to be a localization tester, you need to be native in the language in which the game must be translated and at least fluent in the original language of the game.

- **Stress testing (monkey testing)**: This is meant to check how the application responds to chaotic and unpredictable events. Mobile phones are subjected to several kinds of such events: incoming calls and messages, updates, undesired button presses, screen locks, automatic standby, and so on. It takes a lot of time to carry these tests over, especially if they need to be repeated on different devices.
- **Compliance testing**: This is required to check if a game meets standards, license agreements, and terms of use that are specific for each developing platform. To ship a game on the Apple Store, for example, it must have a unique name, refer to a certain category, must provide a link to the developer for customer care issues, it must not contradict the Human Interface Guideline, and so on. All these aspects are the responsibility of the tester.
- **Beta testing**: This is done during the final stage of development; it refers to the first publicly available version of a game. Public betas are effective because thousands of fans may find bugs that the developer's testers did not. Mobile games don't usually go under beta testing though. It is a very time consuming process and it needs licenses to be exchanged between developers and testers in order to allow their devices to run the tests. We mention this practice here mainly for the sake of completeness to describe the role of the game tester.

Skills of a professional player

A tester first of all needs exceptional linguistic skills, both written and spoken, to be able to write clearly and in concise ways. He must be proficient in writing clear algorithms that exactly explain how a series of gaming actions determine an in-game bug, and that describe that bug in detail. Getting used to explaining hard\technical stuff to not-proficient people is a good way to improve these skills.

There are also several kinds of tests that a potential tester can be asked to fulfill in order to be considered for a tester position, such as the paper clip and the building block exercises. You can search on the Internet to find out more about them.

The game tester needs to be good at any kind of game and must be able to play them professionally at any difficulty setting. Game content may vary depending on the difficulty, so the tester needs to be capable of beating games in conditions most players can't. He also must be very proficient with installment and update procedures on different devices and operating systems, in order to check the accuracy of system messages text.

Being proficient in two or more languages, written and spoken, is definitively an advantage, because many tester positions, especially entry level ones, are available for localization testers. Showing the right attitude as a localization tester can give a chance to more desirable functional testing openings within the same company.

A tester must be a very sharp observer and must demonstrate exceptional attention to detail. He needs to be like some kind of bulldog that never gets tired of repeating a game sequence, until he knows for sure what happened in a specific game situation and why. He must have an iron will to keep playing the game again and again, examine the same part over and over, trying everything that can be done in order to trigger any outcome and thus, thoroughly test any fold of the game logic, even after 18 hours of playing the same game. At the same time, he must be an excellent lateral thinker, because he needs to force himself to think out of his own mental schemes in order to exploit all the opportunities offered by the gameplay of the title he's working on.

Localization testing requires a great attention effort, because with speech and writing, we have several cognitive mechanisms that tend to automatically correct errors, such as repetitions and typing errors. You must force yourself to always put all your attention and resources at maximum levels to such cognitive biases.

One example of tester endurance and patience was during the beta test of Faceball 2000 for the original Gameboy. It was the only multiplayer first person shooter for Gameboy. We handed a build over to a colleague's four year old son who dived right into the game. The boy came back a while later, saying he was stuck. Indeed he was in a room with no exit. Upon further analysis, the boy had been running into a corner where two walls met, over and over. Eventually, he popped through the intersection between the walls, into the interior of a pillar. None of the other testers had tried this.

University of Gamestop

Differently from the other roles in a mobile dev team, the testers are not expected to achieve a specific academic formation to accomplish their tasks. For entry testing positions, a high school diploma is enough.

Instead, we could say that games are the school of choice for a tester. Having played tons of them, on different platforms, genre, and input devices is a must. The more games and gaming devices a tester has experience with, the better he is at playing them and at fully exploring their features, in order to find out what doesn't work as expected.

It is also important for a tester to have a glossary on essential gameplay and bug reporting definitions. Terms such as alpha, beta, QA, gold master, and bug definitions are much appreciated by those who decide if you are worthy of a full time tester position.

As a professional player, the game tester needs to resist the temptation of playing for fun to experience games from an objective perspective. For a tester, playing is not fun; it is a means to accomplish his/her job! He is requested to play games regardless of whether he likes them or not.

There is a very interesting and detailed article about the role of the game tester that we suggest you check out at the following link:

`http://www.sloperama.com/advice/lesson5.html.`

The game producer

The producer is responsible for keeping the project on time, in budget, and top quality. The term producer was introduced by Trip Hawkins to Electronic Arts in the 1980s. His vision was to bring some of the qualities of music and video producers to the video game industry. Today, a producer manages schedules, costs, and resources, keeping the team on track. The producer will take the design document and build a timetable with milestones, as well as a list of assets needed to complete the game. He is also responsible for getting what the team needs in a timely manner.

Typically, the producer is the liaison between the team and any corporate entities, such as a publisher, marketer, and financier. This may involve negotiating contracts, licensing, and the like. The producer coordinates the actions of the dev team to hit milestones, he checks the quality of work, and manages the testing team. He will oversee any localization that is needed.

Even if no third-party publisher is involved in a project (as it usually is for a mobile indie team) the producer covers a vital role for the success of the game.

Indie development is subjected to the most unexpected events: other paid jobs could take time away from game development, money could be scarce until the game is shipped, the game could fail for some reason and not provide income, team members could become undisciplined if they are not hired with a contract, difficulties could arise when working remotely if an office for all team members to work together is not available, and so on. If the producer can deal with such issues, only then can an indie team can reach its goal of making games for a living. The producer should be prepared to live in crisis management mode: he is the chief fire fighter and train's the engineer, keeps the project on track by fighting fires as they arise and preventing them as much as possible.

Keeping things organized

A good spread sheet or database program will help with this task. Microsoft Excel and Filemaker both can serve in this purpose. Another option is to use a project planning program, such as Microsoft Project. If you are working remotely, with team members in different locations, be sure to pick a software package that allows you to publish to the web.

Filemaker also provides web hosting with their server software. Both Filemaker and Project will require you to set up your own host server. There are pre-configured hosting servers, such as `FMGateway.com`, that provide complete hosting services for a monthly fee.

Another inexpensive solution is to use a spread sheet in MS Skydrive (formerly Windows Live) or Google Docs. They are free, but lack the robustness of dedicated project management software packages.

Key questions of a producer

The producer must keep three questions clear in his or her mind to fulfill his/her duties:

- What are we building? It is important to have an exact answer to this question throughout the development process. The team should have access to up to date documentation at all times.
- Who is building it? The quality of the product is directly related to the skills and talents of the team building it. Be honest and objective when evaluating the team's skill sets. Although, traditionally the producer does not hire and fire team members, it is the producer's responsibility to keep upper management informed of any personnel change recommendations.
- How will we build it? Software development, including games, has proven procedures: we suggest you do some research on the most popular techniques and talk to your team. They may have used one or two in the past and may have suggestions.

As we will see in the next section, the producer needs several distinctive skills to accomplish those duties!

Skills for all!

The skills required by the producer to accomplish his/her duties are as follows:

- **Cat Herding**: The producer's key skill is that of cat herder or human relations management. A development team is made up of a wide variety of personalities that think about solutions to problems in a very different way: a programmer may have a different approach to an artist. The producer's primary goal is to keep this group of individuals functioning as a team. A good catchphrase is "commitment over ego". The producer can't let personal pride cloud their judgment or let a dispute with a team mate derail the project.
- **Scheduling**: The producer writes and maintains the project schedule, so it is very important he/she understands how successors work: task A is dependent on task B which is dependent on task C. He/she must be able to arrange a correct and effective working pipeline.
- **Budgeting**: Along with making a schedule, the producer will write up a budget. This is especially important when using outside parties or independent contractors to supply assets, such as graphics and sound. It will fall on the producer's shoulders to negotiate bids with these suppliers. The producer must monitor costs to make sure the project stays in budget. A typical problem is that a team requests numerous changes to an asset, such as the graphic of a character. Sometimes, it is the producer's job to say "it's good enough".
- **Production Management**: After the schedule and budget are set, the producer makes sure milestones are hit, and that the game's quality is as high as the schedule and budget allow. A useful tool for this is regular team meetings, where completed work can be reviewed by the team and milestones set for the next meeting.

  A word of warning on team meeting: have an agenda written up ahead of time and circulate this to the team prior to the meeting. This will help keep the meeting on track and as brief as possible. Remember, while in a meeting, little or no actual work is getting done.
- **Arbitrate**: As with any group effort, there will be disputes within the team. The producer needs to be on top of any possible conflict and should find a resolution as quickly as possible. Remember that you have a team of brilliant people who may not have the best social skills. Be kind, but firm in your decisions. The success of the project rests with your management skills.

- **Negotiating**: The producer is responsible for any contract negotiations with publishers, marketers, financiers, and the like. Learn how to read a contract; lack of this skill alone can turn a great project into failure. When in doubt, do research! Talk to a lawyer if you can afford one. An entire book could be written on this subject: look online for sample contracts. If you don't understand something in the document, ask.
- **Quality Assurance expert**: The producer will be responsible for finding competent testers, as well as scheduling the testing around project milestones. The producer is responsible for getting the testing results to the correct people so that any necessary fixes can be implemented.

All the tasks the game producer accounts for, is shown in the following figure:

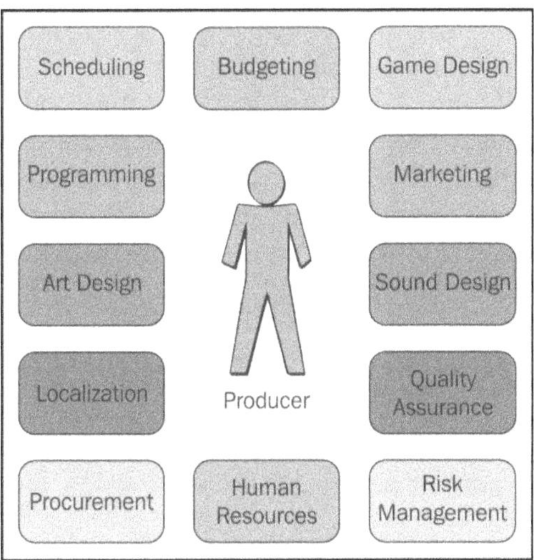

Who is the producer?

You may have deduced that there is a lot to learn on the job. Luckily, other professionals have figured this out and education in this role is available through institutions of higher learning. Many colleges and universities offer certification in Software Production Management as well as Computer Science.

Business administration is an obvious choice, but also training in game design and development, production and more specialized courses in animation, music, or scriptwriting can help to gain a foothold in the industry.

It is definitely worth considering spending the time and money on nailing down the basic skills before joining the school of hard knocks. It will save you money and can pay for itself during your first project from the mistakes you've avoided.

As a producer, be prepared for a high level of stress, lack of sleep, and possible burnout. You are everything to the team and they will look to you for solutions, resolutions, and endless snacks and drinks. Along the high demands come great rewards; however, the satisfaction of a successful product is priceless.

So keep smiling, get as much sleep as you can along with some exercise and a healthy diet. Take up a sport, learn to meditate, find some old comedies on the tube. Find healthy ways to relax and stay balanced.

There is a prime example of this from a project one of the authors worked on, a few years ago. He took the position of producer with a couple of fellows who had financing, but little game production experience. He arranged for a seasoned team with many games under their belts to handle all aspects of the project.

Unfortunately, the partners decided that they would save some money by handling some of the asset production themselves. They tackled a challenging area: motion capture, and character rigging. After they delivered the goods, the programmer determined that formats were wrong for a mobile app; the game choked on all the data in the files. Fixing the files raised the cost over what the developer was going to charge; a classic example of false economy. Eventually, the game did go to market and it was fun, but it was late and over budget. This could have been avoided by checking with the developer on what their requirements were, instead assuming that the bosses knew best.

More on the role and tasks of a game producer can be found at the following link:

`http://www.gamecareerguide.com/features/1009/producing_a_videogame_products_people_and_processes.php?page=3.`

The sound designer

The sound designer is the person responsible for creating all music and sound effects for a game.

The thing that is most expected from the sound designer is to provide the game with a unique and distinct sound that can make a difference in the player's involvement in the game he's playing.

There is one distinctive factor that makes the job of a game sound designer different from that of his closest relative, the audio designer for movies, which is randomness.

In games, there is never (or should never be) a total control on the exact sequence of events that will be triggered by the player. This is the reason why sound design in games tends to be based on things that may or should happen, rather than what will happen next. As a fact, sound in games is usually broken down into chunks that can then be played as needed.

Though audio is an important feature in games, there are two main reasons to consider the sound designer role less relevant for the purpose of this chapter on the mobile development team.

The first is that the sound designer is rarely a permanent member of the development team working on a game, and audio in games is generally added during the final steps of production. For the most part of development, games are worked on and tested with just audio placeholders. More likely, the audio designer is hired as a contract employee during the last phase of development.

The second is that audio is not as important as other features of a mobile game due to the distinctive kind of fruition of mobile games. As they run on handheld devices, mobile games are likely played outdoors or in crowded locations, such as bus and metro stations. Unless the player wears headphones, the music and sound effects of the game are not very much appreciated. In many cases, the player himself/herself will deactivate sound and sound effects to not bother other people around him/her (or be caught playing by his/her teacher, for example!).

Creating music and sound fx

It is not very easy to make a full list of the tools of a sound designer. Sounds can be produced with many different techniques and tools and their creation requires operations, such as playing musical instruments, recording from a source, mixing, and then editing the sounds with software.

A sound designer works with several tools, such as musical instruments, everyday objects that produce specific sounds, microphones, recording devices, sound libraries, and digital audio workstations.

Sound libraries are an important asset for a sound designer, because they provide already made sound effects that can be mixed together to get original sounds and music. Some of these include the East West Quantum Symphonic Library, Sonic Implants, Garritan, and ProjectSam Symphobia.

The following is a list of basic equipment that a sound designer should have at his/her disposal:

- A multi track **digital audio workstation** (**DAW**) for PC and or MAC. There are several such programs and it is impossible to list all of them. We can mention: Garage Band (which is very cheap), Logic Pro, Reaper (which is very cheap) or Sound Forge, Magix, Pro Tools, and Cubase. You can search on the Internet to find out more about the specific features of each of them.
- A two track audio editor, such as Audacity (free license).
- A portable hard disk recorder, if you can afford it.
- Sound libraries of pre-made music and sounds.
- Software to keep libraries organized, such as iTunes.

The following figure represents the working station of a professional sound editor:

Audio skills and tasks

As a freelance audio contractor and the one and only person on the team who knows anything about sound, the sound designer is expected to cover all aspects of sound for games: composing music, creating special effects, mixing, scripting audio events, managing problems of audio formats, and memory allocation issues related to the game audio. The sound designer must be ready to deal with different kinds of problems every day to accomplish his/her task. He/she is also expected to discuss with other team members about any decision that can have an impact on the audio assets he is delivering for the project. As you may understand, this means a lot of responsibility for a single person!

It goes without saying that, the sound designer must be a person with music talents. He/she needs to know how to play at least one musical instrument, how to compose original music, how to record sounds, how to edit them and most importantly, he must be able to convey emotions through music and sounds.

A less obvious, but still very useful skill is that the sound designer must possess some basic programming capabilities, especially the most commonly used APIs.

Scripting proficiency is a very valuable resource too. It can be of help in better understanding the needs of the programmer for specific tasks and help him/her (or the game designer) with the implementation of audio events in the game, should they be overburdened with other tasks.

Schools of sound production

Though music talents and a strong interest in music are necessary to trigger the career of a sound designer, a background in audio from an accredited college or university is very important to be considered for a position on a project. Music production, sound engineering, recording techniques, post production and editing are the necessary theoretical requirements to be able to work on a game development team and take care of audio.

Then experience comes into play, which is, as usual, the most important thing! Try to get involved in projects, and experiment with tools and musical instruments if you are interested in making audio for games, or find someone who can prove his\her skills with a good portfolio of self made sounds and music for your team.

Audio personality

As with any other creative personality, a good sound designer should possess an attitude for experimenting. Sound editing, in particular, requires a lot of creativity in the way different (and sometimes unexpected!) sounds are mixed together to obtain that specific "door crack" effect you are searching for. A sound designer should never be scared of trying something completely new.

He must also have that special sensibility to help him create sounds and music that convey the right emotions for any specific in-game situation as he must be empathetic with people, in order to use music and sounds to get to their hearts and take control of their emotions.

Being a good communicator is also fundamental to discuss with the game designer and understand his requests about the specific kind of sounds and music he desires for the game. There is an interesting article about the communication between designer and audio expert we suggest you read, from Gamasutra at: `http://www.gamasutra.com/view/feature/175427/getting_the_most_from_your_sound_php`.

If you are interested in finding resources for audio (game) designers, you can begin with the following link:

`http://www.gamesounddesign.com/articles.html`.

Summary

We have described the composition of the mobile development team, the key roles that need to be covered, and explained the commitment required to develop games.

Then we analyzed each role in the team, providing information on the tools and duties of each one, and examined the characteristics of their personalities.

We also provided Web references to examine in more depth each role and tables with salary expectations for key roles in a mobile indie development team.

In the next chapter, we will delve into the intricacies of the creation of graphic assets for mobile games. What are the tools and the techniques used by game artists? What kind of 2D and 3D assets must be created and how? What are the tricks to save system memory when producing graphic assets?

Follow us to the next chapter to find the answers to these questions!

3
Graphics for Mobile

Videogames strongly rely on graphics. The production of graphic assets for mobile games poses several challenges to game artists, mostly dependent on the necessity to both create nice-looking and appealing graphics while dealing with reduced screen dimensions and limited memory allocation. In this chapter we will describe how to create 2D and 3D assets for mobile games, what software packages and techniques can be used and what file formats support graphics for mobile games.

In this chapter, we will cover the following topics:

- Raster and vector graphics
- Graphics file formats
- Game videos and cinematics
- Software to create graphics for games
- 2D game assets
- 3D game assets
- Character design for mobile games
- Interface and HUD for mobile games graphics

After gameplay quality, graphics are the most important factor in selling a game. Some have argued that good graphics are the most important factor in impulse buying, since most of the time a gameplay demo is not available. It sure looks good, it must be good.

This has been an ongoing discussion for decades, notably with the release of two games in 1990: *Wing Commander* by Chris Roberts and *Balance of Power* by Chris Crawford. Wing Commander had cutting edge graphics with light game play and storyline.

The following figure represents a screenshot from Wing Commander (source: *Moby Games*).

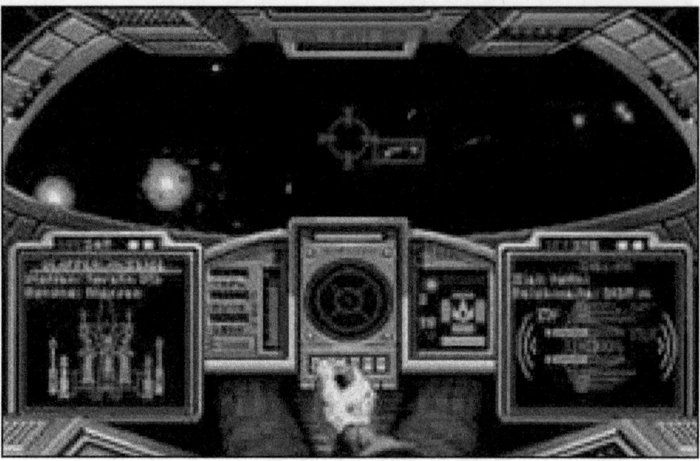

Source: Moby Games

On the other hand, Balance of Power had brilliant and deep game play but amateurish graphics. At that year's Game Developers' conference, a debate (to put it mildly) ensued between the the two developers. Given limited resources, which is more important: content (game play) or context (graphics and sound) to the success of a game?

The following figure is a screenshot from Balance of Power (source: Moby Games):

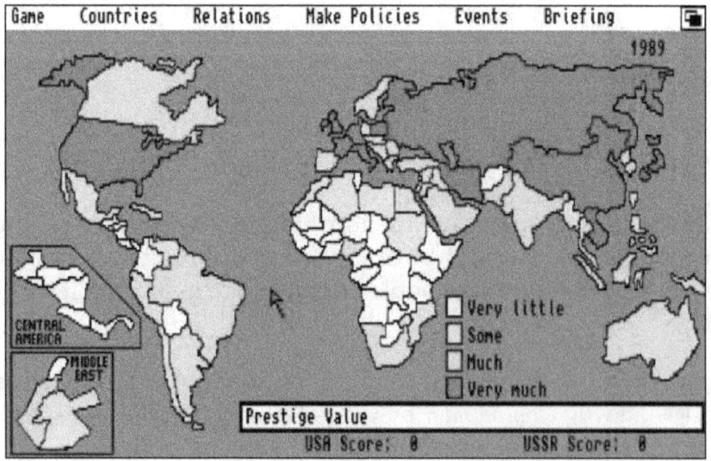

Source: Moby games

At present, hardware capabilities have increased enough to allow both, with proper planning. The production of graphic assets for mobile games requires several gimmicks to make things work properly. Mobile devices have, in fact, relatively limited hardware capabilities: they lack the computational power of PCs and consoles. Since games give the most stress on the hardware capabilities they run on, it is very important to have assets that minimize the requirements while providing an optimal result.

Another important aspect that must be taken into consideration for mobile games is that, differently from home consoles and PCs, handheld devices rely on their battery. The more computationally expensive the app (or game), the shorter the battery life.

There's no point in having a beautiful game running on the device, if it runs for a few minutes and then the device shuts off. Again, optimization of a game's system requirements is a key factor, starting with graphics.

The hardware of today's devices varies very much from one model to the other, so that for a game to run smoothly on the highest number of devices, it must have the lowest possible computational requirements.

With so many different mobile phones available, each with its own hardware configuration, it can be a hard struggle to have your game running smoothly on the highest number of devices, which is mandatory for it to be profitable.

Fortunately, there are ways to overcome such obstacles. A good starting point is comparing the hardware of different mobile phones. The following link points to one such site:

`http://www.mobiledia.com/phones/compare/compare.php`

First, several techniques have been developed to allow the production of quality graphics that minimize the hardware requirements for games.

Second, technological development constantly pushes forward the hardware capabilities of mobile devices, and there are several models today that are equipped with a **Graphic Processing Unit** (**GPU**), a piece of hardware that specifically takes care of computing graphics. This way, the mobile phone's CPU is relieved from taking care of all the calculations required by a game, and as a result, games can run smooth and have excellent graphics at the same time.

Pixels and vectors

As we said in the *The game artist* section in *Chapter 2, The Mobile Indie Team*, a game artist's duties involve the creation of graphic assets with both 2D and 3D techniques. The decision whether to use 2D or 3D graphics is made at a game design level.

Generally speaking, most mobile blockbusters are 2D games. There are several reasons for that: 2D games tend to be easier to play and rely on simple mechanics, which is a plus when targeting occasional players. Playing mobile games is usually a time-limited diversion, something you do while you are waiting for something else (a person, a bus, your turn in a line, and so on). Simple gameplay mechanics better fit such occasions and that's why mobile games, such as Doodle Jump, Fruit Ninja, or Angry Birds are so popular.

2D games also require less computational power and they can run smoothly on low-end devices. Even though developing a high-end-device-only game with excellent photorealistic graphics is a good way to show the potential of a new technology and the ability of a team of developers, when going to market, the higher the potential number of people who can play your game, the better the chances that you can get a profit from it. Not all the people out there possess the latest and most powerful devices available.

When drawing 2D assets, an artist has two options to consider. 2D graphics can in fact be created using two different techniques: pixel art (or bitmap art) and vector graphics.

Pixels

The pixel art refers to a technique used since the early stages of videogame making, and consists of drawing characters, game objects, and backgrounds by drawing on every single pixel of the final bitmap.

Since the computational power to manage graphics was reduced and the drawing tools were not very sophisticated at that time, this was an optimal choice to produce nice graphics in small sized files. The main drawback with this technique is that bitmap images cannot be scaled without losing the details and quality, due to a phenomenon called **anti-aliasing**. You can find more information on this on Wikipedia at: `http://en.wikipedia.org/wiki/Aliasing`

The following is a screenshot of a popular mobile game called Sword and Sorcery made with pixel art technique:

Vectors

As the computational power of gaming devices improved and better drawing tools became available, artists turned to a different technique called vector graphics. In vector graphics, every line drawn by the artist is transformed into a mathematical function. As such, vector graphics can be scaled at will without any loss of details. Software, such as Illustrator and Flash, work with vector graphics to suit the needs of developing digital artworks for the Web and print use and almost all web-based games make use of vector graphics to allow full scalability of the graphic assets. On the other hand, vector graphics files tend to be larger than their bitmap counterparts.

The advent of mobile games gave new life to the earlier technique of pixel art. The reduced dimensions of mobile phone screens and the smaller size of graphic files made with this technique turned pixel art into a useful tool to produce nice looking graphics of smaller file size, when compared to the more advanced vector graphics.

The graphic file formats

There are literally hundreds of image file types. The PNG, JPEG, and GIF file formats are most often used to display the most common image types. They are listed as follows, divided by family.

Raster graphics

The following file formats are from the family of raster graphics:

- **Joint Photographic Experts Group** (**JPEG**): This is a compression method; JPEG-compressed images are usually stored in the **JPEG File Interchange Format** (**JFIF**) file format. JPEG applies lossy compression to images, which can result in a significant reduction of the file size. The amount of compression can be specified, and the amount of compression affects the visual quality of the result. When not too great, the compression does not noticeably detract from the image's quality, but JPEG files suffer generational degradation when repeatedly edited and saved.
- **Tagged Image File Format** (**TIFF**): This is a flexible format that normally saves eight bits or 16 bits per color (red, green, and blue) for 24-bit and 48-bit totals, respectively, usually using either the TIFF or TIF filename extension. TIFF's flexibility can be both an advantage and disadvantage, since a reader reads for every type of TIFF file that does not exist. TIFFs can be lossy and lossless; some offer relatively good lossless compression for bi-level (black and white) images. TIFF image format is not widely supported by web browsers. TIFF remains widely accepted as a photograph file standard in the printing business. TIFF can handle device-specific color spaces, such as the CMYK color model defined by a particular set of printing press inks.
- **RAW:** This refers to a family of raw image formats that are available as options on some digital cameras. These formats usually use a lossless or nearly lossless compression, and produce file sizes much smaller than the TIFF formats of full-size processed images from the same cameras. Although there is a standard raw image format, (ISO 12234-2, TIFF/EP), the raw formats used by most cameras are not standardized or documented, and differ among camera manufacturers.
- **Graphics Interchange Format** (**GIF**): This is limited to an 8-bit palette, or 256 colors. This makes the GIF format suitable for storing the graphics with relatively few colors, such as simple diagrams, shapes, logos, and cartoon style images. The GIF format supports animation and is still widely used to provide image animation effects. It also uses a lossless compression that is more effective when large areas have a single color, and ineffective for detailed images or dithered images.

- **BMP**: This file format (Windows bitmap) handles graphics files within the Microsoft Windows OS. Typically, the BMP files are uncompressed, hence they are large; the advantage is their simplicity and wide acceptance in Windows programs.
- **Portable Network Graphics (PNG)**: This file format was created as the free, open-source successor to GIF. The PNG file format supports 8-bit paletted images (with optional transparency for all palette colors) and 24-bit true-color (16 million colors) or 48-bit true-color with and without alpha channel; while GIF supports only 256 colors and a single transparent color. Compared to JPEG, PNG excels when the image has large, uniformly colored areas. Thus lossless PNG format is best suited for pictures still under edition, and the lossy formats, such as JPEG, are best for the final distribution of photographic images, because in this case, the JPG files are usually smaller than the PNG files.

  PNG provides a patent-free replacement for GIF and can also replace many common uses of TIFF. Indexed-color, grayscale, and true-color images are supported, plus an optional alpha channel.

  PNG is designed to work well in online viewing applications, such as web browsers, so it is fully stream able with a progressive display option. PNG is robust, providing both full-file integrity checking and simple detection of common transmission errors. Also, PNG can store gamma and chromaticity data for improved color matching on heterogeneous platforms. For more details refer to `http://en.wikipedia.org/wiki/Graphics_file_formats`.

Vector graphics

As opposed to the raster image formats discussed previously (where the data describes the characteristics of each individual pixel), vector image formats contain a geometric description which can be rendered smoothly at any desired display size.

At some point, all vector graphics must be rasterized in order to be displayed on digital monitors. However, vector images can be displayed with analog CRT technology, such as that used in some electronic test equipment, medical monitors, radar displays, laser shows, and early videogames. Plotters are printers that use vector data rather than pixel data to draw graphics.

- **Computer Graphics Metafile** (**CGM**): This is a file format for 2D vector graphics, raster graphics, and text and is defined by ISO/IEC8632. All graphical elements can be specified in a textual source file that can be compiled into a binary file or one of the two text representations. CGM provides a means of graphics data interchange for computer representation of 2D graphical information independent from any particular application, system, platform, or device. It has been adapted to some extent in the areas of technical illustration and professional design, but has largely been superseded by formats, such as Scalable Vector Graphics (SVG) and Drawing Exchange Formats (DXF).
- **Scalable Vector Graphics** (**SVG**): This is a 2D graphics format with properties similar to CGM that uses an XML-based text format. Like CGM, it supports vector and raster graphics as well as text. SVG is supported by many popular graphics applications, such as Inkscape or Adobe Illustrator. All major web browsers and most smartphones include SVG rendering support.
- **Drawing Exchange Formats** (**DXF**): This is a computer-aided design (CAD) data file that provides a bridge from Autodesk's AutoCAD DWF format to other CAD programs. DXF supports both ASCII and binary versions. It shares many of the properties of CGM, including interactivity, portability, and compressibility. Due to inherent limitations in the file structure, DXF is being phased out in favor of DWF and SVG.

Videos in videogames

The following are the techniques for creating videos in videogames:

- **Full motion video** (**FMV**): This is a videogame narration technique that relies upon pre-recorded video files (rather than sprites, vectors, or 3D models) to display action in the game. While many games feature FMVs as a way to present information during cut scenes, games that are primarily presented through FMVs are referred to as full-motion videogames or interactive movies.

- **QuickTime**: This is a complete cross-platform multimedia architecture that supports creating, producing, and delivering a broad variety of media. QuickTime provides support for the entire process including real-time capture, generating media programmatically, importing and exporting existing media, editing and compositing, compression, delivery, and playback.
- **MPEG-2**: This is a standard for the generic coding of moving pictures and associated audio information. It describes a combination of lossy video compression and lossy audio data compression methods which permits storage and transmission of movies using currently available storage media and transmission bandwidth.

Software to create game graphics

The following software are used for creating the game graphics:

- **Photoshop**: When dealing with image editing tasks, Photoshop is universally considered the best available software. It can work with and export to any kind of image format, it offers the largest selection of tools to edit images and an endless number of tutorials are available on the Internet to learn anything you may need to do with it.

  All this power, on the other hand, comes at a price. The full Photoshop C6 license costs $699!

- **DeBabelizer**: Photoshop is not the only choice, naturally. Other options are available. One that may be not popular but which is very good, especially for compressing images, is DeBabelizer (`http://www.equilibrium.com/debabelizer/`). It is an image editing software with almost the same capabilities of Photoshop, but it creates lighter `*.png` files.
- **GNU Image Manipulation Program** (**GIMP**): Another interesting possibility for those who follow the path of open source software is GIMP. GIMP (`http://www.gimp.org`) is a free image manipulation package that offers anything you may need to produce high quality graphics. It even supports distinctive image formats of its competitors!

  The main advantage of GIMP is that it is completely free, and as any other well-done open source software, it is supported by a large community of aficionados who provide plugins, hints, and tutorials. The main disadvantage is that GIMP does not have the ease of use of Photoshop. When you work with Photoshop, you understand where all the money you spent for its license went.

- **Adobe Flash**: This is a multimedia and software platform used for authoring vector graphics, animations, games, and Rich Internet Applications which can be viewed, played, and executed in Adobe Flash Player. Flash is frequently used to add streamed video or audio players, advertisement, and interactive multimedia content to web pages.

  Flash manipulates vector and raster graphics to provide animation of text, drawings, and still images. It supports bidirectional streaming of audio and video, and it can capture user input via mouse, keyboard, microphone, and camera. Flash applications and animations can be programmed using the object oriented language, called ActionScript. Adobe Flash Professional is the most popular and user-friendly authoring tool for creating the Flash content, which also supports automation via the **JavaScript Flash language** (**JSFL**).

- **3D Studio Max/Maya**: When 3D graphics come into play, 3D Studio Max and Maya are the obvious choices, as they are recognized as industry standards. They are well-known by artists, their export formats are included in most popular game engines, and they allow production of the best 3D graphics and animations available. They have a price, too: both 3D Studio Max and Maya license costs €3,900 each, VAT excluded!
- **Milkshape 3D**: For those who are not willing to pay for 3D software, there are two options available. One is Milkshape 3D (`www.milkshape3d.com`), a shareware software which only allows low-poly 3D modeling, and is a favorite for indie game developers. It doesn't have the capabilities of more professional tools, but it's free and the community supporting it is strong and offers several tutorials.
- **Blender**: The other option is Blender (`www.blender.org`), an open source tool which is getting more and more popular and has almost the same capabilities of 3D Studio Max. The main difference is that Blender cannot be exported in `*.fbx` format. The `*.fbx` format is a very useful graphics format which allows to export a 3D model together with its materials, animations, and other useful stuff. Popular game engines, such as Unity 3D, support the `*.fbx` format; so lacking this option is a disadvantage for Blender. But at least it it's free!
- **Zbrush\Mudbox**: These software packages consist of digital sculpting tools that are used to create extremely detailed high-poly models. They basically use brushes, like the ones of Photoshop, to add polygons and create details on a 3D model. The details of the high-poly models are then exported as normal maps (explained later) or displacement maps and then used on low-poly models to fake a large number of details on a model with few polygons.

Both ZBrush and Mudbox allow full integration with software, such as 3D Studio Max and Maya, among others. The license cost is $699 for ZBrush and $825 for Mudbox.

Resolution issues with mobile games

When dealing with resolution, mobile phones present the highest variability. Classic phones, those which used to be the most common devices some years ago, had screen resolutions of 176x208 pixels, while recent iOS and Android based smartphones can range anywhere between 320x240 to 1920x1080 pixels for the latest Samsung Galaxy S4.

There are even more options when taking tablets into consideration. Apple iPad screens range between 1024x768 of first generation models to the 2048x1536 of third and fourth generation. The Asus Transformer Pad Infinity TF700, the fastest Android-based tablet available as we write this book, has a screen resolution of 1920x1200 pixels; the Samsung Galaxy Tab and the Google Nexus 7 have both a screen resolution of 1280x800 pixels. The list of options is very long.

This exceptional variety within mobile devices poses two problems.

The first is with smaller screens of older cell phone models: when the screen size is so reduced, every pixel is important. An artist must be very careful when deciding what to draw and why, since inefficient use of graphics can create noise on smaller screens which negatively affects gameplay.

The second order of problems arise when porting games designed to run on a specific set of phones to other devices, and mainly affect the user interface of your game. As we said, Android devices offer the highest variability: if you don't plan in advance and take some precautions when designing your game for Android, you can find yourself spending a lot of time adapting graphic assets and user interface from one device to another.

Fortunately, Google offers several well documented tools to help developers deal with such problems, and starting from Version 3.0, Android introduced elements called fragments which support a more dynamic and flexible UI design for larger screens.

You can find what is considered the Bible of Google's UI design documentation at `http://developer.android.com/guide/practices/screens_support.html`.

iOS devices, on the other hand, are much more consistent and have limited variability when compared to Android devices. Designing separate UI for iPhone and iPad and using vector graphics is enough to ensure that your games will work on either device.

2D graphic assets

In the following section, we will describe the most important types of 2D assets used in the game development.

Sprites

Sprites can be defined as game objects that have a role in the gameplay of a title: the main character (we use the word character here in its broadest meaning: a space ship is a character), enemies, bullets, and collectibles are all examples of sprites. Sprites are usually animated, which means that the artist draws a sequence of frames representing the key positions the game object assumes during the animation for each animated character and for each specific animation. The final result is an image called spritesheet that contains all the animations of a game character. The following figure represents part of the spritesheet of Super Mario Bros for the NES.

Once the sequences are made, it's up to the programmer to invoke the correct sequence for each desired animation through code. The 2D-oriented game engines, such as GameMaker (`http://www.yoyogames.com/studio`), provide easy sprite animation management tools. We will discuss the topic of game engines with more detail in *Chapter 8, Mobile Game Engines*.

To reduce the size of the file of images used in a game, there is a very popular and long-used technique which consists of cutting down the number of colors (color depth) used in the image: the fewer the colors, the smaller the file size. Such an operation can be automatically done by common image editors, such as Photoshop. Since cutting down the number of colors of an image can result in a speckled image, it is a good practice to hand-retouch the image before reducing the number of colors to get the file size reduction while keeping a good image quality.

The following figure represents the result of a progressive so called palettization of an image from full-color to only two colors. With some additional hand-retouching, it is possible to obtain a smaller file size without losing too much quality.

Source: http://en.wikipedia.org/wiki/Color_depth

Backgrounds

Backgrounds are the images that stay behind the game objects of a game. They are very important because they represent the environment where the game action takes place and strongly affect the visual appeal of a title. If your game doesn't have nice backgrounds, players may be turned off and they won't download it and play it.

Depending on the gameplay characteristics of a game, it can have fixed or scrolling backgrounds. Fixed backgrounds are generally used on puzzle games or titles where the game action takes place in a single screen. Tetris, Puzzle Bobble, and Pang are examples of games with fixed backgrounds.

In this definition, the term "fixed" only refers to the fact that the background of the game doesn't scroll. It is possible in fact that animation occurs in the background of the game. Anyway, if no scrolling is involved, we call it a fixed-background game.

Scrolling backgrounds, on the other hand, is a feature of a game where the screen represents only a portion of the total game level. Super Mario Bros, R-Type, or even soccer games where only a portion of the playfield is represented at a time, are examples of scrolling games.

In a 2D game, scrolling can both occur on the horizontal and vertical axis or both at once. In Super Mario Bros, for example, the character can run from left to right (and vice versa), but he can also jump on platforms to climb to a higher section of a level. As Mario navigates the game level, the game camera follows his movements, showing a portion of the level corresponding to the character's position at any time.

When scrolling backgrounds are involved, there are several techniques that are used to obtain the effect of continuity of the background image and to give the illusion of depth to players.

Tiles

Tiles are images that are cut so that they can be put one close to each other without the player noticing the end of the first image and the beginning of the second. All images are then put close to one another to obtain a larger composition, called tileset, which contains all the elements needed to create the backgrounds of the game. Most available game engines allow using tiles to create seamless backgrounds for your games. The advantage of this technique is that it saves system memory for the creation of your game levels; a tileset is a relatively small image that can be used to create endless levels through the repetition of its elements.

The following is a figure that shows a tileset to create a Zelda-like 2D game (courtesy of WesleyFG from `http://wesleyfg.webs.com/tiles.html`).

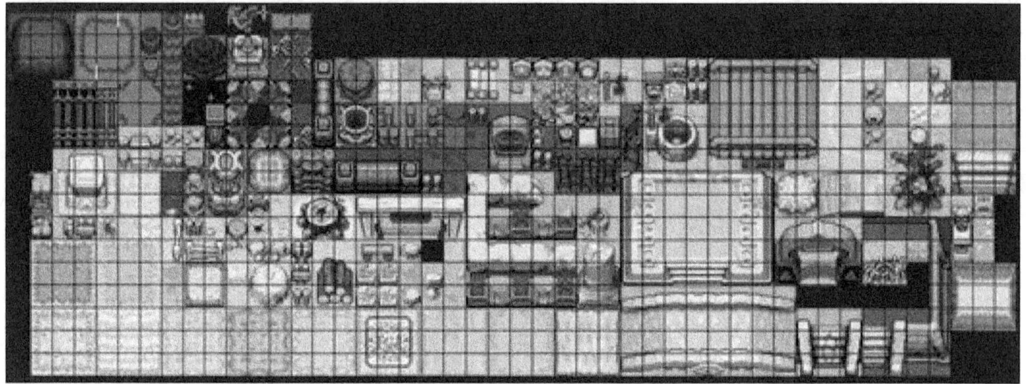

The parallax motion

The parallax motion is a technique that consists of putting different images on separate layers and then letting the code scroll those layers at different speeds. The layers closer to the player character scroll faster, while those farther from the character scroll slower. The final effect is that the character and the elements close to it move at a different speed than the more distant elements. If you have ever travelled in a train or in a car watching the landscape from the window, you know what we are talking about. When used correctly, this simple technique grants a very nice looking illusion of depth for a 2D scrolling game.

Masking

The last technique we would like to describe for the creation of nice 2D assets for your games is masking. Masking is a technique to edit images that allows the game engine to display parts of those images as transparent.

It consists of putting your sprites on a homogenous background of some specific color that is not used for any other graphic asset of the game, then setting that color as transparent in the game engine. The engine will show the sprite, hiding the transparent part of the image.

There are actually two kinds of transparency which are used in game development.

- **Full transparency**: This means that each part of the image is either visible or invisible. To use full transparency, it is necessary to reduce the number of colors of the image to 256 and then set one color as the transparent one in the game engine. The engine will show all the colors of the image, except the one you set as transparent.
- **Alpha transparency**: This is a more refined technique that allows having a full range of transparency for an image, from fully opaque to fully transparent. For example, it allows representing part of an image as if you were looking at it through a colored glass. To obtain the effect, a fourth channel, called the alpha channel, needs to be added to the already existing channels of an image (red, green, and blue). A value of zero (black) in the alpha channel means that that pixel is fully transparent, while a value of one (white) means that it is fully opaque. Any intermediate value represents semi-transparency. A semi-transparent pixel is composed partly with the image color and partly with the background color, depending on the specific value set in the alpha channel of that pixel.

Both full transparency and alpha transparency are supported by the `*.png` image format, so save your graphic assets as `*.png` when you need part of them to be transparent.

The following figure represents a texture for a plant and its alpha channel:

Now that we're done describing the fundamental techniques for creating 2D assets for your games, we can delve into the more complex field of 3D modeling, animation, and skinning (the process of defining which part of a 3D model is covered by which part of a 2D texture).

Much additional and useful information about the creation and editing of 2D assets can be found on the Internet. You can begin your research from: `http://www.gamedev.net/page/index.html`

3D graphic assets

The advent of 3D graphics offered a brand new set of possibilities for game developers and posed new problems for the production of graphic assets.

As mobile phones incorporated the hardware required to run 3D games, mainly Graphic Processing Units designed to take care of graphics, mobile game developers turned to this new technology and began developing successful 3D games for mobile devices.

3D models

The production of 3D assets for games begins with the creation of a 3D model of a game object using software, such as 3D Studio Max, Maya, Blender, or any other you like. This is usually a basic 3D model with no detail. This model is then exported in a sculpting software, such as ZBrush or Mudbox, to convert it into an extremely detailed 3D model, or high poly, a very detailed asset, thanks to the use of thousands of polygons (depending on the importance of that specific game asset).

In the following figure, a beautifully detailed 3D model made with ZBrush is shown:

The high-poly model is first used to create a normal map (or a displacement map) and then turned into its low-poly counterpart: a 3D model that uses fewer polygons and thus, requires less computational resources to run in real time and produces a smaller file size.

This is where the artist's skills come into play. He must be very good to obtain an optimal result when producing a low-poly model that visually matches the quality of its high-poly counterpart.

There is a specific software, such as Polygon Cruncher, that automatizes the conversion of a high-poly model into a low-poly, but to obtain an optimal result it is always best to do such things manually!

The following figure, taken from Wikipedia (`http://en.wikipedia.org/wiki/Low_poly`), represents the procedure to get a detailed low-poly model using a normal map created from the high-poly counterpart.

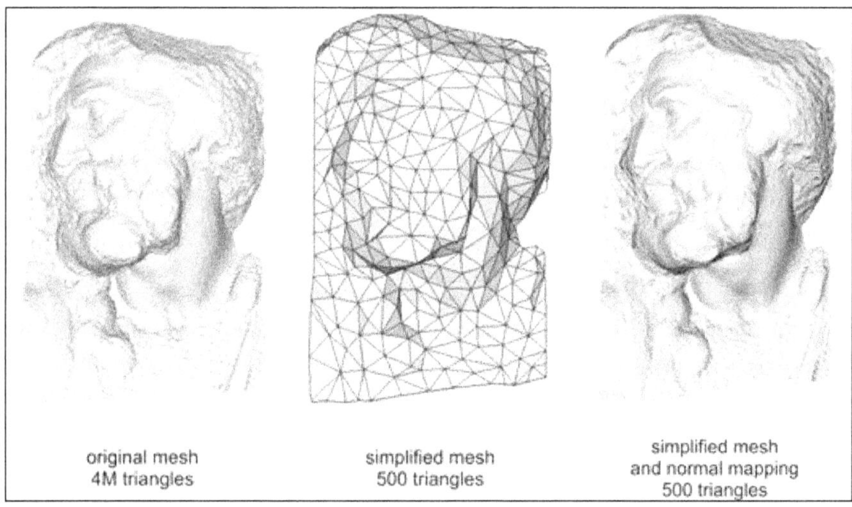

Source: http://en.wikipedia.org/wiki/Low_poly

Texturing

Once a model has been created, it is necessary to put one or more textures on the mesh. The mesh of a 3D model only represents its basic geometry which constitutes a collection of polygons. The texture is the image that covers the 3D mesh to give it its correct aspect for the game.

The following is the figure of a simple, flat texture for a wall made of bricks:

Materials

Texturing a model is not enough to bring it to life. As we said, textures represent the visual aspect of a 3D model and generally, don't take into consideration the way light interacts with the surface of the model.

To make a 3D model look nicer, it is also important to represent the way light interacts with its surface. A vest doesn't reflect light as a metal weapon does, for example. As we said in *The game artist* section in *Chapter 2, The Mobile Indie Team*, to recreate the interactions of light with the surface of a mesh, artists make use of assets, called materials.

A material is a collection of data that define both the generic visual aspect of a model and the way its surface interacts with light.

A material is usually a collection of at least two maps. The first map is the texture of the mesh and the second is the bump map, a black and white texture that defines where the surface is concave and where it is convex. With just two such maps, the look of a 3D model can definitely be improved.

Bump mapping is also a technique that saves system memory for a 3D model, reducing the number of required polygons to make it look like it is actually modeled.

Let's take the example of the wall texture displayed previously. By adding a bump map to the material of the wall, as we said, it is possible to fake the concaveness and convexity of the wall.

You first model the wall as a flat parallelepiped (a three-dimensional figure formed by six parallelograms). Then you create a material for the wall, which makes use of two maps. The first is a texture where the bricks of the wall are simply drawn. The second is a black and white bump map that represents the protrusions and indentations of the bricks composing the wall. Both the maps are included in the material and then applied to the 3D mesh. The final result is a wall that looks like it is fully modeled, but instead, it's just a flat parallelepiped with a nice looking material.

The following figure represents a bump map that can be added to the wall material to make it look more realistic:

To get a better result when using low-poly models, game artists, as we said, use normal mapping. It is an improvement over simple bump mapping because it creates a map of how light bounces on the surface of the high-poly model, which is more detailed, and apply that map to the low-poly model. The main difference between a bump map and a normal one is that normal maps represent the refraction of light in the 3D world, because they allow the re-direction of light bouncing on a surface according to the orientation of its pixels in the 3D world. Normal mapping is very useful to fake the details of a high-poly model on a low-poly one, but requires the original model to get the normal map to be fully detailed (as we said, these high-poly models are created with sculpting tools like ZBrush or Mudbox).

The following figure represents a normal map to be added to the material of the wall instead of the bump map:

The creation of normal maps is a basic skill for any 3D artist and it is a feature available with any modeling software we mentioned. You can learn more about it at `http://en.wikipedia.org/wiki/Normal_mapping`.

The use of materials for 3D models could cover several books by itself. Modeling software and 3D game engines offer a plethora of tools to create amazing materials for your models, for example, animating materials that represent the way snow slowly covers objects in a game environment.

You can find more about it starting from http://www.3d-tutorial.com/.

UV Mapping

It is very likely that the game objects your artists create for a game will not be as simple as a brick wall. Most of the time, they will need to create complex models of irregular game objects, such as cars, space ships, or humanoid characters.

To put a flat texture on a complex 3D model, there is a very popular technique used by artists called UV Mapping. It basically consists of converting the configuration of the polygons of a 3D mesh into a flat plane. The image representing the texture of the model is then aligned to this map, so that each part of the texture covers the corresponding part on the 3D mesh. If you think of a six-faced die and the way you can unfold its faces to get a flat representation of it, you can understand what the UV Map of a 3D mesh is. The operation of converting a 3D model into a plane is commonly called unwrap.

The following figure represents the unwrapping of a cube:

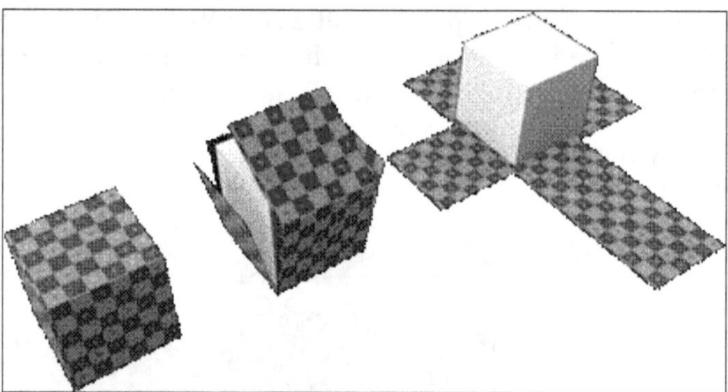

Unwrapping and UV Mapping of a 3D model can be a labor intensive operation, depending on the complexity of the 3D model. It takes time, but still it is a required skill for any 3D modeler. If you want to be a 3D artist, you'd better learn to do it well.

More about the technical aspects of UV Mapping can be found on the Internet at http://en.wikipedia.org/wiki/UV_mapping.

More on textures

Textures do not always need to be simple flat images. To get the final touch for your 3D models in addition to using bump and normal maps, the texture of an important game object, such as the main character of your game, can be "painted" by a 2D artist to represent things, such as the folds and shading of their vest or its pieces of armor. By painting the texture of a 3D model, it is possible to generate a lot of detail for that model which would not be possible to achieve by conventional lighting methods.

In the end, the final decision about which specific techniques to use for detailing 3D models for a game depend on the artistic direction of the project. To recreate realistic objects, such as guns and rifles for a First Person Shooter, you will need several maps for each game asset to get full detailed objects, while for a more cartoon-looking style you can sacrifice details in favor of colors. The producer and game designer, together with the leading artist of your game, are in charge of such matters.

An important aspect that we haven't mentioned yet is that textures must always have dimensions which are a power of two and conform to regular dimensions. There are reasons for that, which depend on how computers manage and process data which we won't explain here. Remember that computers only understand zeros and ones. It is important to stick to this rule!

Though textures don't necessarily need to be square images, still their size must be in the range of 8, 16, 32, 64, 128, 256, 512, 1024, or 2048 (though we suggest, for most mobile devices, to make small use of textures above 512 or 1024 pixels in size, to save system memory. Small screens don't need extra detailed textures.).

Baking

A technique to save computational power to calculate real-time lights for game environments is called baking. It consists of "printing" the shadows generated by the elements which populate a game environment in real time directly on the textures which cover floors and walls and then apply the texture with the baked shadows to the game environment. This way, they can be put in the game engine as objects that don't generate real-time shadows, thus saving power to keep the frame rate of your game as high as possible.

It is important to remember that, to use baking, the objects with baked shadows must be static objects. If you move a crate with a baked shadow, the trick will be revealed to your players and will result in a poor and inconsistent visual experience.

Animations

The techniques to animate 2D and 3D characters are similar and very different at the same time. They both require breaking up each animation in a given (hopefully small) number of key frames and then inserting each frame into a sequence.

The difference is that in 2D animation, the brain of the player fills in the blank spaces between two successive frames at a typical rate of 24 frames per second, creating the illusion of continuity in the animation, while in 3D animation, a tool, usually provided with the modeling software, takes care of interpolating the positions of each part of the model according to a set of rules and parameters between two subsequent positions.

To animate a 3D model, you first need to make its bones, which are the part of the model that is actually animated. Once the model is provided with bones, the mesh of the model is rigged to the bones. This is a delicate operation which can take a lot of time, depending on the importance of that model in the economy of your game and its complexity. Rigging a model means to define which points on the surface of the 3D model follow the movement of each specific bone and the strength of their connection. If a model is not correctly rigged, once you animate it you will see the mesh messing up badly!

For animating humanoid characters, special tools are available, for example, 3D Studio Max has a tool called biped.

The biped is basically a humanoid skeleton made of a given number of bones and their connections. It saves the time needed to create a humanoid skeleton from scratch and allows the user to define both the number of bones and their size.

The following figure represents the 3D Studio Max biped in a typical karate position:

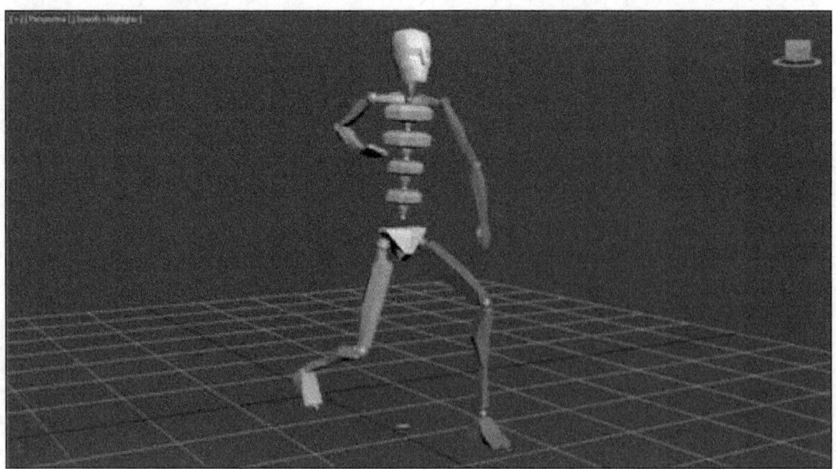

The number of bones is important to define what kind of animations can be created for the character: the number of fingers in the hands, for example, the number of segments for the spine, or the bones to animate a tail, should the character have one.

Scaling the size of the bones, on the other hand, is important to fit the size of the mesh in order to better rig the mesh to its biped.

Once the mesh is provided with bones and is rigged, a model is animated through a sequence of key frames. Each animation is broken down into a number of key positions which represent it. For each key frame, the model is put in a specific position, acting on its bones (the mesh follows accordingly, thanks to its rigging). The software takes care of interpolating the movement of each bone in the model according to a set of rules called inverse kinematics and a set of parameters defined by the user.

Animating 3D characters is no joke! It requires both talent and knowledge of anatomy and the rules of body language. Take a look at any Disney movie to get an idea on how to make objects express emotion through motion.

To stick to the scope of this book, we won't go into further details with regard to 3D animation. Big developers have teams of animators who not only work with modeling software, but also make use of techniques, such as motion capture, if they need to create detailed animations for humanoid characters. It is a branch in the field of 3D computer graphics by itself and we suggest searching on the Internet starting from `http://www.animationarena.com/`.

Designing a character for mobile

As we said, the look and feel of your game will influence your potential players before they even start playing your game. It is thus a general rule to have your graphics match the game's genre: this rule addresses both the creation of the graphic assets for your environments and the character design.

The character design process

The process of designing game characters always starts with the definition of its basic qualities, both visual and character. Use a list of adjectives to create a mental map of both the character and the visual aspect of your character.

The next step is to search for visual references which can represent the adjectives in the mental map. Anything can be a visual reference: shapes, materials, landscapes, and kinetics. Anything that can visually describe a concept related to your game character is a source for the visual aspect of that character.

Once you have a small library of visual references for your character, it is time to start drawing it. A general rule is to begin by drawing basic geometric shapes and compose them to create the outline for your character.

Since the most important thing for small characters that populate mobile games is to have a strong silhouette, don't focus on the fine details of your design at this step: just work on getting a well-balanced, nice-looking outline for your character.

Once you are satisfied with the outline, you can then begin working on its fine details to make it even more distinctive. On the other hand, too many details can add nothing but noise to your design, not to mention the additional time needed to model such details in the case of 3D characters.

Balance is the key; as we said, for mobile games running on small cell phone screens every pixel is important. Put in any detail you feel is important to define your game characters and get rid of everything you don't actually need!

Silhouettes

When designing the character for your game, you want players to immediately differentiate it from anything else in the game and (hopefully) identify with it. A basic way to achieve this goal consists of creating a strong silhouette for your character. A strong silhouette helps your player quickly identify the main character against the backgrounds and tell it apart from the other game objects in the scene. As human beings, we recognize patterns. A strong silhouette represents a pattern that our brain can easily spot so to perceive it as different from anything else in the game to positively affect the gameplay of your title.

A very useful technique to check if your character fits the requirements of good character design is to shade the character black and check if it can be recognized by its silhouette. If the silhouette looks nice and distinctive, you will know that once it will be scaled down to fit the size of the screen of a mobile phone, it will still be well recognizable by your players.

The following figure is the silhouette of a very popular game character. Can you recognize him?

Colors for mobile

The next trick in creating strong characters is to smartly use colors. Since drawings are made of shapes and colors, you cannot create a good drawing if its colors don't match the quality of the shape.

Use a unique palette for your game characters and make their color different from those of the other less relevant game objects of your game. If the main color of your game character is a tone of blue, don't use blue for your game enemies. Once things start moving on screen, the better the player can tell his controlled character apart from the rest, the better the gameplay of your title.

It is also a good practice to create game backgrounds that help the players spot the relevant game objects and focus on them. By using background colors which strongly contrast with the game objects, your players are provided with an optimal gameplay environment to make the best of the game mechanics of your game.

Once you have succeeded in defining the basic shape and palette for your characters and have made them distinctive from other game objects and backgrounds, you can then choose to create the game objects to intentionally get your players confused. You can, for example, have enemies that hide in the background or have a shape or colors similar to that of elements the player must collect. It is an easy and cheap way to add gameplay to a title, but it works if the visual style of your game is designed following the good practices we mentioned.

The user interface and HUD

The user interface is a core aspect of games which is sometimes overlooked until the end of a project. Instead, it has a fundamental role to assure that both the flow and the playability of your game appeals to players and encourages them to keep playing.

For mobile games, the interface requires even more attention. Despite the fact that it is not practical for any game to get players lost in its menus, mobile games run on screens that are both small and different in size from one another, and thus require to display useful gameplay information clearly in a quite small space.

The number of screens that compose the interface of the game must be adequate; it should avoid repetitions and the structure of the screens map must be reasonable and intuitive. Also, you must choose the right font for each menu item.

Another important element of the game interface is the **Head's Up Display** (**HUD**). The HUD is both the graphic frame for the game and the set of information that is constantly displayed on screen to provide the player with the information needed to succeed playing: available ammo for his guns, time left to complete a race or reach a checkpoint, score, available lives, and more.

As this information is constantly displayed on screen during gaming sessions, it is important to be sure that the info is clearly displayed and it doesn't hinder the playability of the game due to the reduced device screen.

The following figure is one of the best HUD ever: the helmet of Samus Aran from Metroid Prime!

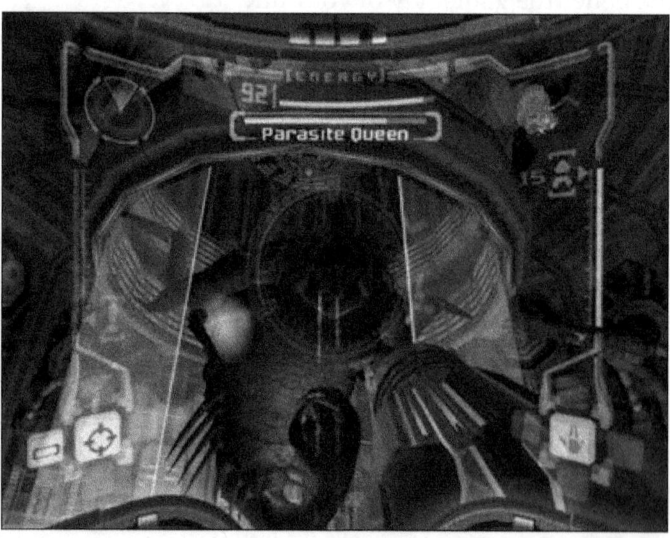

When designing a HUD for a mobile game, game artists not only need to deal with placing all interface elements correctly on screen, so that the info provided is clearly readable; they also have to deal with technical problems, such as scaling the interface appropriately, depending on the different screen resolution of the device the game could run on.

The first order of problems can be resolved at a design level. Creating the right user interface for your game is a matter of studying your game with the designer to set the limits of what specific information the player needs to have permanently displayed on screen, then deciding how to display it smartly, without distracting the player from the actual game.

The second order of problems requires planning in advance. We have said many times that mobile phones have the maximum number of variability with regard to screen size. Planning prevents your artists from having to redraw the interface of your game every time a different device is supported.

Easily put, for iOS devices, which only introduce one new standard with each generation of devices, it is enough to create two different interfaces: one for the iPhone/iPod touch and one for the iPad/iPad Mini. Create it for retina resolution, and then scale it down for non-retina models.

For Android games there's no official standard, so the best choice is to take two or three reference models and design the game interface to fit those models perfectly. When running on screens different from the reference models, the game graphics won't be perfect, but will still work and won't demand too much effort.

Keep a different interface design for Android tablets, also.

Vector graphics automatically scale without any loss of quality and we suggest using them whenever you can.

Summary

In this chapter, we covered the importance of graphics in videogames in general and the challenges specific to creating mobile game graphics.

We reviewed the most common file formats for raster and vector graphics.

We discussed the creation and application of 2D and 3D assets, animation, and the software needed to create them.

Chapter 4, Audio for Mobile, will cover audio for mobile games, including music and sound effects, and we will cover the most effective uses of sound in games and the most popular software to create sounds.

4
Audio for Mobile

Sound design involves specifying, acquiring, manipulating, or generating audio elements. It is employed in a variety of disciplines including video game development. Sound design generally involves modifying recorded audio, such as music and sound effects. In some cases, it may also involve the composition or manipulation of audio to create a desired effect or mood. A person who practices the art of sound design is called a sound designer. For information on sound designer, visit `http://en.wikipedia.org/wiki/Sound_design`.

Sound was once an afterthought in terms of game design; now videogame music is a legitimate industry of its own. Music is one of the many elements of the overall sound design of videogames, where huge leaps have been made in a relatively short time. With the advent of directional and simulated surround sound, game audio became integral to the action itself. Stealth-based games, such as the popular Assassin's Creed series turned the art of listening and eavesdropping into a survival skill in itself. Even early games, such as Tetris and Pac-Man (wacka wacka), earned much of their addictive appeal by getting into your head with thumping, repetitive sound schemes. Every Tetris player will recognize its theme song in the first few bars. Well-designed sound and graphics complement each other to produce rich and enjoyable game play. In this chapter will will cover:

- The history of videogame music
- Recording
- Playback
- Videogame sound types
- Digital audio editors
- Issues of mobile game audio design
- The best practices of mobile game audio design

Digital sound technology

Musical Instrument Digital Interface (MIDI) and digital technology helped to drive the rapid evolution of sound design during the 1980s and 1990s. Also, the Internet is a great resource for sound designers, allowing them to acquire source material quickly, easily, and cheaply. Advances in digital audio editing software have enabled sound designers to create and modify samples on their own.

Analog versus digital

Sound recording involves recording an original set of sound waves and reproducing those waves in a variety of ways. The two basic recording methods are called analog and digital. Both types of recordings require a sensor, such as a microphone or an electric guitar pick-up. With analog recording, a physical record is created by moving a phonograph stylus to imprint a pattern on a vinyl record or fluctuating a magnetic field via a magnetic tape recording head.

Digital recording bypasses the physical element and creates a record directly on a hard drive or other digital medium as a series of binary numbers representing samples of the amplitude of the audio signal at regular intervals. An advantage of digital over analog recording is the ability to make an exact replica of the file. Analog duplication often results in a degraded quality replica.

Both the methods use analog playback by vibrating the head of a speaker or headphone to replicate the original sound waves.

Recording and playback

This section covers the recording and playback technology involved in sound design.

Recording

The process of capturing an analog audio signal and converting it to a digital format is done with an analog-to-digital convertor (ADC). This is a piece of hardware that measures electrical input and records in binary format. The fidelity of the conversion process is dictated by several factors: the sample rate, the word length, and compression.

The sample rate

The frequency at which the ADC measures the level of the analog wave is called the sample rate. The higher the sampling rate the higher the upper cutoff frequency of the digitized audio signal. Sample rates are measured in frequency of samples per second; the higher the frequency, the better the audio quality.

The word length

Word length is the amount of data in an individual sample. The longer the word length, the more accurate the sample. Word size is measured in bits of data.

The number of bits used to represent a single audio wave (the word size) directly affects the signal. Increasing a sample's word length by one bit doubles its possible values; the practical limit of which is 24 bits, since that is the maximum that today's sound equipment can detect.

Compression

Compression is a process to reduce the size of the stored audio file. There are three basic types of compressions: uncompressed, lossless compression, and lossy compression.

Uncompressed

An uncompressed (raw or PCM) audio file requires about a megabyte of storage per second of playback. This format is generally used only for archiving original master studio recordings.

Lossless compression

This format removes data that is generally unperceivable by audio equipment and the listener. A good example is the FLAC format, which, while having a smaller space footprint than PCM, is still too large to be used in the game development.

Lossy compression

This format sacrifices a varying amount of fidelity for a game-friendly space requirement. A typical example is the `*.MP3` format which uses on an average about one megabyte per minute of playback time. This is the format we will focus on in this chapter.

Playback

The sequence of numbers is transmitted from a storage medium into a digital-to-analog converter (DAC), which converts the numbers back to an analog signal by sticking together the level information stored in each digital sample, thus rebuilding the original analog waveform.

This signal is amplified and transmitted to the speakers or headphones.

Types of game sounds

There are a number of sound types, including dynamic, adaptive interactive, diegetic, non-dynamic, adaptive, and non-diegetic versions. The classification is based on the perspective we assume to consider sounds in games. From the point of view of the player's actions, sounds can be divided into Dynamic and Non-Dynamic.If we, on the other hand, consider the sounds from the perspective of "where" they occur, we have Diegetic sounds, which happen in the character's space, and Non-Diegetic sounds. In the following sections we provide explanations for each of these categories.

Dynamic audio

Dynamic audio is any sound which is designed to be changeable, encompassing both the interactive and adaptive audio. Dynamic audio is the sound which reacts to the changes in the gameplay environment and/or in response to the user's actions.

Adaptive audio

Adaptive audio occurs in the game environment, reacting to gameplay, rather than responding directly to the user. An example is during timed gameplay, the music may speed up as time runs out.

Interactive audio

Interactive audio refers to the sound events occurring in reaction to gameplay, which can respond to the player directly. For example, in Tetris, when the player drops a piece into place there is a thump sound. The thump is an interactive sound effect.

Non-Dynamic linear sounds and music

Non-Dynamic linear sounds and music usually occur in movies or cut-scenes. These will play in a set series without input from the player.

Diegetic sounds

Diegetic audio are sound effects or music that occur in the character's space. There are three types of diegetic sounds: non-dynamic, adaptive, and interactive.

Adaptive

Diegetic adaptive audio occurs in the game space and may change based on conditions in the gameplay. For example, during the daylight conditions, birds may chirp, while during night, crickets chirp.

Interactive

Interactive diegetic sounds occur in the character's space, with which the player's character can directly interact. The player's actions trigger the sound effect but the player can't directly affect it. Examples include the character's footsteps, the creaking of an opening door, or choosing a tune on a juke box.

Non-Dynamic

Non-Dynamic diegetic occurs during gameplay, but the player's actions have no effect on playback. Examples would include the background music and sound effects, such as traffic noise.

Non-Diegetic sounds

Non-Diegetic audio takes place outside of the character's space. There are two types of non-diegetic audio: adaptive and interactive.

Adaptive

Adaptive Non-Diegetic sounds are sound events occurring in reaction to gameplay, but which are unaffected by the player's direct movements, and are outside the diegesis or game narrative. An example would be the different background music for day and night conditions.

Interactive

Interactive Non-Diegetic sounds can react to the player directly, but are also outside of the game narrative. An example would be the music changing or starting when the character enters a cafe where a jukebox is playing.

Kinetic gestural interaction

Kinetic gestural interaction can occur in both diegetic and non-diegetic sound, in which the player (as well as the character, typically) physically participates with the sound on screen. This usually involves a specialized controller, such as the Nintendo Wii controller, MS Xbox 360 Kinect, and the guitar in Guitar Hero.

The audio editing software

There are literally dozens of **Digital Audio Editors** (**DAE**) available in the market. The following are a few of the more popular ones:

Avid Pro Tools

Arguably, Avid Pro Tools is one of the best DAE in the market. It is an industry standard with a full range of features. Developed by Avid Technology, Pro Tools is available for both Microsoft Windows and Mac OS X operating systems. The suite is widely used by professionals for recording and editing across music production, film scoring, film and television post production, musical notation, and MIDI sequencing. Pro Tools can run as standalone software, or operate using a range of external A/D converters and internal PCI or PCIe audio cards with onboard DSP. Pro Tools can be purchased and downloaded from `http://www.avid.com/US/products/family/pro-tools`.

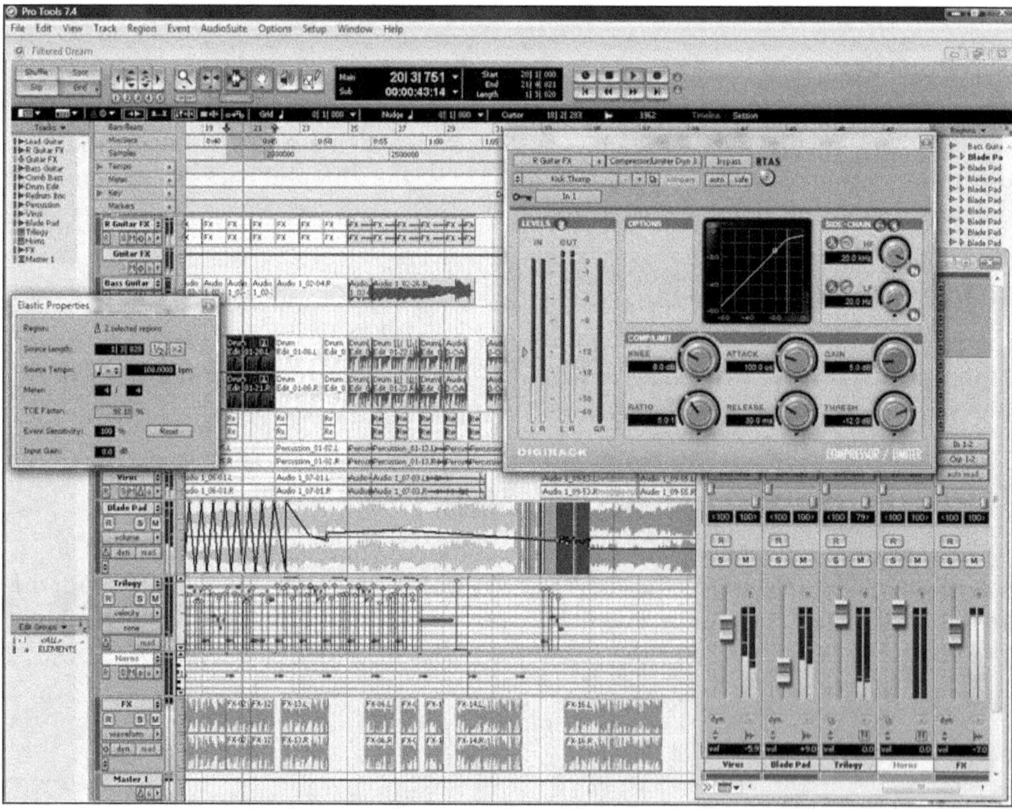

Avid Pro Tools screenshot

Sound Forge/Sonic Foundry

Sony Sound Forge by Sony Creative Software is a digital audio editing suite which is aimed at the professional and semi-professional markets. It is capable of recording, editing, and reformatting sound files in a number of formats including WAV, AIFF, and MP3. A limited version, sold as Sound Forge Audio Studio, provides an inexpensive entry-level digital audio editor. Sound Forge can be bought and downloaded at the following website:

`http://www.sonycreativesoftware.com/audiostudio`

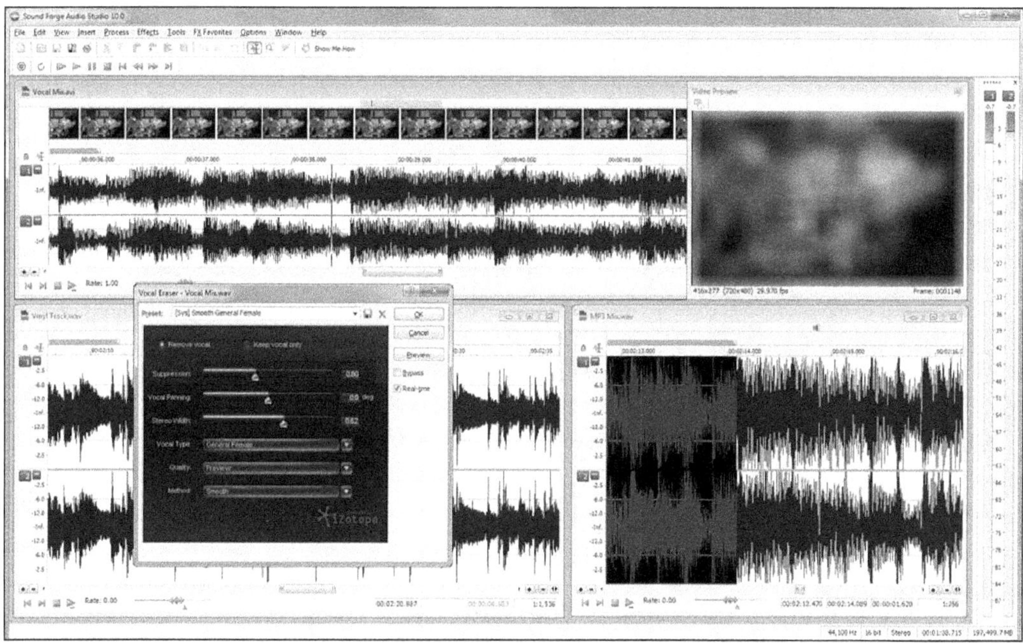

Sound Forge screenshot

Audacity

Audacity is a powerful, open source free digital audio recorder and editor available for Windows, Mac OS X, Linux, and other operating systems. Audacity has been available on Source Forge from October 2011 with over 76 million downloads. Audacity has won multiple awards, including the SourceForge 2007 and 2009 Community Choice Award for Best Project for Multimedia. Audacity is available for download here:

`http://audacity.sourceforge.net/`

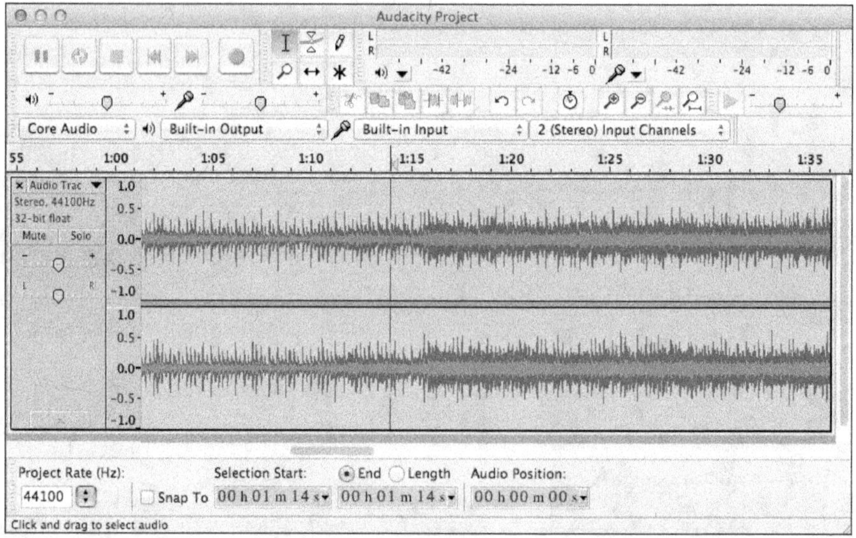

Audacity running on MacOS screenshot

Ableton Live

Ableton Live is a software available for both Windows and iOS which is especially good to rapidly and easily create sound effects. The basic suite of upcoming Version 9 is quite cheap and you can try the free trial version before deciding if it is the right software for your needs (`https://www.ableton.com/`).

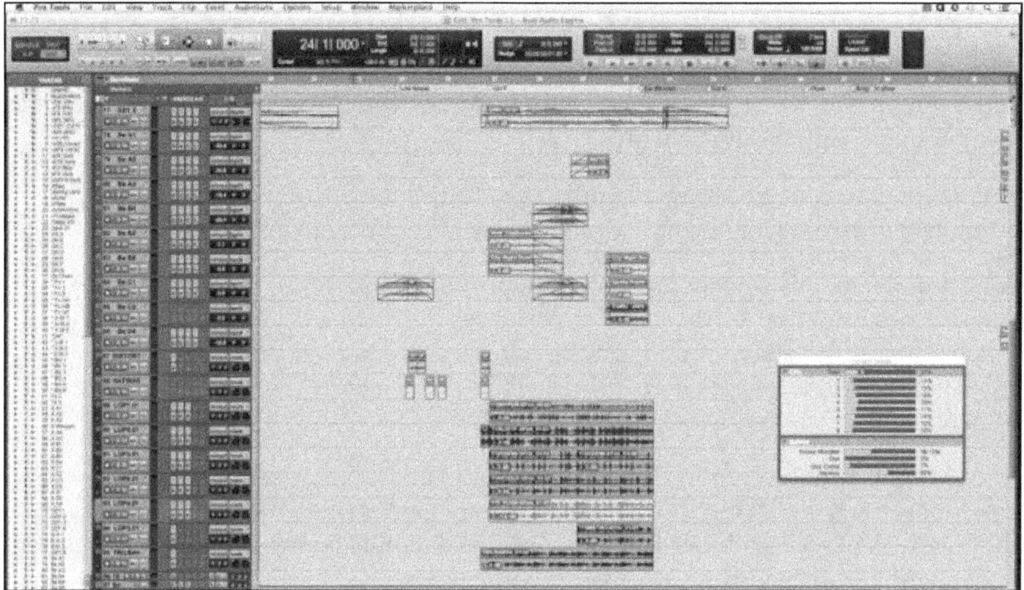

Ableton Live screenshot

Designing audio for mobile games

The creation of good audio and sounds for mobile games poses specific problems to audio designers that depend on both the technical characteristics of mobile devices and the distinctive conditions at which mobile games are played.

In the following sections, we will discuss the most important considerations which specifically relate to the creation of optimized audio for your mobile games.

Planning the audio in advance

The speed at which the mobile games are developed usually means that music and sounds are often the last element to be added to a game. However, poorly designed audio can negatively affect the appeal of a title to its target audience and thus its sales.

Therefore, if you want your title to sell well, we suggest taking care of sound as any other crucial element of your game from the beginning of the development process. Of course, gameplay must be fun, but poor sound can hurt an otherwise high quality game.

Hardware limitations for mobile games audio

As far as the hardware capabilities of mobile phones constantly evolve, users expect better audio for their mobile games and developers can go beyond the standard of a few kilobytes for their music scores.

Still, mobile devices have limited audio capabilities when compared to PCs and home consoles that mobile audio designers need to take into account.

For example, mobile phones are generally provided with a single speaker. Using headphones can improve the audio experience, and with additional hardware the iPhone can output stereo sound (on Wikipedia, you can read that *Stereo audio was added in the 3.0 update for hardware that supports A2DP* `http://en.wikipedia.org/wiki/IPhone`).

In any event, as a developer, you can't rely on your audience to always use headphones when playing mobile games. Many games these days, advise that they are best played with headphones, but this depends on the gameplay and how dependent it is on sound cues.

Another technical obstacle is that the audio capabilities of a mobile device are usually optimized for speech and don't necessarily work as well for other audio purposes. It takes experience, a good sound editing tool, such as those we mentioned, and a lot of fine tuning to deliver an adequate sound experience for your games.

Fortunately, creating audio for mobile games doesn't only mean dealing with limitations. High-end devices allow pretty good audio performance that can be exploited by audio designers to improve the overall experience of a mobile game. For example, iPhone and iPad developers can make use of advanced APIs, such as Open AL, to create excellent sounds for their games. These libraries even allow simulated audio positioning in the 3D space or giving players the option to choose the music played in their games.

The role of audio in mobile games

Generally speaking, mobile audio design follows the same rules of audio design for any other game platform. The goal of the game audio is to immerse players in the game world and improve their gameplay experience.

Typically, your mobile title will require the following audio elements: looping background music, in-game sound effects, dialog, and interface sounds.

A key aspect is that those sounds that are most often played don't bother players even after being heard hundreds of times. Work with volume, pitch, and sound modulation over time (game engines usually offer tools to do that) and test as much as you can to be sure that the final experience should always be pleasant to players, rather than annoying.

Listening conditions for mobile games

Mobile gaming has distinctive characteristics of its own that need to be taken into account by audio designers with regard to the kind of experience that mobile games deliver to the players.

For example, the listening conditions for a mobile game are hardly comparable to that of a title you can play on a home console or PC. The spatial sound available for house speakers, as well as the difference between left and right channels, may not be available on a mobile phone when playing on a bus or in the doctor's waiting room. As we said, headphones could help here, but you cannot rely on players using them.

Then there's noise! When playing outdoors, all kinds of noise can interfere with your game sounds: background sounds, other people's conversations, dogs barking, and the like, which will negatively affect your game audio, if not masking it at all. Testing your game audio in different environments and with or without headphones, is crucial to find the optimal setting and tuning for your game audio.

Another aspect to be taken into account is the social aspect of playing in public. People around our player shouldn't be bothered with audio coming from his mobile phone or the player may not want people to know what he is doing. Those facts imply several decisions to be taken at a design level, for example, setting the ideal volume game sounds should be played at or the conditions at which audio starts and stops playing.

As you can see, sound design for mobile games should not be seen as a task independent from the more general design of a game as a whole!

Best practices for mobile games audio design

In the following sections we will suggest a few basic practices that can help audio designers to address the most common problems when creating audio and sounds for mobile games.

Scripting skills for a mobile audio designer

Due to the reduced size of mobile developing teams, a very useful skill for your audio designer to have is the capability to use the scripting language of your game engine of choice to manage in-game audio. This will have two main advantages: the first is that the other team members won't have to take care of this specific aspect, as they will already be overburdened with the other elements of game development: designing, programming, or artwork production. The second advantage is that, as the sound expert takes care of putting audio and sounds in the game, the overall quality of the project will improve.

Most game engine scripting languages, as we will see in the following chapters of the book, are Java or JavaScript-based (UDK and Unity among the others). If your audio designer can deal with such tools, not only the overall quality of your game will be better, but it can also help meet the deadlines of your project.

File compression

As mobile devices lack the memory capabilities of home consoles and PCs, it is fundamental to use compression algorithms to reduce the size of your audio files, while keeping an acceptable quality. For example, in order for your iPhone game to be downloadable under the 3G standard, its size cannot exceed the threshold of 20Mb.

As we said, the lower the bitrate of an audio file, the lower its quality. Fortunately, when developing audio for mobile games, there is no need to produce optimal 5.1 sound quality. It is thus easier for the audio designer to balance the reduction in the bitrate of the audio files and yet have those sound good on a mobile device. For example, with MP3 compression, which is generally accepted by most popular game engines, stereo audio file size is almost the same as their mono counterparts.

Looping background music

A very annoying problem that may arise when creating audio for mobile games is with looping background music. When an uncompressed file is converted into an MP3, the algorithm generally adds samples that can make it impossible to create seamless looping music backgrounds. Game engines provide solutions to this issue. As an audio designer, you'd better be ready to face such problems.

To learn more

Further details on the development of audio and sounds for iOS mobile games can be found in this very good article on Gamasutra:

`http://www.gamasutra.com/view/feature/134597/ios_audio_design_what_everyone_.php`

Final advice

We mentioned several times that adding audio to a game only in the final steps of the development process is a bias of mobile game development and we stressed the importance of considering audio and sounds for as part of the general design of a game. We would like to say more on this topic.

Since game developers and sound experts don't share very much common knowledge and hardly possess a common terminology, if the game designer and audio expert don't discuss their opinions on what kind of audio and sounds are required for a game, a lot of confusion may arise, with the consequence that time and money can be wasted.

Communication is crucial in this matter. Always take your time to instruct your audio designer on what exactly is expected from him/her and make every effort to be sure that you two share a common vision on the audio and sounds desired for your title. Provide your sound designer with a full list of the audio and sounds for your game early on during the development process and also send him examples and references of what you have in mind. This will reduce the number of iterations the sound expert has to go through before creating the perfect sound asset and will help him to fulfill his tasks while meeting the deadlines, thus saving time and money.

With some practice, you will see that developing a communication channel with your sound designer will provide your game with better audio and sounds and improve the overall quality of your project.

A very interesting article on this topic can be found at: `http://www.gamasutra.com/view/feature/175427/getting_the_most_from_your_sound_.php`.

Summary

In this chapter we discussed the history of videogame music. We reviewed how sound is recorded and played back. We listed the sound types for games and the most popular digital audio editing software.

Finally, we described the main issues and best practices when dealing with the creation of audio and sounds for mobile.

During the course of the following chapter, we will delve into the details of mobile game programming.

We will describe the most popular coding and scripting languages and their characteristics, the development environments that are most commonly used, and the best practices of mobile games programming.

5
Coding Games

In this chapter, we deal with programming languages to create mobile games. It is a very rich topic that cannot be entirely discussed in a single chapter dedicated to mobile game development, though we will give you all the information needed to approach the matter, and provide useful hints to find the programming language that best fits your needs to develop mobile games.

We begin with a general discussion on the characteristics of programming languages and then we describe the most useful languages to create games for the mobile market. We end the chapter with the description of the program structure of a game.

In this chapter, we will cover the following topics:

- Main features of programming languages
- C++
- Java
- Scripting languages
- Game programming for mobile
- Objective-C
- HTML5
- The game structure

Main features of programming languages

A programming language is an artificial language used to create programs that express precise algorithms to make a computer perform computations.

Programming languages allow the manipulation of data structures and the flow of execution of a program.

There are several different kinds of programming languages, which differ in many aspects, the most important of them being the computations they are capable of, also known as the **expressive power** of a programming language.

Each programming language provides a basic set of elements, which describes data and the processes and transformations which can be applied to them, also called **primitives** of that language.

A very important element of programming languages is their syntax. Most programming languages are textual and their syntax includes words, numbers, and punctuations. However, there are other programming languages that make use of a graphical approach, where programs are created by a visual representation of symbols, for example, a flowchart.

The syntax of a program defines the possible combinations of symbols that constitute a syntactically correct program.

Another way to differentiate between programming languages is whether they require **static typing** or allow **dynamic typing**.

Static typing means that all expression types of that language are predetermined before the program is executed. If an expression expects a string data type and you pass them integers, the output is an error message.

In the category of static typing, we can also distinguish between programming languages that require types to be specified at the beginning of a program (variable declarations) and languages which can infer the type of data passed to a function by the context in which the operations occurs.

A mainstream language such as C++ is an example of statically-typed languages, while C# (C sharp) and Java make use of variable declarations, but can also infer data types in limited cases.

On the other hand, dynamically-typed languages do not require types to be explicitly defined at some point of a program and allow a variable to refer to different types of data at different points of the program's execution. This could be both an advantage and a problem; it allows a more flexible approach to programming, but it also makes debugging difficult. Lisp, Perl, Python, and JavaScript are examples of dynamically-typed languages.

Orthogonal to the dichotomy between static and dynamic typing, there is the one between strong and weak typing.

Strong-typing languages don't allow operations to be carried out on wrong types of data, such as multiplying a string by a number. Weak-typing languages allow these kinds of operations with the same risks we mentioned previously; it is a more flexible way to create computer programs, but it is also more prone to generate errors that are hard to detect as well.

Libraries

The core operations that are available for a programming language are contained in libraries. Libraries include definitions for algorithms, data structures, and input and output operations. Programming languages such as C++ or Java cannot work at all if such core libraries are not included as a part of any program written with them.

Abstraction

The capability of a programming language to perform operations strongly depends on its abstraction level. Early programming languages were tightly related to the hardware they ran on, thus limiting the utilization of programs written for different hardware. However, more recent programming languages are designed so that programmers can write programs that are less tied to the complexity of the computer for which the program is written, thus requiring less effort from programmers to write computer programs that can run on different hardware configurations. The process of converting a program to run on a different hardware platform is called **porting**.

Implementation

The abstraction level of a programming language is directly related to its implementation. Implementation provides a way to execute a program on different hardware and software configurations. Programming languages can be implemented in two ways: by compilation or by interpretation.

Compiled programs are directly executed by the hardware of the computer they run on, while interpreted languages are executed by an interpreter, software that takes care of converting the instructions of the program into machine code, the lowest-level programming language. As such, interpreters can be considered as an interface between a programming language and the hardware of a computer.

Generally speaking, compiled languages allow for operations to be carried out faster when compared to interpreted languages, as they take direct control of the operations carried on by the computer hardware.

For example, the technique of Just-in-Time compilation speeds up the execution of a Java interpreted program, by using a so-called virtual machine that translates specific chunks of code called bytecode into machine code just before the execution of the program.

Usage

There are thousands of different programming languages available and not all of them are able to carry out the same kind of operations or treat the similar kinds of data.

When we use spoken languages, we can commit small errors, and still expect to be understood by our listener. Programming languages, on the other hand, don't allow such flexibility because we cannot expect the computer to understand what we intended to write. A computer program can only work if the programmer is absolutely precise when writing the code. This is why programming languages provide very structured mechanisms to define the data they can deal with and the operations that can be carried out on that data. This is also the reason why debugging a piece of code can be a hard task if the program is not written according to the syntax, the abstraction rules, and the best practices specific to that programming language! Programmers have a phrase for this: **Garbage in, garbage out** (GIGO).

There are several books and online resources that you can refer to delve further in the details of programming languages. A good starting point is the Wikipedia page at `http://en.wikipedia.org/wiki/Programming_language`.

Game programming

When developing video games, the decision on which programming language to use cannot only be dictated by the proficiency of your game programmer. As a developer, you must also take into consideration the libraries and APIs which best support the design characteristics of your game. For example, there are libraries entirely focused on managing game AI tasks, such as path finding. If you plan to develop a game whose gameplay strongly relies on AI, you'd better consider which programming language offers libraries that perform such tasks, before starting development. This is the reason why it is so important for a game programmer to be at ease with more than just one programming or scripting language.

When graphics come into play, there are several APIs available designed to manage 2D and 3D graphics for games. OpenGL and Direct3D are the most popular 3D graphic APIs, which offer native support for Microsoft Windows OS. If you want to know more about OpenGL and Direct3D, we suggest the following links:

`http://www.opengl.org/`

`http://social.msdn.microsoft.com/search/en-US/windows/desktop?query=direct3d&Refinement=181`

With regard to mobile game development, the decision about the programming language to use also depends on the target platform of your game.

We already mentioned that Java should be your choice when developing games for the Android platform, while Objective-C is the programming language for iOS game development. There are other options as well, naturally. C++ can be used to program games for the iOS, using the game engine of your choice (game engines will be discussed in *Chapter 8, Mobile Game Engines*) and for the Android with the Android Native Development Kit, available at `http://developer.android.com/tools/sdk/ndk/index.html`.

If you plan to use a game engine, and we recommend you to do so, get proficient with JavaScript if you intend to use Unity3D, learn UnrealScript if you are oriented towards the Unreal Engine, or LUA if you want to develop games with Corona SDK (among others).

For multiplatform browser games, HTML5, featuring dedicated engines such as ImpactJS (`http://impactjs.com/`) and Canvace (`http://canvace.com/`) is a good choice too. Though this standard is not yet fully featured as we write this book, when compared to the game engines we mentioned (for example, HTML5 doesn't fully support audio and sounds), still it is considered a standard for upcoming browser-based games and the most promising alternative to the already popular Flash ActionScript.

C++

C++ is a statically-typed, compiled, intermediate-level language and is actually the most used programming language for game programming. It can be considered, easily put, a version of the popular C language with object-oriented features, which include the ability to create classes.

C++ is implemented on several hardware configurations and operating systems, and being a very efficient way to compile native code, it is used to develop system software, applications, device drivers, data servers, and naturally, video games.

Renowned companies such as Microsoft and Intel offer C++ software compilers (for example, the popular Microsoft's Visual Studio) to create and manage programs written with C++. You can check the latest version (at the time of writing) Visual Studio 2012 Express at `http://www.microsoft.com/visualstudio/eng/products/visual-studio-express-products`.

Being such a versatile programming language, C++ has influenced several other languages that are used for game programming, such as Java and C#. If you are about to decide which programming language to learn to begin with, C++ should be your first choice!

Memory management

When programming mobile games, memory management is a crucial aspect to enhance the performance of your code, while keeping the hardware requirements for your applications as low as possible.

C++ offers four types of memory management techniques:

- **Static memory allocation**: This means that values are assigned to variables once and for all inside a program, so that these values do not change during the execution of the program. To achieve that, the `static` keyword is put inside the variable name in the variable declaration section of the code.
- **Automatic memory allocation**: This implies that the amount of memory allocated to store a variable value is automatically freed once that variable goes out of use in the program. This operation is performed by a special method available in C++ called destructor.
- **Dynamic memory allocation**: This happens when the memory allocation for a variable value is manually assigned using the `new` and `delete` keywords.
- **Garbage collection**: This is a very useful operation that we already mentioned when discussing the basics of iOS game development in *Chapter 1, Operation Systems – Mobile and Otherwise*. It is a way to automatically manage memory allocation that relieves the programmer from doing it manually and is performed by dedicated software such as the very popular **Boehm-Demers-Weiser garbage collector** (`http://en.wikipedia.org/wiki/Boehm_garbage_collector`).

Memory management is one of the most important aspects of the C++ programming language. It is both a welcome feature, as it gives full control to programmers over the execution of a piece of code, and a blamed characteristic, for it requires extra work of programmers when compared to other languages such as Java or Perl, which don't require any memory management at all. It is a classical situation of balancing the pros and cons of control over efficiency!

Objects

C++ is an object-oriented programming language that uses classes. Classes are definitions of types of data structures and the functions that operate on those data. Thanks to the use of classes, C++ allows abstraction, encapsulation, inheritance, and polymorphism.

We already mentioned that abstraction allows a piece of code to work independently of the hardware it runs on.

Encapsulation means that all data are contained and hidden in a class, and are only accessible to members of that class, so that classes work as some kind of black boxes. The advantage of this technique is that it prevents human errors, since the class can't be accidentally modified or corrupted while writing a piece of code.

Inheritance means that when a new class is declared, which extends a pre-existing class, it automatically gets all the attributes and behaviors that were available to the class it extends. Inheritance saves development time and efforts. For example, when programming game objects for your application, the programmer can create a general class which defines the basic properties common to each game object, and then extend other classes from that which will share the same so-called members.

Polymorphism, as some say, can be considered as the feature of object-oriented programming that fully expresses the potential of such programming languages. It means that the same code or operations behave differently in different contexts.

A full explanation of this feature goes beyond the scope of this section about C++. We suggest visiting `http://www.cs.bu.edu/teaching/cpp/polymorphism/intro/`, which provides examples to clear the concept of polymorphism.

Complaints about C++

Being a multi-paradigm and all-purpose programming language, C++ is blamed for being too generic and for not enforcing a well-defined programming style. There is a very funny satirical article where *Bjarne Stroustrup*, developer of the C++ language, is portrayed as confessing to the complexities of this programming language. You can check it out at `http://harmful.cat-v.org/software/c++/I_did_it_for_you_all`.

Java

Java is an object-oriented, multi-purpose programming language based on classes. It's main feature is portability and its motto is "write once, run anywhere!". Java is designed to be as platform-independent as possible, so that Java programs will run regardless of the platform. This is achieved thanks to the **Java Virtual Machine** (**JVM**), a program which compiles programs written in Java into bytecode. Bytecode is analogous to low-level machine code, so that programs can run with different operating systems or hardware configurations.

Java derives most of its syntax from C and C++, though it is considered to be far easier on its users!

Unfortunately, portability has its price; as with any interpreted program, Java code tends to be slower and requires more memory than software written with compiled languages such as C++. Anyway, since Just-In-Time compilation was added in 1998, the execution speed of programs written with Java has improved.

The Java SE platform, which is derived from the original implementation by former developer and owner, Sun Microsystems, is the current implementation of the Java platform and it is available for Mac OS X, Windows, and Solaris. The Oracle implementation is distributed into two versions: **Java Runtime Environment** (**JRE**), which is required to run Java programs and **Java Development Kit** (**JDK**), intended to develop software and contains the usual development tools (compiler, debugger, and so on).

Several platforms offer direct hardware support to Java code; not only computers, Microcontrollers, TVs, but even video-recorders are controlled through Java code!

More important for the scope of this book, ARM-based processors can implement hardware support for Java bytecode, and 95 percent of today's smartphones host an ARM processor.

Memory management

Besides portability, the other main feature of Java is its automatic garbage collector. Java doesn't allow explicit memory management. Once the programmer creates an object, the garbage collector takes care of freeing the memory allocated to it, if no references to that object remain as the code is executed. This cannot entirely prevent memory leaks, though. It is still possible that a reference to an object that is no longer needed remains, as it is part of another structure, such as an array, which is still active.

Nonetheless, the automatic garbage collector of Java spares a lot of effort to programmers, as they aren't forced to explicitly manage memory. Manual memory management in other languages can be a source for errors that can cause instability or make a program crash, it is very hard to identify the causes unless complex methodologies are adopted.

Syntax

The Java syntax is basically derived from C++, and similar to C++, Java is an object-oriented language. Java differs from C++ in the fact that it is less structured than C++. In Java, every piece of code is written inside a class and everything, except the usual language primitives (strings, integers, Boolean variables, and so on), is treated as an object. Java also lacks some low-level features of C++ we discussed, such as inheritance.

Java for mobile – Java ME

Java Micro Edition (**Java ME** or **J2ME**) is a subset of Java SE, designed for use on mobile devices such as cell phones. Java ME is embedded in millions of dumb (non-smart) devices around the world. For most smartphones, it is possible to download and run Java-ME-based games that have been approved by their carrier.

As we already mentioned in *Chapter 1, Operating Systems – Mobile or Otherwise*, Android-based smartphones run Java ME and the Android SDK, used to develop mobile games for the Android platform, uses Java ME as well.

Gaikai is a very useful Java application for those of you that are interested in playing video games demos. It is a cloud-based application, which allows playing PC and console games on any computer or mobile device (provided it has access to an Internet connection).

Since Gaikai was acquired by Sony, their cloud gaming system has been offline. At the time of writing, their website says this will change in the near future.

There are many Java-based game emulators online, including ones for classic console, arcade, and mobile games. **Mobile9** (`www.mobile9.com`) has all three platforms and more.

Objective-C

Objective-C is the main programming language used by Apple for the OS X and iOS operating systems and their respective APIs: Cocoa and Cocoa Touch. Based on the C programming language, it adds object-oriented programming via a thin layer of interface similar to Smalltalk.

It was developed in the early 1980s by NeXT for its NeXTSTEP operating system. It was selected by Apple as the main language from which OS X and iOS are derived. Generic Objective-C programs that do not use the Cocoa or Cocoa Touch libraries can also be compiled for any system that can run basic C and vice-versa.

Cocoa

Cocoa is Apple's native object-oriented API for the Mac OS X operating system. Most OS X and all iOS applications are built using Cocoa. Combining Xcode and Cocoa provides an excellent set of development tools for both operating systems.

Cocoa Touch

Cocoa Touch is a UI framework for building software programs to run on the iPhone, iPod, and iPad from Apple Inc. It's mostly written in Objective-C and adds features to OS X that are targeted specifically at iOS devices. Cocoa Touch provides a Model-View-Controller software architecture, just like Cocoa. Tools for developing applications based on Cocoa Touch are included in the iOS SDK.

Xcode

Developed by Apple, Xcode is an SDK for developing software for OS X and iOS. Initially released in 2003, you can download the latest stable release (version 4.5.2) for free from the Mac App Store. If you are a registered developer, you can download preview releases and previous versions of the suite through the Apple Developer website.

The suite includes the Xcode IDE and the Interface Builder. It also has most of the Apple's developer documentation; the Interface Builder is used to construct graphical user interfaces.

Working with objects

When building apps for OS X or iOS, you'll spend most of your time working with objects. In this case, objects are instances of Objective-C classes, some of which are provided for you by Cocoa or Cocoa Touch and some of which you'll write yourself.

To create your own class, you need to start with a description that includes its public properties and a list of methods. Methods must include what kind of messages it can receive, what happens when the method is called, and the necessary code to implement the method.

Extending classes with categories

Instead of creating an entirely new class to provide minor additional capabilities over an existing class, you can define a category to add functionality to an existing class. You can use a category to add methods to any class, including classes for which you don't have the original implementation source code.

With a class' source code, you can add new properties or change its current properties with class extensions. Class extensions are particularly useful when customizing a framework.

Protocols define messaging contracts

Generally, the work in an Objective-C app happens when objects send messages to each other. Usually, the construct of messages is determined by the methods defined in a class. At times you will find it helpful to define a set of related methods that are independent of a specific class.

Objective-C provides protocols that are used to define a group of related methods; either optional or required. Any class can use a protocol, which means that it requires implementations for all of the methods in the protocol.

Values and collections

In addition to primitive types defined by the C language, such as int, float or char, Objective-C can also use Cocoa or Cocoa Touch classes to represent values. These classes include:

- Strings of characters are defined with `NSString`
- Different types of numbers use the `NSNumber` class
- The `NSValue` class for other values such as C structures.

Collections are generally represented as instances of one of the collection classes, such as `NSArray`, `NSSet` or `NSDictionary`, which are used to collect other Objective-C objects.

Blocks

In C, Objective-C, and C++, blocks are a feature that represent a unit of work; which makes them similar to closures in other programming languages. They include a block of code along with a captured state, blocks can be used to simplify common tasks such as:

- Collection enumeration
- Sorting
- Testing
- Concurrent or asynchronous schedule tasks

Error Objects: Cocoa and Cocoa Touch handles programming errors, which need to be fixed before an app is submitted to the App Store.

All other errors are represented by instances of the `NSError` class. Be sure to plan for errors and decide how best to handle them in such a way that does not negatively impact the user experience.

Please note that Objective-C includes internal exception handling.

Objective-C conventions

Objective-C code has a number of established coding conventions. For example, method names start with a lowercase letter and use camel case for multiple words such as `doThis` or `doThisInstead`. Make sure that method names are easily understood but not too long.

Also, there are a few conventions that are required if you want to use the language or framework features. For example, property accessor methods must follow strict naming conventions in order to work with technologies such as **Key-Value Coding** (**KVC**) or **Key-Value Observing** (**KVO**).

Apple Developer documentation can be found at `http://developer.apple.com/library/ios/#recipes/xcode_help-documentation_organizer/BrowsingDocumentation/BrowsingDocumentation.html`.

Getting started

To get started with programming Objective-C, you will need a Mac running OS X Version 10.7 or later. If you have an earlier version of Mac OS X, you need to upgrade.

We need to follow the ensuing steps for getting started:

1. Download the latest version of Xcode.
2. Open the Mac App Store app on your Mac, search for Xcode, and click on **Free to download Xcode**.
3. Enroll in the Mac Developer Program.

After you enroll in the program, you have access to the tools and resources you need to distribute your app. You will learn more about these tools later in the road map.

For more information on getting started, go to `https://developer.apple.com/library/ios/navigation/#section=Resource%20Types&topic=Getting%20Started`.

HTML5

HTML5 is a markup language, which extends the capabilities of former markup languages and introduces new APIs to create complex web apps, so that it can be used to create cross-platform applications and games. Among its features, HTML5 is designed to run on low performance devices such as smartphones and tablets, this is the reason we decide to mention it in this chapter about programming languages for mobile games. Have you ever heard of a game called **Cut the rope**? Well, it has been developed with HTML5!

Well known by web developers for years, the decisive push towards popularity of HTML5 was given in 2010 by Steve Jobs, who stated that since Flash was not open platform, as it is controlled by Adobe, it could no longer be the standard for multimedia applications.

At Cupertino they believed that HTML5, with its open platform, could become the new standard for web applications and overcome Flash. As a consequence, iOS devices don't support Flash and this is the reason why many developers turned to HTML5 to develop games for the iPhone and the iPad.

Canvas

The main feature that allows HTML5 to be used to develop games is its APIs, which can be controlled with JavaScript to create interactive, multimedia applications.

Among the APIs, the most important for game development is an element called Canvas, defined by the `<canvas>` tags.

The canvas block can be added to a web page and then manipulated through JavaScript to paste images, set compositing modes, manage alpha, transformations and scaling, and to draw basic shapes.

The drawback of the canvas element is that, though it is well supported by both desktop and mobile browsers, the rendering speed varies very much, depending on each specific platform.

HTML5 and Flash

While HTML5 is often compared to Flash and is considered as its main competitor, the two technologies differ in many aspects.

They both allow to play audio and graphics inside web pages and to manage vector graphics. On the other hand, Flash is a complete tool of its own, thanks to its scripting language called ActionScript, while interactions between elements of web apps created with HTML5 can only be implemented through JavaScript. In the end, many features of Flash have no counterpart in HTML5 yet!

We mentioned that Apple gave a decisive push towards the spreading of HTML5 instead of Flash. The reason is that Flash-based apps cannot be directly rendered by web browsers. A freely available component called Adobe Flash Player is required. But, Adobe Flash Player is supported by any platform, excluding the iOS (and Android Version 4.1 and higher)! The result is that no Flash-based application can run on iPhones, iPad, iPod Touch, or even Apple TV.

On the other hand, the HTML5 standard is supported by all major web browsers, both desktop and mobile. This is why some game developers turned to HTML5 to develop iOS games and why HTML5 is considered the optimal choice for true multiplatform game development.

Issues with HTML5

The debate on whether HTML5 is the ultimate tool to create cross-platform web application, and thus games that can equally run on different mobile phones, is still developing.

There are in fact two main issues when using HTML5. One is that different browsers implement HTML5 in different ways, so the performance of a HTML5 game can dramatically differ, depending on the specific browser it runs on.

The other is that the implementation of HTML5 games rely on the use of a complex chain of tools: WebGL to have 3D graphics rendered by the GPU in the browser window, SVG for vector graphics, NaCl to compile C/C++ native modules, WebSockets to support multiplayer, WebAudio, Canvas, DOM, and obviously, JavaScript; it is a quite long list!

HTML5 games

We guess you are asking yourselves which kind of games can be developed with HTML5?

Desktop: There are obviously desktop browser games, which also include Facebook games. As we said, HTML5 is supported by all major web browsers, though all web users are very likely to already have the latest Flash Player installed on their PCs.

Mobile web browser: More importantly for the goal of this book, HTML5 is supported by mobile web browsers. Generally speaking, when referring to mobile gaming, one's likely to have apps in mind, stand alone programs that can be downloaded and then run on a mobile device. Developing games that run in mobile web browsers, on the other hand, is a viable alternative, as it is a growing market which already offers dedicated portals to buy high profile games. There are obviously issues related to performance when your game runs on different iPhone models and even more due to Android devices variability. But this is an issue of mobile development in general, regardless of the specific technology you intend to use. You shouldn't forget that HTML5 is a rather new technology and still under development; the issues you face today could be resolved tomorrow!

Mobile apps: Mobile games in the form of downloadable apps can also be developed with HTML5, though in this case, you will need a third-party development framework such as PhoneGap. Using PhoneGap, HTML5 and a little bit of JavaScript, it is possible to create games that natively target all mobile platforms with a single codebase. Since 2012, in fact, the **PhoneGap Build** service allows source code to be cloud-compiled and generate apps that can run on any desired mobile platform: iOS, Android, Windows Phone, Blackberry, and so on.

Even tablets such as the Blackberry PlayBook offer support for HTML5 games.

If you want to know more about PhoneGap we suggest to check `http://phonegap.com/`.

Conclusions

In conclusion, HTML5 is both a viable option to develop mobile games and a source of problems and performance issues.

On one hand, it allows true cross-platform games development. For example, using a framework such as PhoneGap, the same JavaScript code can target any platform you may decide to develop your game for.

On the other hand, since HTML5 is implemented differently on each platform, your game will very likely perform differently, depending on the specific platform it runs on. Moreover, when compared to Flash, HTML5 games development is no easy task, as you need several side-tools to implement the required features for your game, JavaScript being the glue between all such tools.

Finally, HTML5-based games are generally slow, while at the same time, HTML5 offers very easy debugging solutions.

So, is HTML5 the right choice? It depends on your needs and what you want to achieve. Right now, HTML5 still seems immature when compared to other languages and the tools you need to create HTML5 games are still buggy and not perfected. But HTML5 is also considered by many developers as the future of mobile game development.

As *Morpheus* says to *Neo*: "I told you we can only show you the door, you have to walk through it!"

Scripting languages

Scripting languages are programming languages used to create programs that run in another software application. They are usually interpreted from source code or bytecode, while the environment in which they run is programmed with a compiled programming language such as C++. This is a way to prevent scripts from causing fatal errors, since users cannot access the original source code or modify it.

Generally speaking, scripting languages are easier and faster to pick up, when compared to true programming languages, thanks to the implementation of a simpler syntax.

There are several kinds of scripting languages; some are domain specific, with very specific design and implementation goals while others address more general purposes. Scripting languages are usually meant to automate a specific set of actions; many popular software packages offer internal scripting languages to perform user actions. For example, 3D Studio Max, Maya, or Blender have an internal scripting language to program so-called macros that automate operations available in the software environment. Scripting, in this case, is a way to save time when the user has to carry out repetitive operations.

With regard to the scope of this book, we discuss scripting languages as programming languages supported by game engines such as Unity, UDK, Corona SDK, and so on. They are used to program the game logic, the behavior of game objects, the user interface, and any other aspect involved in the creation of the gameplay inside a specific game engine. ActionScript, JavaScript, UnrealScript, and LUA are the examples of scripting languages that are supported by popular game engines.

Structure of a game program

Regardless of its destination platform or complexity, each game has a basic structure made of three sections: initialization, the game loop, and termination. Let's describe each one of them.

Initialization

The initialization is where you set anything that the game needs to get going, mainly variables. You set the starting position and parameter values of the main character, the number and starting position of enemies, collectibles and bonus, the difficulty settings, activate data sharing, and run connection protocols; the list may be pretty long, you got the idea.

The game loop

The game loop is the heart of the game, the fundamental routine that keeps going as long as the player keeps playing. In this part of the game program, you get the input from the player, compute the consequences of his actions, and draw the results on screen. Then repeat.

The following script represents the basic structure of a game loop:

```
int main()
{
    bool gameEnded=false;

    while(!gameEnded)
    {
        HandleInput();  //Reads keyboard, mouse or any other
                        //kind of input used by the player

        Update();       //Updates game logic and, based on info
                        //gathered with the previous step

        Draw();         //Draws graphics on screen,
                        //a process called Render.
    }
}
```

In this piece of script, the loop given by the `HandleInput()`, `Update()`, and `Draw()` functions is repeated as long as the `gameEnded` variable remains `true`.

At some point that variable turns its value to `false`, likely due to the main character death. The loop then stops, the **Game Over** message is displayed, and the game gets ready to start a new match.

Termination

The final section is termination. The player decided to quit playing, so it is time to clean up the system memory from any residual of the game routines and perform any shut-down operation required.

This phase is especially important for smartphones, which are kind of omnitools that solve many different tasks. You surely don't want a game that keeps running on your device, sucking down system resources, and slowing down its performances.

Conclusion

This is the basic plan all games stick to, regardless of platform and programming language. The internet is full of resources to develop the game structure of a game in any language you may want to use.

We thus close this section with a few pieces of advice. One is to draw on screen only after all other operations regarding the game logic are performed. Otherwise, the player could experience errors, for example, on the position of game objects.

The other is to learn to manage the time-related functions of the programming language of your choice because they allow to keep the frame rate of your game stable, both during gameplay sessions and across different devices.

Summary

In this chapter we discussed the general characteristics of programming languages and examined the two most popular ones: C++ and Java.

We described what a scripting language is and provided basic details of two programming languages used for game development today: Objective-C and HTML5.

Finally, we provided an example of the basic structure of a game program and its main sections.

In the next chapter, we will discuss today's smartphones and tablets as gaming devices.

We will analyze their I/O characteristics and their technical features such as touch screen, gyroscope, proximity, and light sensors, and describe how these features can be exploited to design games that perfectly fit the mobile platform.

6
Mobile Game Controls

The control system, together with graphics, is the factor that most affects the gameplay experience. If game controls are not intuitive and easy to learn, or don't respond promptly to players' actions, players won't enjoy playing that game and it won't sell much.

We thus dedicate a chapter to describing the available input methods and technologies available on today's mobile devices, including keypads, touch screens, and sensors that can enhance your gameplay experience. By knowing the strengths and weaknesses of each input method available on today's smartphones, you will be able to make the right choice when designing the control system for your next mobile game.

In this chapter we will cover the following topics:

- Input technology
- Touchscreens
- Keypads
- Touchscreen gestures
- Built-in devices
- Future input technologies

Input technology

What is the difference between passive (video) and active (games) digital entertainment? The answer is being able to control the outcome of the experience. And how does one control the game's outcome? Well, with the controls, also known as input. The two most common forms of input are via the keypad of traditional phones featuring physical buttons, and the touchscreen and sensors that smartphones are equipped with. As smartphones featuring touchscreens and sensors represent the latest technology, which is replacing traditional cell phones, this chapter concentrates on the touchscreen and the many input options available on today's smartphones.

Touchscreens

The touchscreen is the natural evolution of the icon-based operating systems we are used to. Instead of selecting data represented by icons and then issuing commands to manipulate them with a mouse, with touch interfaces there is a direct manipulation of the data through a set of predefined, touch-based actions performed with our fingers on the screen.

Mobile devices can use lots of different methods to detect a person's input on a touchscreen. Many use sensors and circuitry to monitor changes in a specific state. Many monitor changes in electrical current. Others monitor changes in the reflection of sound waves or beams of near-infrared light. Some measure changes in vibration caused when your finger hits the screen's surface, or cameras to monitor changes in light and shadow.

Contemporary devices can process more than one touch at a time. This makes it possible to use multitouch gestures, which we will discuss later in the chapter. Earlier touchscreen devices may or may not be able to process more than one touch.

For example, the Apple iPhone has a multitouch user interface that requires touching multiple points on the screen simultaneously. One example is called spread and pinch, where the thumb and forefinger touch the screen at the same time; bringing the fingers together (pinching) zooms out the image while moving the fingers apart (spread) zooms in.

The iPhone is not the only device that allows multitouch operations: Android and Windows Phone-based devices do that too. To allow multitouch operations, screens have capacitors arranged on a grid. When a touch occurs, the device detects its location and direction of movement. A feature of this configuration is the ability to process more than one touch simultaneously.

Generally, two methods are used to detect touch; mutual capacitance and self-capacitance. Mutual capacitance requires two distinct layers of material; one carries electrical current and the other has electrical sensors. Self-capacitance combines the current and sensors into a single layer.

The following figure shows the basic construction of most touchscreens. The processor detects changes in state between the two conductive layers and then calculates where the cursor should be displayed on the LED screen.

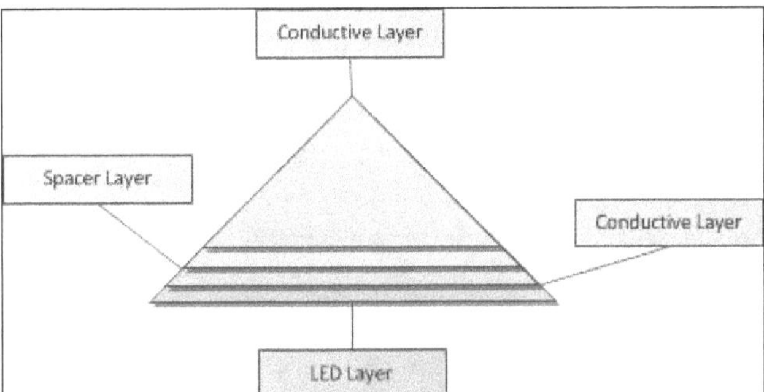

Keypads

These are most common in older mobile devices, although some smartphones have a keypad and a touchscreen, such as the Blackberry. There are three configurations: numeric, alphanumeric, and directional. Following is a figure of the Blackberry Bold, a smartphone featuring all three configurations and that is also equipped with a touchscreen. (This screenshot has been taken from `http://us.blackberry.com/smartphones/blackberry-bold.html?lid=us:bb:devices:blackberrybold&lpos=us:bb:devices#!family=Bold`.)

Touchscreen gestures

Touchscreen smartphones allow a variety of operations to be performed by users, both single and multitouch. Multitouch gestures refer to touchscreen input that uses two or more fingers at a time. The following is a list of the most common touch-based operations available with Apple, Android, and Windows Phone devices.

Single–tap

Touch the screen with one finger, once. This is the fundamental operation required to type text messages and notes, and to launch applications.

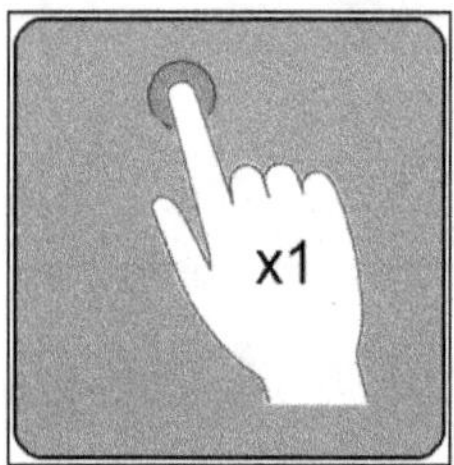

Double–tap

Tap the screen twice, with one finger. This is usually done to select a piece of text to edit it.

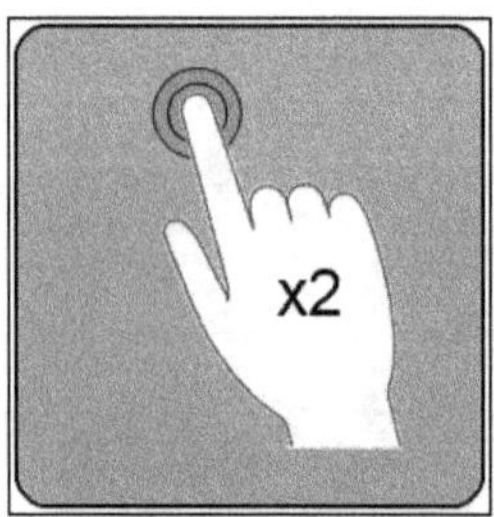

Long press

Press the screen with one finger, and hold. This operation is generally used to select and move icons around the screen.

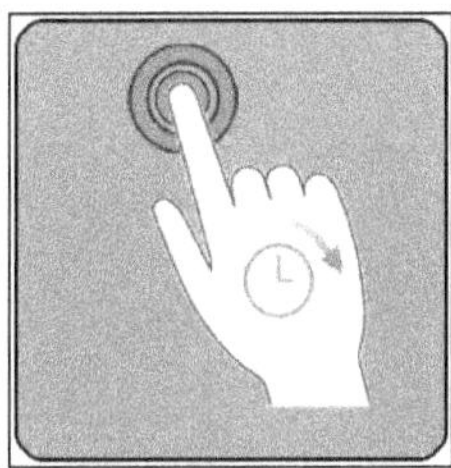

Scroll

Touch the scroll with a single finger, and move it up and down, or left and right. You do this when, for example, you need to find a contact in your list.

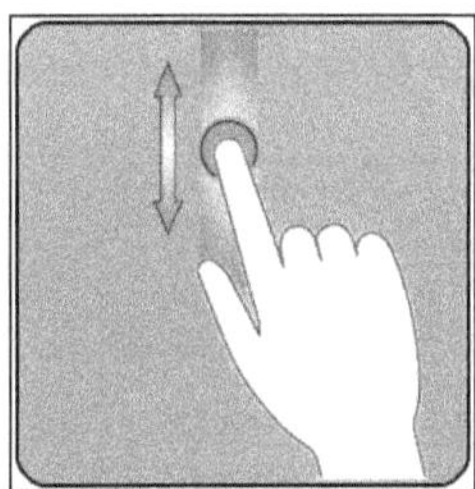

Spread and pinch

To "spread" means to touch the screen with thumb and forefinger and move the fingers apart, an action also known as "pinch in". This is often used to zoom in.

Pinch (or pinch out), on the contrary, means to touch the screen with thumb and forefinger and move the fingers together. This is usually done to zoom out.

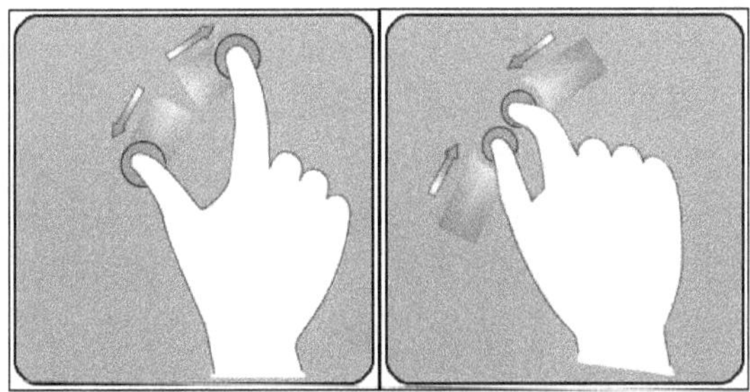

Pan

Touch the screen with one finger and move in any direction. This operation is used to pan the view when an application offers an interactive area which is larger than the available screen, as is the case, for example, when playing strategic and management games.

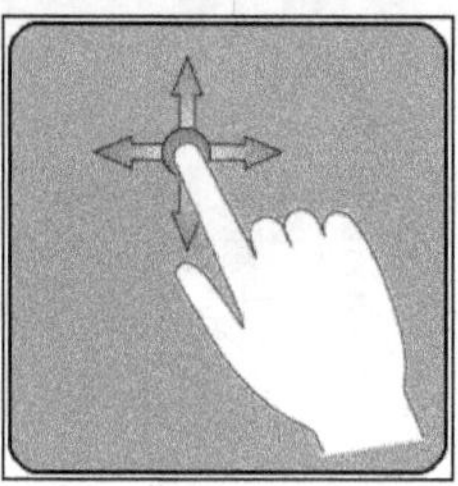

Flick

Touch the screen with one finger and move it rapidly side-to-side or up and down. In games this is used to kick things away, like the ball in soccer games.

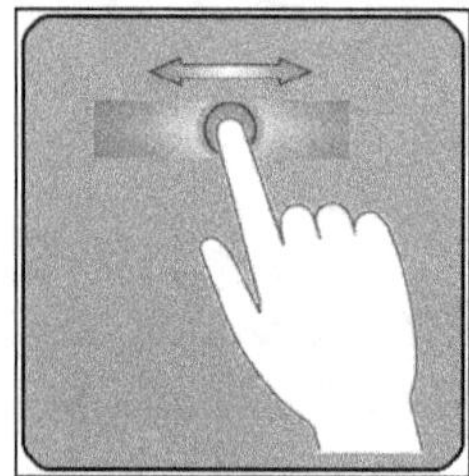

Multifinger tap

Touch the screen briefly with two or more fingers. Different applications implement this action to perform specific tasks, such as resizing an image, zooming in, or zooming out.

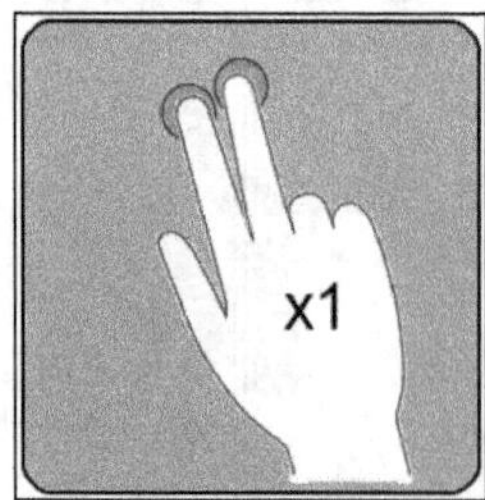

Multifinger scroll

Touch the screen with two or more fingers and move them side-to-side or up and down. For example, the latest Google Map application allows the use of this action to change the inclination of the plane with respect to the user's view.

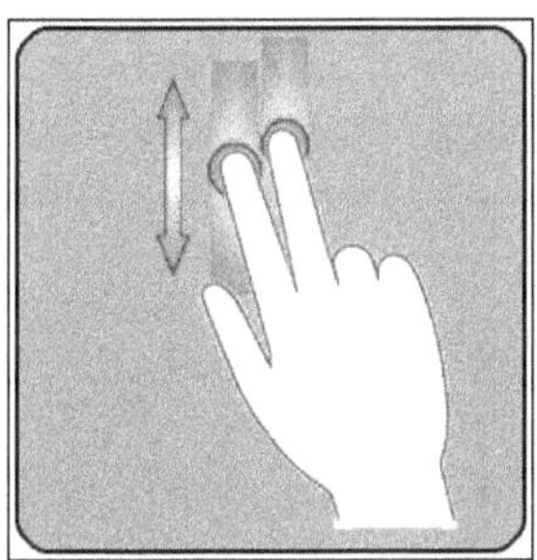

Rotate

Touch the screen with thumb and forefinger, and rotate the forefinger around the thumb. This is often used to rotate an image on screen and is a popular touch operation in puzzles and investigation games.

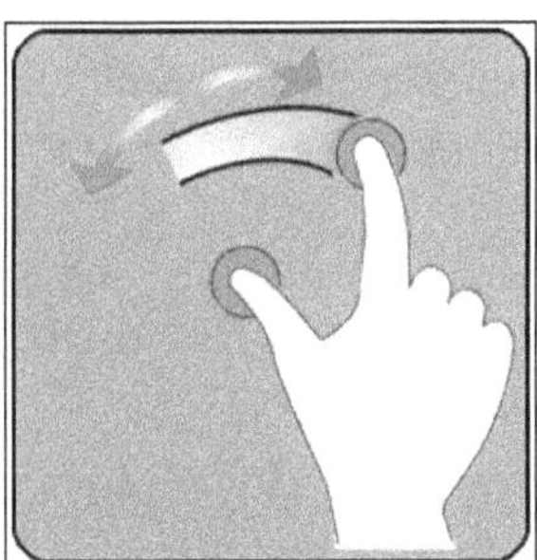

(Images courtesy of Wikipedia)

`http://en.wikipedia.org/wiki/Multi-touch_gestures#Multi-touch_gestures`

Input interfaces for mobile games

The advent of the iOS and its revolutionary touch user interface is responsible for one of the most interesting aspects of mobile game development: the possibility of creating games that rely on very innovative input control systems.

Not only the usual touch actions, such as swiping and tapping, have been exploited to create the mechanics for innovative and popular games belonging to various genres, such as Fruit Ninja, Spider the Secret of Bryce Manor, Angry Birds, or Temple Run.

As the iPhone and the majority of smartphones are provided with sensors to detect movement, proximity, light, a camera, a microphone, and a headphone jack, these pieces of hardware have been taken into consideration by game developers to create games that were simply not possible before the advent of the touch interface and today's smartphones.

In the following sections, we examine the distinctive features of mobile devices from a mobile game designer's perspective. How can we exploit the potential of built-in and external components of today's smartphones to design games?

Built-in devices

We begin our tour with the features of a smartphone which are the built-in features. Modern smartphones include a variety of built-in sensors that can be accessible for mobile games, and we encourage you to exploit these whenever you can in your games.

There is more than one reason for this. The successful built-in features of one device tend to be adopted by competitors over a period of time. In fact, the most popular smartphones tend to share relevant and appreciated features, such as the accelerometer. The accelerometer is featured by any smartphone we can think of today, and it is a piece of hardware that any smartphone owner expects to have on his device.

If you design a game mechanic around the accelerometer, you can be pretty sure that your game can reach the largest audience possible, which is a good start for any indie game.

GPS

The **Global Positioning System** (**GPS**) is a space-based satellite navigation system that requires an unobstructed line of sight to four or more GPS satellites. The GPS can provide very accurate location information to the device, for itself and its surroundings. For example, it is possible to search for nearby restaurants, landmarks, and so on.

GPS games usually include an element of **Augmented Reality** (**AR**). One example of a GPS game is Shadow Cities by Grey Area. Players team up to conquer their neighborhood, street by street, using magic spells. One of the few **MMORPGs** (**Massively Multiplayer Role Playing Games**) on mobile devices, Shadow Cities is free to play and is available on the App Store on `www.shadowcities.com`.

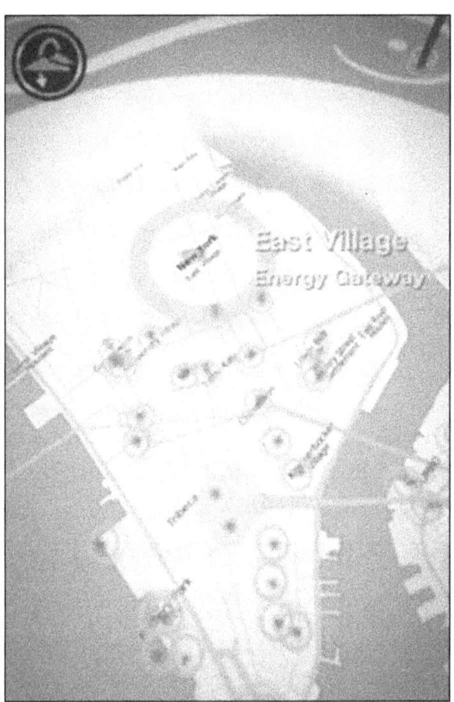

Accelerometer

Smartphones are provided with a 3-axis accelerometer which detects the orientation of the phone in the space and changes the screen orientation accordingly. Most applications take advantage of this feature by swapping between landscape and portrait view, for example, when viewing a photo.

With regard to games, the accelerometer (and the gyroscope) are exploited by tons of games; generally all games which simply weren't possible on any other kind of device.

So many games use the accelerometer for driving, that there's no need to mention any. Tilt the iPhone left/right to turn your vehicle accordingly.

Doodle Jump is a completely different kind of game, still popular regardless of its age, which requires the player to tilt the iPhone left or right to control the jumping direction of the game character as he climbs an endless series of platforms.

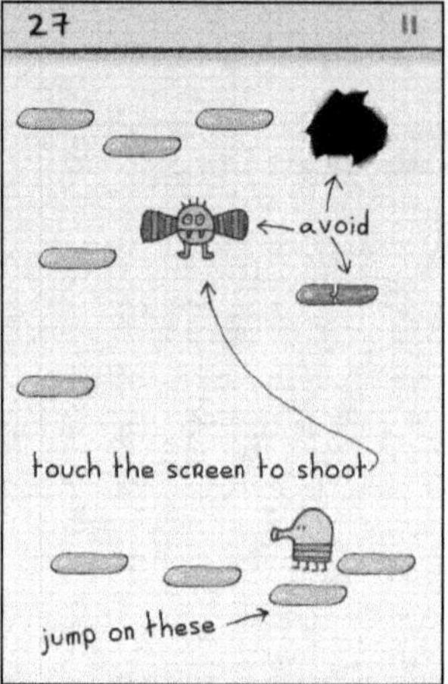

Rolando is a very smart physics-based platformer where you control a spherical character by tilting the iPhone to exploit gravity, and to get momentum to overcome obstacles and get to the end of each level.

Camera

All smartphones have a built-in camera which is often used for games based on Augmented Reality. AR is a technique which allows enhancing the real-world environment by overlaying computer generated elements such as 3D characters that are visible in the real world when watching through the camera. It provides interactive and digitally manipulatable information about the real world of users and has many uses, not only in architecture, tourism, and entertainment but also has uses in medicine, the military, and obviously, in gaming. More on AR can be found at `http://en.wikipedia.org/wiki/Augmented_reality`.

Among recent popular titles that use AR to enhance gameplay, we would like to mention Star Wars: Falcon Gunner and AR Defender.

Falcon Gunner is a classical **First Person Shooter** (**FPS**) in which the player is asked to shoot incoming enemy ships. The distinctive feature of the game is that, thanks to AR techniques, the player can see the enemy ships attacking him as they fly in his actual environment.

AR Defender is a tower defense game where the player controls a defensive tower as it fires against enemies attacking in the kitchen, the bathroom, the bus, or wherever the player decides to land the marker.

Microphone

Speech recognition is an interesting opportunity for mobile developers, since Fonix developed its VoiceIn toolkit for the iPhone. The most important game developers such as EA, Ubisoft, and Harmonix, creators of the Guitar Hero franchise are already licensees for this technology, which means that the number of games which feature speech recognition will grow over time as the technology gets more popular. As we write, there are several applications which offer speech recognition services already available on the Apple Store.

Smartphones, on the other hand, are provided with a built-in microphone which has already been used to develop many quirky games that use the microphone as an input device.

Zoom Zoom is a car racing game in which the car speed is controlled by the player's voice: the more noise you make, the faster the car goes.

iBBQ is a barbecue simulator. As a player, you are requested, among the other things, to blow in the iPhone microphone to blow on the embers to revive the fire.

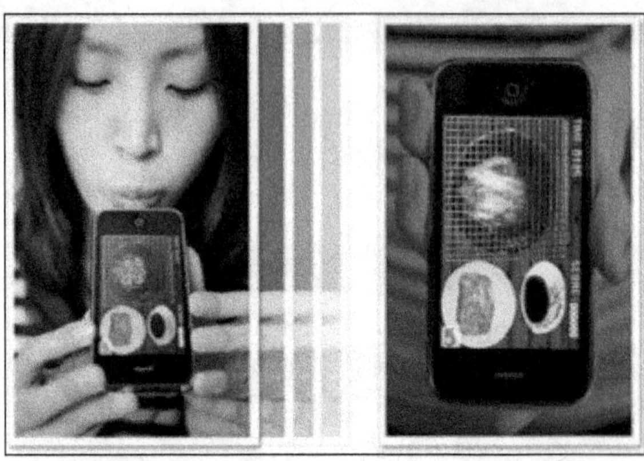

Sonic Lighter is a lighter simulator with a distinctive feature: the possibility of blowing in the microphone to blow out the flame.

But the most popular application using the iPhone microphone as an input device is Ocarina. The player must tap the holes displayed on screen and blow in the microphone to play with this ocarina simulator.

These are just a few examples of creative ways to exploit the technical characteristics of a device to create innovative gameplay without spending millions. Keep these in mind when planning your next indie game or application!

External controllers

A number of manufacturers provide add-on controllers that can simulate classic console controllers, joysticks, and even miniature arcade cases. They are a reasonable alternative to virtual buttons on the screen and generally provide a better user experience, especially for the more retro-styled mobile games.

On the other hand, they are external hardware, and as such you cannot expect them to be a requirement for a game. Designing a mobile game around an external control only makes sense if you are developing the game for the hardware manufacturer in the first place.

Anyway, they exist, and are quite popular too, so why miss the opportunity of supporting them in your next game in order to provide extra value?

Gamepads

These are Bluetooth external controllers consisting in a control pad and a full set of buttons to offer optimal control capabilities for more console-style oriented titles. Such devices offer some advantages and have drawbacks.

The first advantage is that a gamepad is a better controlling device than a touchscreen when dealing with levers and buttons, because a gamepad offers that tactile feedback to the player's actions that the virtual pad on a touchscreen cannot. This is very important for action games. Secondly, the player has his/her hand on the pad and don't encumber the screen area with their fingers. Finally, playing with your iPhone won't leave any oily traces on the screen, which is good anyway!

One disadvantage is that external controllers must be supported by titles, to work with games. This means that game developers are supposed to take care of supporting one or more of these controllers in their games. As a developer, you have to consider the extra time and money it costs to support gamepads and compare it with the popularity of such devices.

Gamepad models range from those that apply to the device itself, offering a better grip on the smartphone and turning it into a true handheld game console, while others are provided with a docking station for the mobile device, so that the player only holds the gamepad in his hands, such as with the debated Duo Gamer, the first gamepad officially approved by Apple, which costs $79 at the time of writing, and is only compatible with the Gameloft titles. There is also the retro style 8-Bitty controller by iCade which is basically a NES controller connected via Bluetooth to your iPhone.

Others are as small as a key holder and only offer a cross-directional pad and a couple of buttons, enough for more arcade-oriented, old-school titles.

For those of you with a steam-punk soul, it is even possible to connect Bluetooth or USB gaming devices to an Android phone. We know of gamers who use their PS3 controller to play mobile games! If you are interested, we suggest you checkout the following link:

`http://reviews.cnet.co.uk/mobile-apps/how-to-play-android-games-with-your-ps3-controller-50004688/`

Analog sticks

For those not interested in playing mobile titles with a gamepad, there are several stick controllers that directly apply to the screen, right above the virtual pads, to offer a better sensibility when playing, such as the well-designed Fling by Targus that attaches to the device with suction cups and is transparent, in order to not obstruct the player's view.

There is even one stick controller that detects the player input through the iPhone camera. It is an analog stick developed by a group of Japanese researchers at the Kejo University (`http://www.keio.ac.jp/`) which uses markers to send input to the on-built camera. The markers on the controller are detected by the camera. As the player moves the stick, the markers move too, and their movement is interpreted through the iPhone camera and turned into movement of an object on the screen, like a game character.

Touch-enabled cases

Another interesting line of external controllers is consists of touch-enabled cases such as the Sensus by Canopy. It is an iPhone case equipped with capacitive back and side areas to control games and the device in general, without obscuring the screen with your hands. As with the gamepad discussed previously, these kinds of accessories help keep the screen free and clean, but need to be supported by developers. The Sensus, in fact, comes with a free SDK to help game developers quickly and easily offer support for the device in their games.

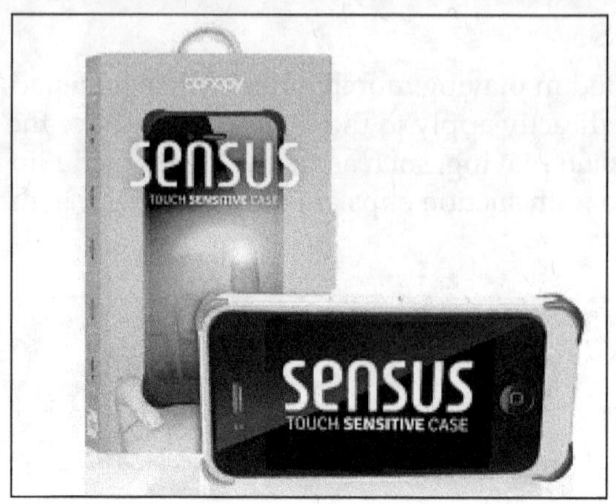

Grip

Here is an example of a touch-enabled device. Docomo has a new technology that it calls the Grip UI concept, which allows users to interact with a smartphone by gripping it in different ways. In addition to sensing where pressure is applied, this technology will detect different levels of pressure applied, and can execute certain functions or shortcuts corresponding to specific input. So for example, it could unlock your phone by gripping it in a certain manner, or launch an application. This has some exciting implications for gaming input.

`http://technology.xin.msn.com/technology-news/techinasia-article.aspx?cp-documentid=250777765`

Cabinets

For those who are really hardcore mobile gamers, the iCade and the iCade Jr are accessories that turn your iPhone/iPad into a true old school cabinet. Though large, the selection of games (mainly Atari titles) supported by the device is still limited, so the same issues that arise from other external controllers occur. We only mention the iCade for its aesthetic qualities.

Headphones

As we switch to the topic of audio-based games, we also move from input to output systems.

Audio-based games are important for two reasons. First is that it is a way to create innovative gameplay.

There's a game called Papa Sangre, where the player is asked to control the direction the game character moves in, to reach specific sound sources. The screen only displays the actual direction the character is facing. The direction it must move to is to be inferred by sound cues, that are delivered to the player through the headphones thanks to positional audio technology. By not displaying anything on the screen and the use of strange, disturbing sounds, this game is capable of providing pretty cool immersion and an uncommon, and almost scary, gaming experience.

In Audio Invaders, the player controls the popular ship from Space Invaders by tilting the iPhone to move left or right. The screen is pretty much black and enemy ships are not fully displayed. The player must infer their position to fire at them using audio cues provided through the headphones to his left or right ear.

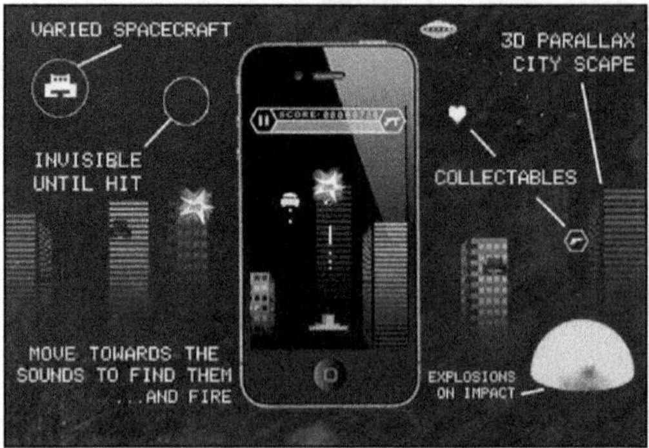

But second and the most important reason in mentioning mobile games and applications that rely on audio as the main output channel is that these kinds of games are accessible to people with visual impairments. Still today, very few games offer such feature, and most of the time this fact is unavoidable, since after all, video games are video games. Whenever you, as a developer, create a game that can be played even by those with impaired vision, you not only show that you are a very smart developer who can design games that target the largest audience, but also prove that you have sensibility towards other people's needs, which is a nice personal quality!

Future technologies

There are some technologies on the horizon that will be widely available very soon. One example is eye tracking; brainwave readers are another. Both have a lot of gaming potential, so we would like to say a few words on each of them.

Eye tracking

Using eye movement as an input device has been around for a long time, but up until recently it was prohibitively expensive. This is rapidly changing, with eye-tracking add-ons becoming cheaper over time.

Senseye is an example that has been designed to allow users to interact with their mobiles through eye movement tracking. Uses include scrolling a web browser, controlling game objects, and turning on the screen as it's looked at.

Starting in 2013, eyetribe.com (Senseye's maker) plans to integrate their technology into new smartphones as well as releasing an add-on device for older models.

Docomo's I Beam invested in this technology and their tablet has eye tracking built in. Still in the prototype stage, there have been no announcements on the specifications or release dates at this time.

Brainwave readers

The second interesting technology that we would like to mention is that of brainwave readers.

It is now available at a reasonable cost; there is hardware that allows us to record the electric signals emitted by areas of our brain cortex using headsets which don't require expertise to be worn, and gels of any sort that are used to improve the conduction of signals coming from our brain.

Such a headset can be connected to a mobile phone with an application running which can read the signal coming from the headset and perform interesting and useful functions, ranging from the field of pure entertainment to more medical or experimental oriented tasks.

NeuroSky (`http://www.neurosky.com/Default.aspx`) is a company which invests in the brainwave reader technology, and they have developed a kit with the headset and a suite of applications to run on your mobile phone, to take advantage of the signal coming from your brain.

The potential for gaming is unimaginable. If you are interested in this topic, we suggest you checkout the following link showing the potential of the brainwave reader technology:

`http://www.ted.com/talks/tan_le_a_headset_that_reads_your_brainwaves.html`

The following figure represents a bluetooth headset for reading brainwaves and sending the signal to a mobile phone:

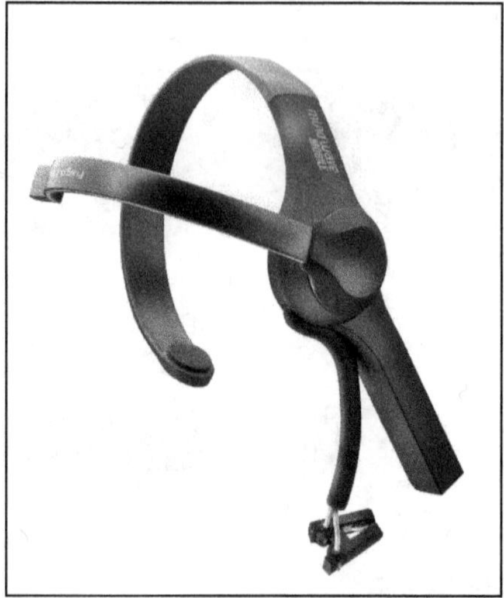

Summary

This chapter covered the basic technology of input devices and the standard gestures used with touchscreens. It also discussed the uses of other built-in sensors and output devices. We covered a variety of external controllers such as joysticks, cabinets, and headphones. We looked at some future technology such as eye-tracking and the brainwave readers.

In the next chapter we will cover the topic user interface design. We will discuss relevant theories about interface design and describe the best practices to design interfaces for mobile games.

7
Interface Design for Mobile Games

In the previous chapter, we described the I/O capabilities of today's smartphones. In this chapter we will analyze the process of creating user interfaces for mobile games which take advantage of such capabilities.

With so many different screen sizes, so little space to work with, and no real standard in the videogame industry, interface design is one of the toughest parts of creating a successful game. We will provide you with what you need to know to address the task properly and come up with optimal solutions for your mobile games. In this chapter, we will cover the following topics:

- Approach to user interface design
- Diegesis theory and videogames
- User interface design
- Icons design
- Best practices of UI design
- "Must-have" game options

The role of the user interface

The user interface is the element that most affects the gameplay of a title, as it defines how the player interacts with the game and accomplishes the task he is presented with.

A well-designed user interface can make a game with simple mechanics feel fresh and interesting, while fully supporting the expectations of the player. It is always a nice surprise for a player when he realizes he can perform some specific action exactly how he imagined it through the game interface: if you can make many players happy like that, your game will climb up the sales charts!

At the same time, the contrary is true as well. No matter the number of innovative game features and mechanics, the quality of graphics and sound, the license you are exploiting, or the story you develop throughout a game, if the interface is patchy, intricate, not intuitive and unappealing, your game isn't likely to sell well.

As we saw in the previous chapter, today's smartphones offer a completely new set of input styles for games. It's up to you, as a mobile game developer, to fully exploit those features to create an interface which optimally fits the needs of your potential players.

Approaching user interface design

When developing a game, there is no official standard or pre-defined set of rules to follow to design its interface. Different games rely on different mechanics and there is always more than one way to implement effective controls for a game.

To approach the task correctly, it is good practice to invest some time in research. A good starting point is to study the general aspects of interaction design. Design affects the shape of the tools we use in our everyday activities at any level and cognitive psychology has thoroughly investigated the means to design effective interactions between humans and the tools and instruments they use. We suggest having a look at *The Theory of Affordances* by James J. Gibson, described in his book *The Ecological Approach to Visual Perception* (`http://en.wikipedia.org/wiki/Affordance`) and reading the book by Donald A. Norman *The Design of Everyday Things*.

The next step is to get proficient with general UI theory. Game engines offer several assets to implement the graphic interface for a game, but how can you make the best of it if you don't know the strengths and weaknesses of a drop-down list compared to a combo box? Which are the pros and cons of each interface element?

Once you understand which interface element is good for what, you can start learning from the success or failures of other developers. Take some time to study the interface of both successful and unpopular games to understand what worked and didn't work for them, what were the reasons they adopted a specific solution for a game mechanic, if there were other options available, and why were they discarded.

Some elements of the UI of a game are shared regardless of the genre, while others are distinctive for different genre. For example, any game should provide the player with info to understand if he's winning or losing. Such info is usually provided in the **Heads up Display** (**HUD**) of a game, in the form of score, available lives\energy, or position of the player in a racing game.

On the other hand, each game genre has its own distinctive UI characteristics that players, especially experienced ones, expect to find in a title. By not supporting such expectations, you enter a risky gray area, as you may find your game frustrates the players, as it contrasts with what they learned during their career. For example, **Real Time Strategy** (**RTS**) games allow selecting a group of units to issue orders. The possibility to drag a selection box around a group of units is an expected feature of any RTS title. By not implementing such feature you basically bet against your players: before you do that, take some time to think if it really makes sense for your game to deny what other games proved to have worked fine. There are other ways to be innovative when designing a game than messing up with the interface, which could result in a total failure for your game!

Practicing is the best way to learn to design effective UI for games, in the end. Approach different genres and try different solutions, then test them. Have both experienced and un-experienced players try your game interface. Ask them what worked for them and what didn't, and why. You may find, for example, that the gaming experience affects the evaluation of a game interface, as experienced players know what to expect, while casual gamers are less likely to make comparisons. To please all of them is hard work of tuning and refinement, which takes time and effort to accomplish. If you do it right, your game will be enjoyed by many gamers and get you good revenue. A good rule of thumb is watch as a player encounters a new feature. If it takes them more than 30 seconds to figure it out and/or they ask more than three questions, the interface needs to be redesigned.

UI in videogames

Throughout the history of videogames, interfaces have evolved according to the evolution of game mechanics, which basically got more complex with time. If you think that an Xbox 360 controller has two analog sticks, a D-pad, and 13 buttons, while the Atari 2600 pad had a stick and one button, you can understand what we mean! The way you take advantage of such potential to develop the proper interface for your gameplay, can make a difference between fame and failure. As we saw in the previous chapter, today's smartphones rely on touch-screen controls and a few sensors for input, so they can't compare to gamepads with regard to in-game controls capabilities. But it is also true that a very interesting aspect of mobile gaming is that it brought simple mechanics that characterized old-school games back to the top. Give all attention you can to converting your game controls in an effective user interface for your target device and your gameplay will very much benefit from it.

When games were basically 2D, there was not too much to question about realism. Games weren't realistic and the interface only needed to show the score, available lives, equipped weapons, or actions available. Interface design only required being effective and consistent, and the suspension of disbelief was not a matter of concern.

With the advent of 3D in videogames, designers had to face the problem of realism and how to preserve the players' immersion throughout the game. If one's playing from the perspective of the game character in a First Person Shooter, is it acceptable to provide him with a HUD? Won't this break his suspension of disbelief? Though a full detailed HUD can fit Crysis, which is set in the future, how can it be adapted to a title set in WWII?

Still, players need plenty of info when playing shooters, especially competitive ones: ammo available, direction they are facing, stance of the character, map, and others. Correctly displayed, these info can make the difference between "life and death" during a multiplayer death match.

With regard to the types of different interface styles adopted by videogames, a very popular theory, adapted from the diegesis theory used in literature and film, defines four categories to classify game interfaces: diegetic, non-diegetic, spatial, and meta.

The classification is based on two dimensions, depending on the answers given to the following two questions:

- Is the interface component part of the game story\narrative?
- Is the interface component part of the actual game space?

The following figure offers a representation of this classification:

		Is the interface component part of the game story/narrative?	
		no	yes
Is the interface component part of the actual game space?	no	non-diegetic representations	spatial representations
	yes	meta representations	diegetic representations

Let's explain these concepts through examples taken from actual 3D games.

- **Diegetic**: A diegetic representation answers "yes" to both the questions of the diagram: the component is part of the game narrative and it is located inside the game world. It is experienced by both the player and his character.

Shadow of the Colossus implements a diegetic representation of the compass which tells the player where he should go. When the player needs to know where to go next, he can make the game character raise his blade in the sun and a light beam appears that shows the direction to take. Check the following figure which represents a screenshot of the game:

Health is represented by a bar on the suit of the game character in Dead Space or the stealth level represented as colored LEDs on the suit of Sam Fisher (Splinter Cell) are other examples of this approach.

The good thing about diegetic representations is that they tell the player what he needs to know without breaking the continuity of the gaming experience. The bad thing is that, if not done properly, it can be very destructive to the game flow and can annoy the players. In Grim Fandango, the inventory can only be scrolled one item at a time. Though realistic, this option frustrates the players and breaks their suspension of disbelief.

- **Non-diegetic**: Opposite to the former definition, a non-diegetic component is rendered outside of the game world and it is only available to the player, not to his character. A non-diegetic component answers "no" to both questions; it represents the approach used by most games which offer a full-optional HUD to their players.
    - **Call of duty**: Modern warfare uses a typical non-diegetic HUD, which perpetually displays several pieces of useful info to the player: the weapon he is wielding and its cross-hair, the amount and types of ammo and grenades available, a map and a compass for directions, and the stance of the character, among the others.

The following figure is a screenshot from the game:

If it is well-designed, a non-diegetic interface goes unnoticed by the players and has no detrimental effect on their experience, as they have adapted with time to the use of such HUDs in games.

HUDs can be very complex or very minimal, according to the complexity of the game mechanics and what is necessary for the player to be aware of to play the game. Tactical shooters, simulations, and RPGs tend to have the most complex interfaces, as players are supposed to be aware of many things to effectively play such games, while more action oriented titles tend to require less stuff to be continually displayed on screen.

A very interesting example of a game with basically no HUD is Peter Jackson's King Kong, an adventure FPS with no ammo, health, or even cross-hair displayed on screen. Aiming with no reticule and the low amount of ammo available in the game made every fighting sequence pretty engaging and full of tension. Think about such examples whenever you are about to decide which components are really necessary when designing the HUD for your user interface.

The following figure represents the absence of HUD in King Kong.

- **Spatial**: These components are elements that live outside the game narrative ("no" to the first question), as they are not experienced by the game characters, still they appear inside the game world to provide specific cues to the players ("yes" to the second question).

  In Fable 2, the player is told the direction of his next objective via a shiny trail that appears on the ground, in front of the game character. Whether we assume that the game character can see it or not, the trail is an artifact created by the game designer to help the player never get lost in the game world, which doesn't actually affect the game story and it is a smart implementation of the compass which perfectly adapts to the look and feel of the title.

  The trail is represented in the following image taken from Fable 2:

  Another example is the brackets which appear on selected units in RTS games. If those brackets weren't put inside the game environment, it would be pretty hard for a player to understand which units he is in control of at any moment. Still, we cannot assume that the brackets are perceived by the game units or affect the outcome of a battle.

Spatial components tend on one side to encumber the game view, as they consist of icons and text displayed on screen and add to anything else which is already in the player's view. On the other side, they are more than helpful; they can be necessary to fully exploit the game mechanics of a title. Ask any WOW player about the configurable interface of their favorite title!

- **Meta**: This is the last category and it stands for all those components of an interface which exist in the game world, so "yes" to the first question, but are not visualized spatially in the game world, so "no" to the second question. The blood splatters on the screen which reduces visibility for a short while in shooters are an example of such components. Another one we would like to mention is Samus' face reflection in the helmet in Metroid Prime, as shown in the following figure:

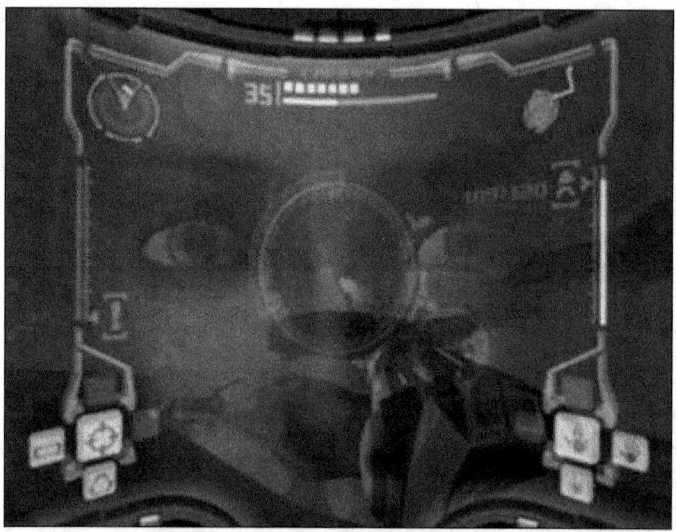

The aim of such components is generally to make the game experience feel more real and consistent for players, they are little touches that help the player sustain the suspension of disbelief as he plays a title.

It's important to note that making the game experience feel more real and consistent doesn't necessarily mean more realistic. Think of the lens flare effect in a racing game. As the lens flare is an effect generated by light refracting on a lens, whenever we are shown a lens flare in a game, the designer is telling us "this is just a game, you are not really driving a car". On the other hand, we as entertainment consumers, are so used to the representation of sports and events on TV, that whenever a game features special effects, such as lens flare, we feel like we are witnessing the real event through a TV camera, not just a game.

The diegesis theory provides us with a useful scheme to make a basic categorization between different game interfaces, though, as any model, it could not perfectly apply to any game we may experience. Definitions are useful, but more important is that the interface that you are designing for your game fits its needs. The most important thing for a game interface is that it serves the purpose of the game mechanics and puts the player in the optimal conditions to fulfill the game goals. Never stick to a model based on a prejudiced assumption or a style manifesto; instead, ask yourself what is the look and feel you want for your game and what kind of involvement you want for your players, then choose wisely the kind of interface that best adapts to your assumptions.

If you want to examine this topic in more depth, we suggest the following articles from Gamasutra:

- `http://www.gamasutra.com/view/feature/4286/game_ui_discoveries_what_players_.php?print=1`
- `http://www.gamasutra.com/view/feature/132475/a_circular_wall_reformulating_the_.php?page=4`

Designing the UI

The UI of a game should be designed while taking two aspects into consideration: what the look and feel of the game is and what are the actions the main character will perform, and how.

Begin by defining a list of functions that must be included in the UI, things such as score, available lives, real and virtual money amount, cross-hair, and mini-map, whatever is absolutely necessary to be displayed in the interface of the game.

Then map these fundamental functions to different interface methods. Take each item on the list and ask yourself which is the interface method that better fits the needs of the game with regard to that specific interface component. For example, assume we need to show the health status of units in a strategic title: will the player better benefit from a spatial method, such as drawing a health bar on the top of the unit, or a diegetic method, such as displaying the health status as actual damage to the unit model/sprite?

When making such a decision, always keep in mind the look and feel you want for your game. If your game mainly relies on immersion, try to manage the most important components with diegetic methods. If efficiency and clarity of the info displayed on screen is what you care most about, it is very likely that a spatial or non-diegetic representation will better serve such purposes.

Iterate the process many times, until you feel like the main components of the interface are displayed with the best method and the way game actions are performed reflect the look and feel of the game and/or the main character style.

Remember that a game interface is not only made of graphics juxtaposed on the screen: audio, animations, and FX can be used as well. For example, the position of enemies in the game world could be displayed as colored dots on radar, but you could also use audio cues and audio positioning techniques to lure the player toward the enemies. Try to mix things up, and as usual, be creative!

Aesthetics

Optimal functionality is not enough for a game interface to be well-designed. The game interface should also be consistent with the aesthetics of your game. If you are working on a futuristic title, there's no question that the interface should be futuristic as well.

As the best interface is the one which the player doesn't even notice, many developers agree that the UI is secondary to the artworks of a game. Always create interfaces that are consistent with the other artwork of your product and that complement them. If you design an intrusive interface, it will pop out of the screen and distract the players from the engagement of playing your title.

More on vectors and rasters

We already discussed the topic of rasters and vectors graphics in *Chapter 3, Graphics for Mobile*. We are now going to delve into the details of these drawing techniques with specific regard to UI design.

The variability of screen sizes and resolutions that (from a game developer perspective) affects mobile devices, especially Android smartphones, requires specific techniques to design game interfaces to deal with such variability.

The risk that must be avoided at all costs is that you need to redesign the game interface every time you target a new device for your game, as scaling up or down an interface can be very problematic.

As we already said, when creating graphics for games, there are two options available: drawing pixel by pixel (raster graphics) or drawing with curves and gradients (vector graphics). Vector graphics result in lighter files but they are less efficient for real-time graphics, as vectors must be converted into raster before they can be displayed on screen. Raster graphics, on the other hand, don't need such conversion, resulting in better game performance.

The important thing here is that vector graphics can be scaled, while rasters cannot. A good solution to address the problem of scaling the game interface to adapt to different devices is to create a basic template for your game UI using vector graphics and working with dedicated software, such as Adobe Illustrator. Scale vectors as needed, until you find the size that best fits the needs of your game.

Then convert vectors into rasters (bitmap, JPEG, or PNG file formats) as you move to the actual interface for the game. This procedure will help you save time and money, should a new device become available with different screen size\resolution, requiring scaling up or down the UI you already designed. In such cases, you just need to scale the template in vector graphics and then recreate the rasterized assets from that template. With raster graphics, on the other hand, you would be forced to re-design every interface component altogether.

Whether to use vector or raster graphics also depends on the artwork styles you chose for your game. For example, vectors rarely suit realistic graphics. As the handheld technology advances, players generally expect more realistic-looking games. In such cases, you should prefer to produce the graphic assets for your interface as bitmaps.

On the other hand, vector art allows creating perfect stylized graphic artworks for those titles with a strong characterization, in terms of creative direction. Kid Vector is one such title: a platformer with excellent controls and vector graphics, as you can see in the following figure:

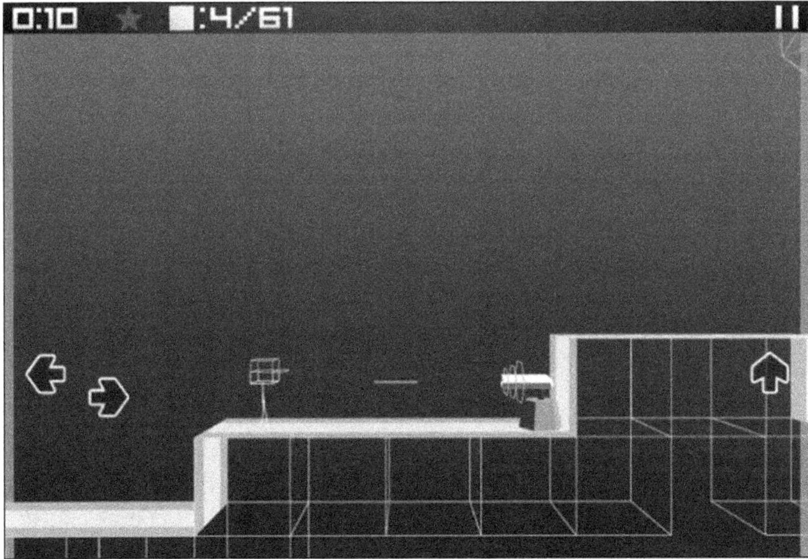

Designing icons

Icons are a very important element of any mobile game from the very beginning of its commercial life. When you upload your new game on the App Store, it's mainly the icon you provide that will convince potential customers to try your game. Badly- designed and crafted icons won't attract many players in the sea of potential apps to download!

Creating the perfect icons for your game is not to be overlooked. But which are the best techniques to create nice, crisp icons? In the previous section of this chapter, we discussed the differences between raster and vector graphics. Now we will apply those concepts to the creation of game icons.

First of all, we need to re-formulate the concept that vector graphics can be scaled at our wish with no quality loss.

Though it is true that vectors can be scaled, when the size of an icon is less than 48x48 pixels, some weaknesses of the vector based approach emerge. If you create a 24x24 pixel vector image and scale it down to 16x16 pixels, some blurring will occur, as there is no way to match the proportions between the two sizes.

As you may notice in the following figure, the first line of icons, created as separate files, are far more detailed and crisp than the second line of icons, obtained by scaling a single vector file.

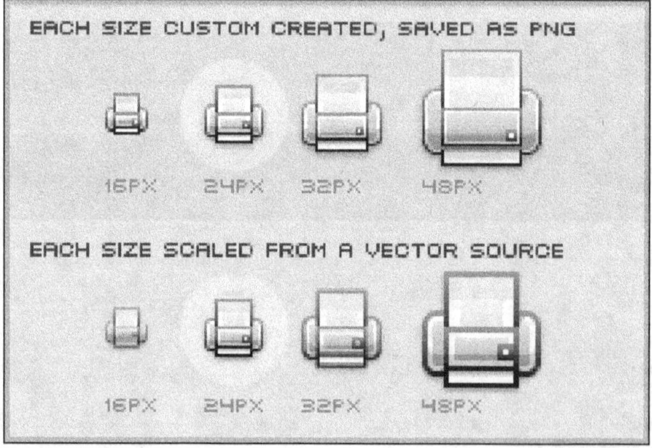

Whenever you need to create small sized icons, the best thing to do is to design separate bitmaps, scaled to match every required size. Even if it takes a little more time to achieve, it prevents the poor results obtained when scaling a single vector to different icon sizes.

On the other hand, you just need to worry about it for small, very detailed icons. If the size of your icons is more than 48x48 pixels and/or your icons are not filled with many fine details, you won't have to worry about the vector scaling problem.

Best practices in UI design

Now that we have discussed the theoretic aspects of interface design for mobile games, in the following section we will provide a list of useful hints to approach the creation of a well-designed UI for your next game.

The first golden rule is that the better the game interface is designed, the less it will be noticed by players, as it allows users to navigate through the game in a way that feels natural and easy to grasp.

To achieve that, always opt for the simplest solution possible, as simplicity means that controls are clean and easy to learn and that the necessary info is displayed clearly.

A little bit of psychology helps when deciding the positioning of buttons in the interface. Human beings have typical cognitive biases and they easily develop habits. Learning how to exploit such psychological aspects can really make a difference in the ergonomics of your game interface. We mentioned *The Theory of Affordances* by Gibson, but there are other theories of visual perception that should be taken into consideration. A good starting point is the Gestalt Principles that you will find at the following link:

`http://graphicdesign.spokanefalls.edu/tutorials/process/gestaltprinciples/gestaltprinc.htm`

Finally, it may seem trivial, but never assume anything. Design your game interface so that the most prominent options available on the main game screen lead your players to the game.

Choose the target platform. When you begin designing the interface for a game, spend some time thinking about the main target platform for your game, in order to have a reference resolution to begin working with. The following table describes the screen resolutions of the most popular devices you are likely to work with:

Device model	Screen resolution (pixels)
iPhone 3GS and equivalent	480x320
iPhone 4(S) and equivalent	960x640 at 326 ppi
iPhone 5	1136x640 at 326 ppi
iPad 1 and 2	1024x768
iPad 3 retina	2048x1536 at 264 ppi

Device model	Screen resolution (pixels)
iPad Mini	1024x768 at 163 ppi
Android devices	variable
Tablets	variable

As you may notice, when working with iOS, things are almost straightforward, as with the exception of the latest iPhone 5, there are only two main aspect ratios, and retina displays simply doubles the number of pixels. By designing your interface separately for the iPhone/iPod touch, the iPad at retina resolution, and scaling it down for older models, you basically cover almost all the Apple-equipped customers.

For Android-based devices, on the other hand, things are more complicated, as there are tons of devices and they can widely differ from each other in screen size and resolution. The best thing to do in this case is to choose a reference, high-end model with HD display, such as the HTC One X+ or the Samsung Galaxy S4 (as we write), and design the interface to match their resolution. Scale it as required to adapt to others: though this way, the graphics won't be perfect for any device, 90 percent of your gamers won't notice any difference.

The following is a list of sites where you can find useful information to deal with the Android screens variety dilemma:

- `http://developer.android.com/about/dashboards/index.html`
- `http://anidea.com/technology/designer%E2%80%99s-guide-to-supporting-multiple-android-device-screens/`
- `http://unitid.nl/2012/07/10-free-tips-to-create-perfect-visual-assets-for-ios-and-android-tablet-and-mobile/`

Search for references

There is no need to reinvent the wheel every time you design a new game interface. Games can be easily classified by genre and different genres tend to adopt general solutions for the interface that are shared among different titles in the same genre.

Whenever you are planning the interface for your new game, look at others' work first. Play games and study their UI, especially from a functional perspective. When studying others' game interfaces, always ask yourself:

- What info is necessary to the player to play this title?
- What kind of functionality is needed to achieve the game goals?
- Which are the important components that need to stand out from the rest?
- What's the purpose and context of each window?

By answering such questions, you will be able to make a deep analysis of the interface of other games, compare them, and then choose the solutions to better fit your specific needs.

The screen flow

The options available to the players of your game will need to be located in a game screen of some sort. So the questions you should ask yourself are:

- How many screens does my game need?
- Which options will be available to players?
- Where will these options be located?

Once you come up with a list of the required options and game screens, create a flow chart to describe how the player navigates through the different screens and which options are available in each one.

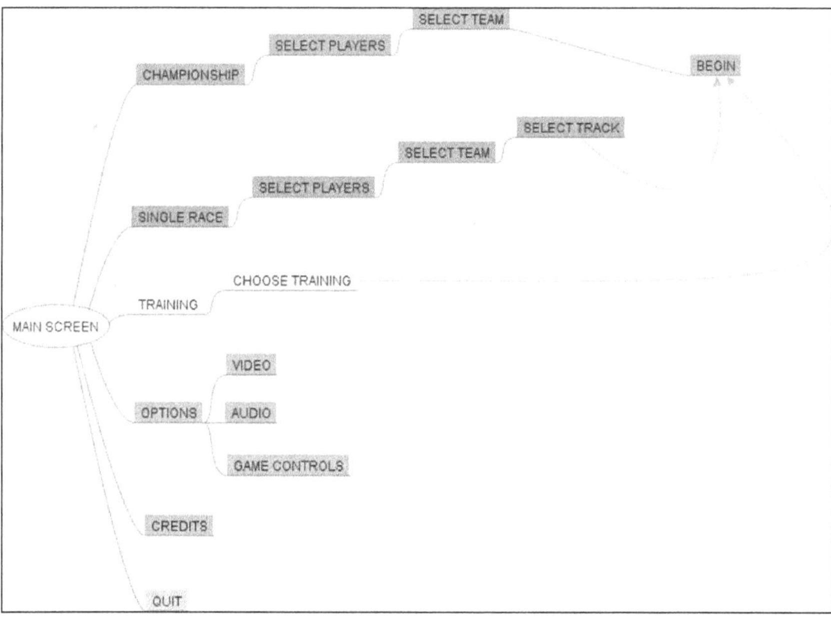

The resulting visual map will help you understand if the screen flow is clear and intuitive, if game options are located where the players expect to find them, and if there are doubles, which should be avoided.

Be sure that each game screen is provided with a **BACK** button to go back to a previous game screen. It can be useful to add hyperlinks to your screen mockups so that you can try navigating through them early on.

Functionality

It is now time to define how the interface you are designing will help users to play your game. At this point, you should already have a clear idea of what the player will be doing in your game and the mechanics of your game. With that information in mind, think about what actions are required and what info must be displayed to deal with them. For every piece of information that you can deliver to the player, ask yourself if it is really necessary and where it should be displayed for optimal fruition.

Try to be as conservative as you can when doing that, it is much too easy to lose the grip on the interface of your game if new options, buttons, and functions keep proliferating. The following is a list of useful hints to keep in mind when defining the functionality of your game interface:

- Keep the number of buttons as low as possible
- Stick to one primary purpose for each game screen
- Refer to the screen flow to check the context for each game screen
- Split complex info into small chunks and/or multiple screens to avoid overburdening your players

Wireframes

Now that the flow and basic contents of the game interface is set, it is time to start drawing with a graphic editor, such as Photoshop.

Create a template for your game interface which can support the different resolutions you expect to develop your game for, and start defining the size and positioning of each button and any pieces of information that must be available on screen. Try not to use colors yet, or just use them to highlight very important buttons available in each game screen.

This operation should involve at least three members of the team: the game designer, the artist, and the programmer. If you are a game designer, never plan the interface without conferring with your artist and programmer: the first is responsible for creating the right assets for the job, so it is important that he/she understands the ideas behind your design choices. The programmer is responsible for implementing the solutions you designed, so it is good practice to ask for his/her opinion too, to avoid designing solutions which in the end cannot be implemented.

There are also many tools that can be used by web and app developers to quickly create wireframes and prototypes for user interfaces. A good selection of the most appreciated tools can be found at the following link:

`http://www.dezinerfolio.com/2011/02/21/14-prototyping-and-wireframing-tools-for-designers`

The button size

We suggest you put an extra amount of attention to defining the proper size for your game buttons. There's no point in having buttons on the screen if the player can't press them.

This is especially true with games that use virtual pads. As virtual buttons tend to shadow a remarkable portion of a mobile device, there is a tendency to make them as small as possible. If they are too small, the consequences can be catastrophic, as the players won't be able to even play your game, let alone enjoy it. *Street Fighter IV* for the iPhone, for example, implements the biggest virtual buttons available on the Apple Store.

Check them in the following figure:

When designing buttons for your game interface, take your time to make tests and find an optimal balance between the opposing necessities of displaying buttons and saving as much screen space as possible for gameplay.

The main screen

The main goal of the first interactive game screen of a title should be to make it easy to play. It is thus very important that the **PLAY** button is large and distinctive enough for players to easily find it on the main screen.

The other options that should be available on the main screen may vary depending on the characteristics of each specific game, although some are expected despite the game genre, such as **OPTIONS**, **LEADERBOARDS**, **ACHIEVEMENTS**, **BUY**, and **SUPPORT**.

The following image represents the main screen of Angry Birds, which is a perfect example of a well-designed main screen. Notice, for example, that optional buttons on the bottom part of the screen are displayed as symbols that make it clear what is the purpose of each one of them. This is a smart way to reduce issues related with translating your game text into different languages.

Test and iterate

Once the former steps are completed, start testing the game interface. Try every option available to check that the game interface actually provides users with everything they need to correctly play and enjoy your game.

Then ask other people to try it and get feedback from them. As you collect feedback, list the most requested modifications, implement them, and repeat the cycle until you are happy with the actual configuration you came up with for your game interface.

Evergreen options

In the last section of this chapter, we will provide some considerations about game options that should always be implemented in a well-designed mobile game UI, regardless of its genre or distinctive features.

Multiple save slots

Though extremely fit for gaming, today's smartphones are first of all phones and multi-purpose devices in general, so it is very common to be forced to suddenly quit a match due to an incoming call or other common activities.

All apps quit when there is an incoming call or when the player presses the home button and mobile games offer an auto-saving feature in case of such events.

What not all games do is to keep separate save states for every mode the game offers or for multiple users.

Plants vs. Zombies, for example, offers such a feature: both the adventure and the quick play modes, in all their variations, are stored in separate save slots, so that the player never loses his/her progresses, regardless of the game mode he/she last played or the game level he/she would like to challenge. The following is a screenshot taken from the main screen of the game:

A multiple save option is also much appreciated because it makes it safe for your friends to try your newly downloaded game without destroying your previous progresses.

Screen rotation

The accelerometer included in a large number of smartphones detects the rotation of the device in the 3D space and most software running on those devices rotate their interface as well, according to the portrait or landscape mode in which the smartphone is held.

With games, it is not as easy to deal with such a feature as it would be for an image viewer or a text editor. Some games are designed to exploit the vertical or horizontal dimension of the screen with a purpose, and rotating the phone is an action that might not be accommodated by the game altogether.

Should the game allow rotating the device, it is then necessary to adapt the game interface to the orientation of the phone as well, and this generally means designing an alternate version of the interface altogether. It is also an interesting (and not much exploited) feature to have the action of rotating the device as part of the actual gameplay and a core mechanic for a game.

Calibrations and reconfigurations

It is always a good idea to let players have the opportunity to calibrate and/or reconfigure the game controls in the options screen.

For example, left-handed players would appreciate the possibility of switching the game controls orientation.

When the accelerometer is involved, it can make a lot of difference for a player to be able to set the sensibility of the device to rotation. Different models with different hardware and software detect the rotation in the space differently and there's no single configuration which is good for all smartphones. So let players calibrate their phones according to their personal tastes and the capabilities of the device they are handling. Several games offer this option.

Challenges

As games become more and more social, several options have been introduced to allow players to display their score on public leaderboards and compete against friends.

One game which does that pretty well is Super 7, an iPhone title that displays, on the very top of the screen, a rainbow bar which increases with the player's score. When the bar reaches its end on the right half of the screen, it means some other player's score has been beaten. It is a nice example of a game feature which continually rewards the player and motivates him as he plays the title.

Experiment

The touch screen is a relatively new control scheme for games. Feel free to try out new ideas. For example, would it be possible to design a first person shooter that uses the gestures we outlined in the previous chapter, instead of traditional virtual buttons and D-pad? The trick is to keep the playfield as open as possible since the majority of smart devices have relatively small screens.

Summary

During the course of this chapter we introduced some basic theory behind interface design with *The Theory of Affordances* by Gibson and the book *The Design of Everyday Things* by Norman.

Then we moved to the specific aspects of videogame interface design, describing the diegesis theory and listing some fundamental problems related to the creation of optimal interfaces for videogames.

In the last part of the chapter, we suggested some of the best practices for videogame interface design and mentioned a few options that no game should lack.

In the following chapter we will discuss game engines, their features, and how to take full advantage of their potential.

8
Mobile Game Engines

A game engine is a software used to develop and run games. It is based on a collection of tools to create or import all assets and elements of a videogame, and pull them together to make them work as a whole. Rendering, materials and lighting, physics, particle effects, collision detection and management, AI and gameplay scripting, GUI design and game controls: a good game engine either allows to directly create such game elements and functions, or offers the possibility to import elements and assets from other software. For example, 3D models are usually created with third-party programs such as 3D Studio Max or Maya, and are then imported with a specific file format (such as `*.fbx` files) in the game engine

In this chapter, we will cover the following topics:

- What a game engine is
- What engines can do
- The main characteristics of the most popular game engines
- The first part of the tutorial to create a game with Unity 3D

For quite a long time, game companies used to create their own game engines and then used that technology to develop a series of titles to recoup the costs and speed up the development process. Lucas Arts' SCUMM engine which powered so many graphic adventures, the id Tech engine developed by *John Carmack* (id Software) for the Quake saga, or the Unreal Engine are examples of popular game engines created and used by game companies to develop their own games.

As the costs to build a game engine from scratch improved with the quick advancement of computer technologies, many developers began licensing their engines or even turned their whole business towards the creation of game engines and other game-related middleware, rather than games. At the same time, smaller companies found the opportunity to invest their money in buying the license of an already crafted and bug-proven engine, rather than developing their own, resulting in saved time and money, and the opportunity to begin development from day one.

This aspect is especially true for mobile indie teams, there are so many full-featured engines available today which target single or multiple platforms, each with its own strengths (and weaknesses), that there is really no reason for not using them. We strongly suggest you to follow this advice, unless your goal as developers is to sell engines and middleware to game developers, spend some time understanding your specific needs, research on the Internet to find the engine that best fits those needs, then get that engine and begin developing your game. You will find this process easier, faster, and cheaper than building your own tools from scratch.

What engines can do

As we said, there are several engines to choose from. Some are very easy to pick up and learn, though limited in their capabilities, which makes them excellent tools for educational purposes. Others target a single platform, as it is with Cocos2D, which in its first versions only allowed game development for the iOS. Most game engines, on the other hand, target multiple platforms, as is a more profitable marketing strategy to widen the potential gamers audience as much as possible. There are even engines which are considered genre-specific, as it is the case with the Unreal Engine, which many people regard as the perfect tool for crafting only 3D shooters, although several unconventional games showed that with good ideas and a little bit of programming, almost any game genre can be developed with a professional tool.

There are several functions that all game engines share. In the following sections, we will list the most important.

Importing graphic assets: All game engines offer the possibility to import graphics assets for games. 2D-oriented engines allow users to import sprites and spritesheets, tilesets, and background images, while 3D engines import 3D models, materials, textures, and animations. Depending on the specific characteristics of each game engine, not all file formats may be supported. When choosing the game engine for your next game, be sure that `*.png` files are supported for 2D assets and that a 3D engine supports the `*.fbx` file format, as this format imports 3D meshes together with materials, textures, and animations, in a single operation.

Creating game levels and environments: Regardless of whether they are 2D- or 3D-oriented, game engines offer the possibility to design game levels with the graphic assets imported from a third-party software. It can be the disposition of platforms for a 2D game or the terrains of a 3D game. Clearly, the creation of game levels with a 3D engine is far more complex than assembling levels for a 2D platform, as 3D requires, for example, to deploy light sources, which is a task of its own. It is not by chance that people working at the creation of 3D game levels are called environmental artists!

Adding audio to a game: Game engines provide tools to implement audio in your game, may it be sound effects, which are played when specific events occur or the background music to make it more immersive. Engines also usually allow users to perform sound editing, such as tuning the volume or changing the pitch to better merge them into the gameplay experience.

Creating the UI for the game: As any game requires a UI, game engines provide the tools to design game controls and the graphic interface for your game. It is generally a set of buttons and labels to display useful info to the player, but the most professional software even offer compatibility with middleware tools to create very advanced, dynamic GUIs, as is the case of Scaleform, used to craft the interface of popular games such as *Batman Arkham Asylum* and *Mass Effect*.

Programming the enemy AI and script game events: Not all engines provide effective enemy AI design tools. For example, in its former free versions, Unity 3D was offered with no built-in tool to create paths for game characters, while the Unreal Engine implemented waypoints and navigation meshes as part of the engine itself, from the very beginning. When a useful function is not natively implemented by a game engine, and pathfinding is one such function, it is very common that a third-party developer created those tools. Such is the case with the *A* Pathfinding Project* for Unity, a package developed by *Aron Granberg* that provides pathfinding and navigation meshes management for Unity. You can check it out at `http://arongranberg.com/astar/docs/index.php`.

On the other hand, all game engines offer the opportunity to code game events triggered by the players' actions. The task is usually achieved through a scripting language that is easy to grasp (when compared to a programming language) and allows quick and easy implementation of game events. Lua is a scripting language implemented by popular game engines such as Corona SDK. JavaScript is another and it is used, for example, to script events in Unity 3D. Other engines may implement their own scripting languages, as it is the case of the Unreal Engine (UnrealScript) or GameMaker (GameMakerLanguage).

Building the executable of a game: The last feature no engine can miss is cooking everything you put inside your game to create the final build, the executable file which will be downloaded by your players. The build of a game is basically the final result you get from a game engine after you spent weeks or months feeding it with graphic assets, script files, audio, and anything else you needed for your game. Depending on the scope of the game you developed, cooking the final build can take minutes to hours. It took us around 14 hours to cook the final build of our FPS *XX The Breach*, developed with UDK!

What engines can't do

Generally speaking, each game engine has a slogan, which more or less tells you that you can achieve everything without doing anything with that engine, the most advertised sentence being "without any coding". Our advice is to distrust such statements if a game engine doesn't allow to add your personal pieces of code in one way or another, maybe it is just a poor tool, probably designed for specific tasks and which may not fit your specific game design needs.

Game engines

Generally speaking, each engine can serve several purposes with regard to game genre and no engine can be described as a single-gameplay-style-oriented one. But it is also true that each engine has its own weaknesses and strengths, which make it more or less fit for a specific game genre, a technology, or gameplay styles. In the following sections, we are going to provide a selection of different game engines, mentioning useful information on their strengths and weaknesses, and analyze which purposes each one serves the best. Our selection won't obviously include all game engines available as we write, we will only focus on the most popular, with regard to their features, target platforms, and professional versus educational purposes.

2D game engines

Generally speaking, there are several reasons why a newly assembled team should begin dealing with 2D games.

One is that touchscreens of today's smartphones offer a better support for 2D-style gameplay. Another is that 2D games are usually easier to develop, as they require less mathematics and algebra to be coded, while sprites and 2D backgrounds are easier to craft. Finally, 2D games have lower hardware requirements to run on mobile devices.

As you are going to begin the development of your first game, we suggest you to go for a 2D game. The following engines can help you fulfill this goal.

Torque 2D

Torque 2D is a 2D game engine, which is based on the popular Torque Game Engine developed by Garage Games (`http://www.garagegames.com/`).

A former version of the engine, called iTorque, was designed to develop games specifically for the iOS platform, though its latest incarnation also supports publishing for Windows OS and thus the development, for example, of browser games. We will now review the features of Torque 2D:

- Torque 2D provides a very intuitive drag-and-drop interface and a robust C++-based scripting language called TorqueScript, which makes game prototyping quick and easy.
- It supports OpenAL libraries for full-featured sound capabilities and a physics engine called Box2D to add physics to your gameplay.
- Its simple WhatYouSeeIsWhatYouGet interface, which supports several image formats, particle systems, and tilemaps among the others, allow even inexperienced users to make their own high-quality games, thanks to a strong community support and very little coding required.
- Torque 2D also features built-in multiplayer and Internet game support to further enhance the gameplay of your titles while keeping performances high.
- As it is based on the popular Torque 3D engine, Torque 2D is a very solid and mature development tool, which has been recently upgraded to support 3D models to create interesting mixtures of 2D and 3D elements, though it is customized for 2D gameplay. If you aim towards the creation of full-3D games, there are better options available, which we will analyze in the following sections of this chapter.
- Torque 2D is based on C++ source code and as such it requires an installed C++ compiler to make the final build of your games. A license is also required to make use of this game engine, which is around $1000 as we write.

Cocos2D

Cocos2D is an open source, free framework, based on an MIT license, which allows development of games for the iOS and Android. Its architecture is based on a pre-existing engine written in Python and first converted to Objective-C for the iPhone, and then to JavaScript to support Android development.

Cocos2D is excellent for the first time developer for the following reasons:

- An intuitive interface
- A full set of libraries including Box2D and Chipmunk physics engine
- It's open source and free
- It allows mixing native and external C++ libraries to extend its capabilities
- It now supports 3D
- It has a strong user community

There are a few disadvantages of Cocos2D:

- You are stuck with iOS. There is no native support for Android, so you will have to port to JavaScript.
- Objective-C has a fairly steep learning curve; so previous experience with C++ is recommended.

Being approved by Apple and with almost 3000 titles available on the Apple Store developed with this tool, Cocos2D is definitely a good choice for any indie mobile team interested in making 2D games.

You may want to check the following link for a list of best practices when using Cocos2D:

`http://www.cocos2d-iphone.org/wiki/doku.php/prog_guide:best_practices`

Corona SDK

Corona SDK is another mobile-oriented engine, which allows developing 2D games for the iPhone, iPad, and Android devices. It is based on OpenGL libraries and C++ programming language, though it also integrates scripting with Lua.

Corona's advantages are as follows:

- The use of Lua makes it easy to compile for iOS and Android from the same code base. This saves time and money for multiplatform development. Lua is a very efficient scripting language, resulting in a fraction of the number of lines of code than needed in Objective-C for example.
- It supports standard physics libraries such as Box2D.
- It has a strong community of people to help with development issues.
- Corona offers built-in support for the distinctive hardware features of today's smartphones, such as the accelerometer, the GPS, the compass, and the camera.

- This engine offers a very interesting licensing policy, you can download the engine and use all of its features for free, and then pay only if you wish to create builds for the iOS or Android (though they have separate costs).

And now the downside of Corona SDK:

- Android support is pretty bad, causing any kind of flaw you can imagine.
- Inconsistency between the performances you get from the simulator (yes, Corona SDK offers a simulator to run your tests!) and the actual device.
- Unexpected crashes without proper reporting, which generated a common statement among the community of developers that Corona is not fit to develop for the Android platform at all. Corona SDK requires your code to be uploaded to Ansca Mobile servers for compilation. You send them your code and they return you the executable. This fact has two main consequences: the first is that, if you are offline, you can't compile your code. The second and more severe problem is that you must send them your code, without knowing what they actually do with it, as Ansca Mobile is known for not being particularly transparent about its internal procedures.
- Finally, many users complain that applications developed with Corona SDK tend to be slower when compared to other frameworks and it doesn't allow integration with external libraries.

3D game engines

Though mobile gaming instilled new life in 2D titles and strongly propelled old-school game mechanics to appeal to the casual audience, as demonstrated by the large popularity of 2D games such as *Angry Birds*, *Fruit Ninja*, or *Jetpack Joyride*, 3D is the players' most expected feature in today's games.

What follows here is a description of the most popular game engines which we recommend to develop 3D games for mobile.

Shiva 3D

Shiva 3D is a 3D game engine developed by StoneTrip (`http://www.stonetrip.com/`), which can be used to develop games for any target platform you may choose, such as Windows and Windows Phone, OSX and iOS, Linux, Android, Blackberry, PSP, and Wii. With the release of the Android SDK in 2010, Shiva 3D was the first engine to support the development of 3D games for the Android platform.

Shiva's advantages are as follows:

- Shiva 3D supports native C++ compilation, which means you can import your own libraries to add functionality to your games
- It uses Lua as its scripting language
- Though it is claimed to work with Mac OS X through parallels, Shiva 3D editor is Windows-only, which means that you don't need to own a Mac to develop iOS titles
- Unlike other engines, what is displayed in the editor windows of Shiva 3D is almost equal to the final rendering you get after building your app
- The lightmapping is generally of high quality, performs pretty well on mobile devices, and dynamic shadows are fully supported
- It includes libraries to manage basic pathfinding and allows control of it through scripting, which saves development time
- The same project file can be compiled for any target platform
- Finally, when compared to its competitors, Shiva 3D is quite cheap, as the editor is free to use and a license is required just to publish games

The flexibility Shiva 3D offers with regard to the target platforms it can address, comes at a price, though:

- Shiva 3D doesn't support popular 3D file formats such as `*.fbx` or `*.obj`, as other engines do, and it only imports `*.DAE` files. Several users also claim that the only way they could import 3D models and their mapped textures in the editor was thanks to a third-party software, namely Ultimate Unwrap Pro (`http://www.unwrap3d.com/u3d/index.aspx`).
- The learning curve to get proficient with the interface is quite steep, and the editor doesn't allow reconfiguring the layout of the different windows of the editor, which can only be set according to a list of predefined layouts.
- The physics engine is claimed to be very limited.
- The error messages, which may occur when building your app are vague and not very helpful (a trait unfortunately shared by its main competitor Unity 3D).
- The documentation is sparse and poor.
- The most frustrating feature of Shiva 3D in the opinion of users is the terrain editor. Differently from its competitor, the terrain editor in Shiva 3D is implemented through chunks, which are a bit tricky to select and keep selected as you sculpt the terrain, with the result that creates terrains with Shiva 3D requires a lot of time and effort.

In conclusion, Shiva 3D is a very good tool that offers a perfect balance between costs and capabilities, which make it especially fit for teams with a low budget. There are better tools available on the market, but they all cost much more than Shiva 3D.

Unity 3D

Unity 3D is a cross-platform engine developed by Unity Technologies, which can be used to create games for desktop PCs, the Web, consoles, and mobile devices. It is the most popular game engine used by game developers today (especially indie teams) and the one that first offered to small, indie developers the opportunity to develop their projects with a professional, almost full-featured tool coming with a low cost, and thus affordable license. It can be said that if we've got so many almost-free engines available today, a big chunk of the credit goes to the success of Unity.

The engine is written in C/C++ (thus allowing extension of its capabilities with external libraries) and supports scripting through JavaScript, C#, and Boo. The Version 4.0 is the latest update to the tool and it comes in two main licenses as we write; the free license with limited capabilities and the Pro license, which costs $1500 and offers all the features supported by the engine. Still, with the Pro version of Unity 3D, separate licenses are required to create builds for Android, iOS, and Adobe Flash Player. You can refer to the following link for a detailed description of the different license available and their costs: `https://store.unity3d.com/`. With a cost of $1500 for the Pro version, the Unity 3D full-featured license, which allows creating game builds for the mobile market is not cheap, when compared to its competitors!

On the other hand, there are several features supported by Unity such as post-processing, physics, bump and reflection mapping, ambient occlusion, dynamic shadows, and render to texture functions, among the others.

The interface is very intuitive and the actions required to create assets and so-called Prefabs (game assets that can be instantiated at will into the game) are handled with extreme simplicity; you perform most of the actions through a drag-and-drop interface, which for example allows adding a script to control the behavior of a game object by simply dragging the script on the game object itself in the editor window.

There are many reasons that help make Unity 3D the perfect tool for a mobile indie team. Its interface is intuitive and very easy to grasp. The editor is quite powerful and allows to quickly prototype game mechanics with few mouse clicks. Unity 3D supports all major 3D file formats, `*.fbx` in particular, so that you can easily work with professional software such as 3D Studio Max or Maya, and then import the result in Unity without compatibility problems. Support is really strong, both by the community of users, which is always ready to provide the answers to any problem you may face in the dedicated forums, and by the developers, as Unity comes with very detailed and extensive documentation.

Unfortunately, there are also reasons why not all developers, especially the true professionals, are so fond of Unity 3D. As it often happens with many engines, once the initial enthusiasm for its intuitive interface goes down, problems start arising. First of all the quality of lights and rendered graphics in Unity is not as good as other tools, unless you know how to code your own shaders. Shadows tend to look low resolution, and as we already mentioned, dynamic shadows are only available with the Pro version. The terrain editor looks dated, as for example, it doesn't allow creating destructible terrains. The physics engine is blamed for creating performance issues and there's no native pathfinding, nav-mesh, or AI support, unless you turn to the latest pro version of the engine or third-party middleware. Finally, as we stated previously, Unity is not cheap for the average indie developer, to create games for the mobile market you are required to invest not less than $3000 in licenses.

Before ending this section on Unity 3D, we would like to mention the Asset Store. It is a collection of asset packages which contain 3D models, textures, materials, sound effects, particle systems, scripts, and networking resources which can be bought and then implemented in your game. The Asset Store allows the community around Unity 3D to share contents and has turned this engine into a perfect tool to begin the game developing business.

In the following screenshot you can appreciate a popular game developed with Unity 3D: *CSR Racing* by Natural Motion for the iPhone.

Top-quality engines

Among so many engines available to create games, there are some which simply are capable of reaching higher standards with regard to quality, visual quality in particular.

The Unreal Engine is one such tool, credited by most users as the only really good engine to develop games which meets the actual industry standards.

In the next section, we will provide a description of the characteristics of the Unreal Engine and its development kit.

Unreal/UDK

The Unreal Engine is the 3D game engine developed by Epic for its popular Unreal saga, available today in its 3rd generation and which powered games such as *Gears of War*, *Batman: Arkham Asylum*, or the *Mass Effect* franchise, just to mention a few. In 2009, Epic released to the general public a free version of the UE3 SDK, called Unreal Development Kit, thus offering the community of indie game developers a tool like they never had before.

Though the engine was designed with shooters in mind (the Unreal games were first person shooters), it has been successfully adapted over time to several other game genre and applications, ranging from 3rd person games (shooters, action games, and RPGs), stealth games, melee fighting games (we suggest you to have a look at the very interesting *Chivalry Medieval Warfare* shown in the following picture. The link to the game is `http://www.chivalrythegame.com/`), and MMOs, but also to create detailed 3D simulations, serious games and training software:

The rendering capabilities of the Unreal Engine are what makes it better than most of its direct competitors, as it supports many advanced features such as HDRR, pixel per lighting, dynamic shadows, and global illumination, as well as advanced physics, destructible environments, and crowd simulations.

The Unreal Engine also offers a complete set of tools to create beautiful assets for your games, featuring a very advanced material editor, the AnimEditor to manage 3D characters animations, and the possibility to create terrains and level geometries, this one in particular being a feature which other engines lack.

The Unreal Engine is written in C++ and offers both a visual scripting tool called Kismet, and a scripting language called UnrealScript to extend classes and code behaviors for the actors of your games.

The editor is offered with a free license, though a fee of $99 is required to sell games and 25 percent royalties must be paid to Epic, if your games earn money above the threshold of $50,000.

In 2010, Epic released its first iOS game called *Infinity Blade*, a sort of tech-demo to show the potential of the engine with regard to mobile development, which reached the top of the iTunes App Store charts, was named by IGN as the Best iPhone Game of the Year and won several other awards in Best Action and Best Graphics categories. With *Infinity Blade*, Epic declared to the world that yes, mobile games could definitely be developed with UDK!

You can have a look at the breathtaking graphics of the *Infinity Blade* in the following screenshot:

On the negative side, there's complexity. Though the editor interface is clear and well-structured, still you need a lot of practice to grasp its full potential. Every tool included in the development kit is a software of its own which requires time and practice to be mastered, given that mastering each one of them is even possible.

The Unreal Engine allows the best graphic quality standards to be reached, but it doesn't do it by itself. It will take a lot of time to learn its intricacies and many attempts resulting, inevitably, in failures, before you get the graphic quality you ever dreamed of for your games.

UDK doesn't offer any access to its source C++ code, which means that whenever you need to implement some specific functionality, you first need to understand how things are done according to its internal logic and to class mutual dependencies, and then adapt. Delving through the classes of UDK can be a painful process (as we showed in a former chapter), which requires unreal patience and which you cannot expect to accomplish before stepping into many failures.

Finally, there is the license cost; giving 25 percent of the revenues to Epic in case your sales go well means that compared to other available engines, UDK costs a lot more.

That said, if you are ready to put time and effort in the learning process, UDK grants the possibility of creating high-end games, which clearly stand out from the mass of titles available for any platform. Many teams, even small indie ones, succeeded in developing well-crafted games and made a name for themselves, thanks to this wonderful tool. Whatever the engine you put your hands on when you begin your adventure in the industry of game development, UDK is the point you should arrive at, sooner or later.

Educational engines

In the last section dedicated to game engines, we will describe two engines that are particularly fit for educational purposes, due to a very friendly visual interface. Despite the fact that some nice games have been created with such tools, no true professional would recommend them, these are software for beginners who can use them to understand what a game engine is and how to create a complete game from scratch.

GameMaker

GameMaker is a very interesting game engine developed by *Mark Overmars* and published by YoYoGames. Its main feature is that it allows to quickly create 2D games without any need to write anything. The interface offers the possibility to define the behavior of game objects (as the actors of your game are called) by a simple procedure based on events (such as creation of the game object, collisions occurring with other objects, or mouse- and keyboard-related actions) and then choosing the actions that must take place when those events occur. The action list provides all the basic things you can expect to happen in a game, such as moving actions, modification to gravity or vertical speed of game objects, destruction or creation of game objects, or drawing score, available lives, or health bars on the screen. It also allows users to perform basic logic and mathematics checks, such as whether a collision occurs, if a position in the world is free, or whether a certain expression is true or false.

Once you learned these basics, you will very likely feel the need for something more flexible and complex to happen in your game, at which point you can turn to its built-in, and quite easy to learn scripting language, called Game Maker Language, to begin coding stuff your own way. GameMaker even allows proficient programmers to extend the capabilities of the engine by programming their own DLL to perform specific tasks they may need.

GameMaker has been used to develop hundreds of 2D games according to many genre, such as platformers, maze and puzzle games, arcade shooters, and strategy games. Even more, YoYoGames offers the opportunity to registered users to upload games made with GameMaker on their site to show and share them with the community. A very popular game called DeathWorm, made with GameMaker, after being largely claimed by the community of users, was eventually converted for the iOS and downloaded from the App Store by almost 5 million people! You can check it in the following screenshot:

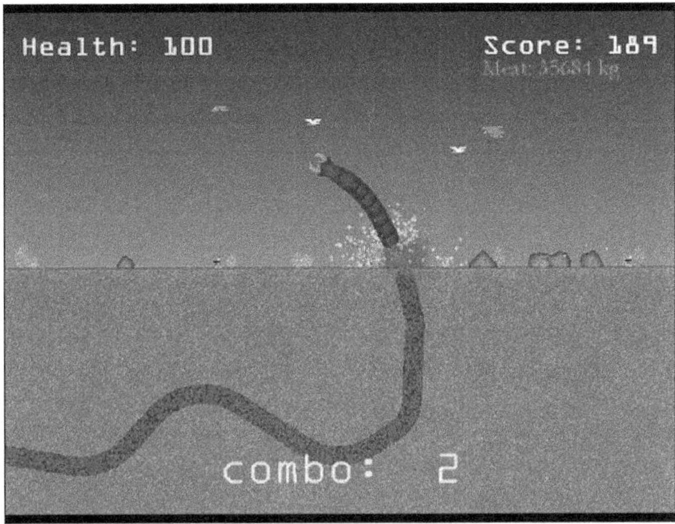

The latest update of GameMaker offers support for Mac and Windows, and separate licenses can be bought to export for the iOS, Android, and HTML5.

With its friendly interface, its very intuitive workflow, the abundant documentation, several easy-to-follow tutorials, a large community ready to help behind it and its cheap price, GameMaker is definitely the best tool to learn how to develop a game for anyone interested in approaching this line of work.

GameSalad

GameSalad is another user-friendly engine developed by GameSalad Inc. which is perfect for beginners, as it doesn't require any coding thanks to a fully implemented drag-and-drop interface that allows users to create games for all mobile platforms such as iOS, Android, HTML5, and Windows Phone. Similar to GameMaker, GameSalad is usually used for educational purposes or by artists and designers to quickly prototype their gameplay ideas.

The implementation of gameplay is based on the creation of behaviors for game actors based on sets of rules, which define how the actor reacts to various events happening in the game. Everything is managed through a clean and clear visual interface, and tutorials, help boards, and forums are abundant, as well as the extensive and easily available documentation.

The GameSalad editor, called Creator, can be downloaded for free, as the $299\ year license is only required to publish your games for Android or Windows 8, or to implement features such as In-App Purchase, iAds, or GameCenter. For the full feature list of the engine you can check the GameSalad Inc. site at `http://gamesalad.com/creator/pricing`.

Though it has been used for thousands of games, some of which made a score on the App Store, GameSalad is considered a tool for starters to get a grip on how things interact with each other in a game environment and for designers and artists without any coding knowledge to quickly prototype gameplay ideas. Again, it is very likely that at some point, as you get more proficient with the subject, you will turn towards something more professional and evolved than GameSalad.

For a full list of tutorials to begin creating games with GameSalad, you can refer to `http://mac.appstorm.net/reviews/games-reviews/become-a-game-developer-with-gamesalad/`.

Unity3D Tutorial – part 1

Now that we have described several game engines, it is time to pick one and start assembling a game with it. As our reference title to develop the tutorial we chose a classic game named *Space Invaders* by Activision.

In this first part of the tutorial, we will create the setup for our game environment. In the next chapter, we will add the main actors for our game: the player's ship and the enemies, and define their behaviors. In the last part of the tutorial in *Chapter 10, Balancing, Tuning, and Polishing Mobile Games*, we will add the final touches required by the game. As the engine to be used to develop the game, our choice is Unity, for several reasons. First of all it is a professional tool, so whatever you learn about it can be useful for your career as a game developer. It is a both an excellent 2D and 3D engine, which means you can develop any game you like with it. Unity is also very user-friendly, which will help grasp the basics with a short tutorial. Finally, the basic user license of Unity is free, which means you can download it and follow the tutorial at no cost!

In case you haven't done it yet, go to `http://unity3d.com/` and download Unity, we suggest Version 4 or 3.5.7. The first is the latest, the second is the more stable.

You may also need a 3D-modeling software to create the assets that will be used for the game. We mentioned several such tools in *Chapter 3, Graphics for Mobile*, of this book, we suggest you to pick one of them to work with, as this will help you to get familiar with software that are considered as Industry standards.

In case you can't or don't want to to model your own assets, we will provide them anyway as part of the contents of this book.

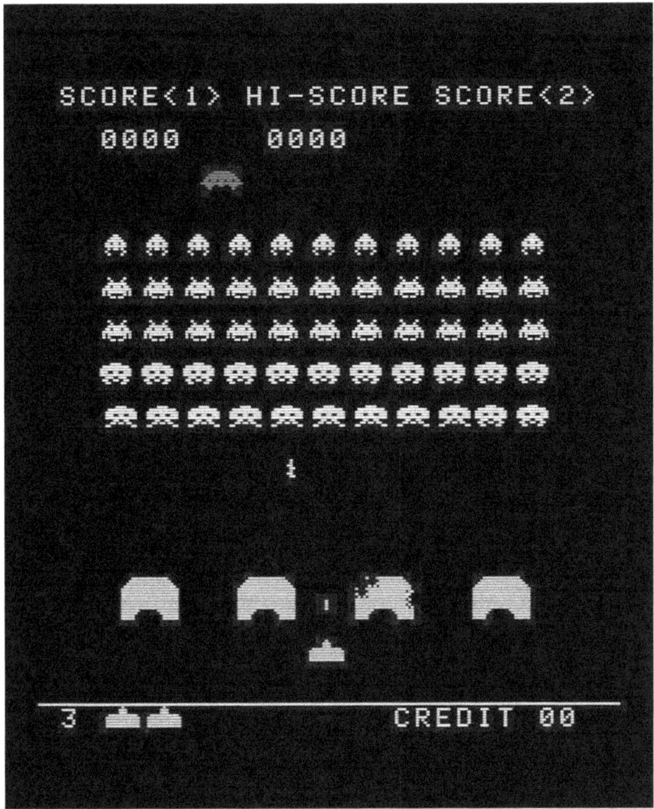

Space Invaders

Though Space Invaders is a 2D title, we will assemble it with 3D assets. Even if we are not going to exploit true 3D features for our prototype, by adopting a 3D perspective, we will have the opportunity to show a broader set of features of Unity 3D.

Anyway, as we have a limited number of pages to show a lot of information, we will assume you are familiar with the basics of the Unity interface.

Let's get to work now!

Tutorial part 1A – importing 3D models

From the reference image, we can define a list of assets we will need for our game:

- Four different models of aliens, one for each line
- One model for the player's ship
- One bullet for the player's ship and one for the aliens
- One asset for the barriers that protect the player's ship
- A basic GUI with scores and available lives

We can import 3D models using the following steps:

1. Let's begin with the 3D models. Open up 3D-modeling software of your choice and create some simple models inspired by Space Invaders like the ones represented in the following pictures. We need four models for the aliens and one for the player's ship, or if you prefer there are several websites that have graphics and sounds from the original game.
2. Since we are only going to make a prototype, you can use any primitive you like. Our main interest is to show you how to import 3D models in Unity. The following screenshot represents the assets we made for this tutorial, using 3D Studio Max. It is very important that you create all the assets for the aliens models with the same size.

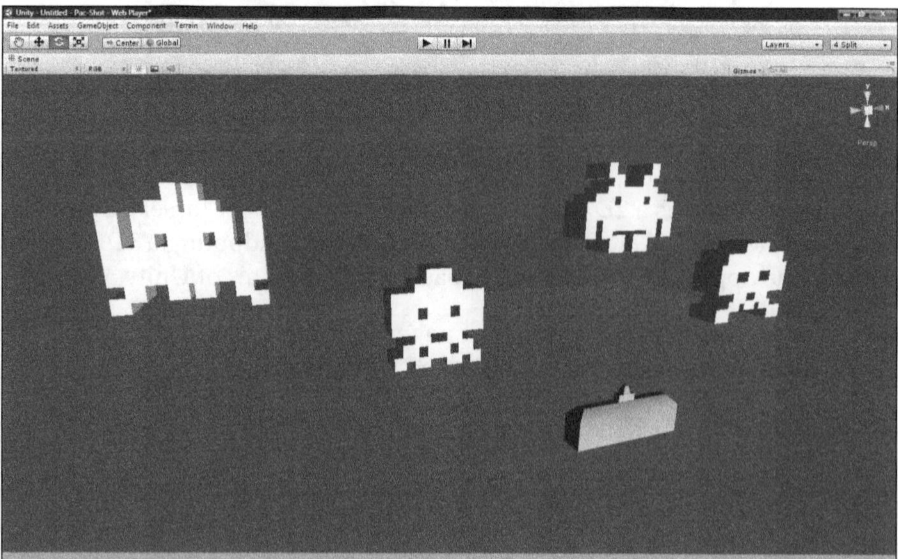

3. Export each model separately as `*.fbx` or `*.obj`, and save it with a meaningful name!
4. Now open Unity 3D and start a new project. A window similar to the following will open where you can set a folder and its path to store our game. The window also allows a list of basic Unity packages to be included in your newly created project. As we don't need them, don't flag any packages from the list:

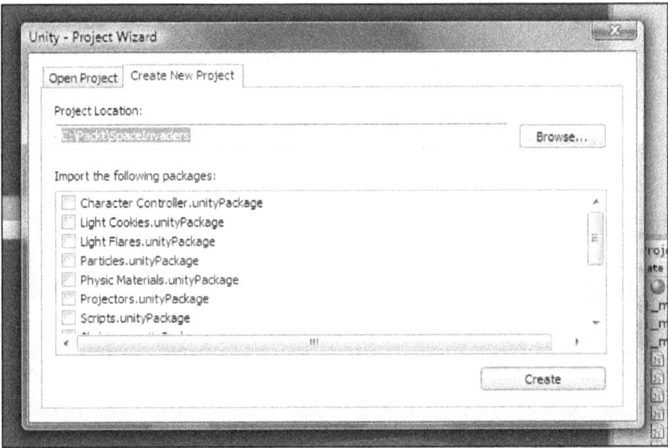

New Project

5. With your new project opened, go to the **Project** panel and create a new folder to store our 3D models. Name the folder `3DModels` as well:

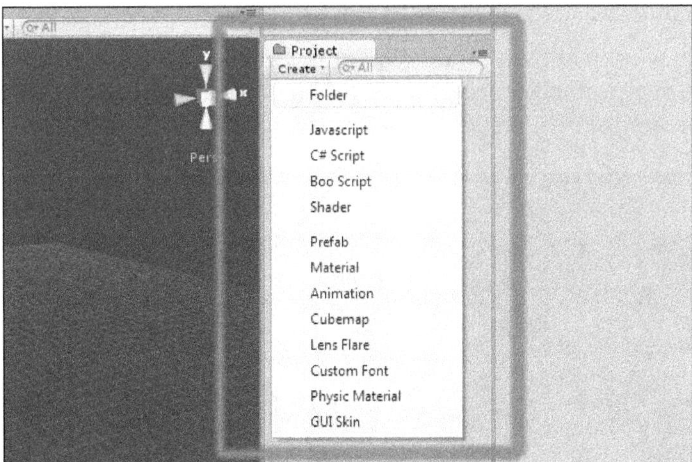

New Folder

6. Now we can import our models. With the `3DModels` folder selected in the **Project** panel, navigate to **Menu Bar** | **Assets** | **Import New Asset**, and from the displayed window, select the 3D models for the aliens and the player's ship. Unfortunately, you cannot import all of them with a single operation, you will have to import them one at a time.
7. A very useful feature with Unity is that you can create so called Prefabs, assets that can be created and instantiated multiple times in the game scene. The advantage of Prefabs is that all its instances are linked to the Prefab they come from, so that you can modify multiple instances of game objects cloned from the Prefab by working on the original Prefab itself.
8. Let's show this feature.
9. Select one of the alien's models and drag it into the scene. Now go back to the **Project** panel and create a new folder. Name it `Prefabs`. If you are wondering why create a separate folder for every type of asset we are working with, the reason is to keep projects well organized. This is going to be a simple game with few assets, but a real game will require many. So we better not get overwhelmed by lack of order!
10. With the Prefabs folder selected in the **Project** panel, click again on the **Create** button and now make a new empty prefab. Assuming you selected the model for the first type of alien, name this prefab `Alien1`. To complete the `Alien1` prefab, drag the model in the Unity Hierarchy panel into the newly created prefab. Now the empty prefab is filled with the 3D model for our first alien asset.
11. You can now delete the alien model from the scene and then drag the alien prefab into the scene instead.
12. Finally, we can show you the power of Prefabs. Create multiple instances of the `Alien1` prefab by pressing *Ctrl+D* to get something like this, where we have created four instances of Alien 1:

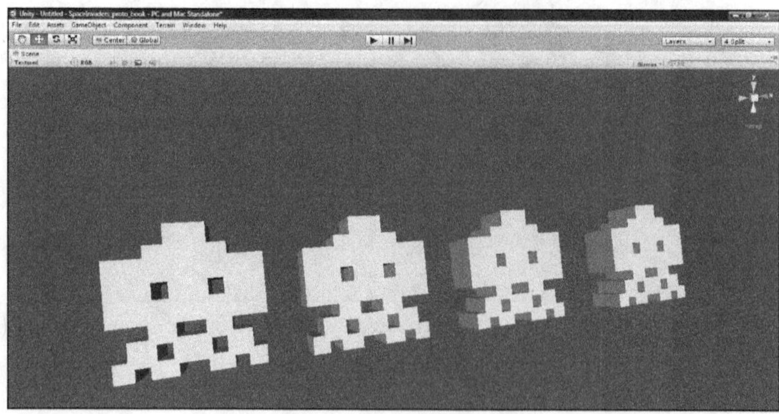

13. Now create a new folder for our materials in the **Project** panel and name it `Materials`. With the `Materials` folder selected, create a new asset, a material this time. Name it `red` (or whatever the color you like) and then, with the material selected, click on the white rectangle in the upper-right corner of the **Inspector** panel in Unity. Refer to the following screenshot for clues:

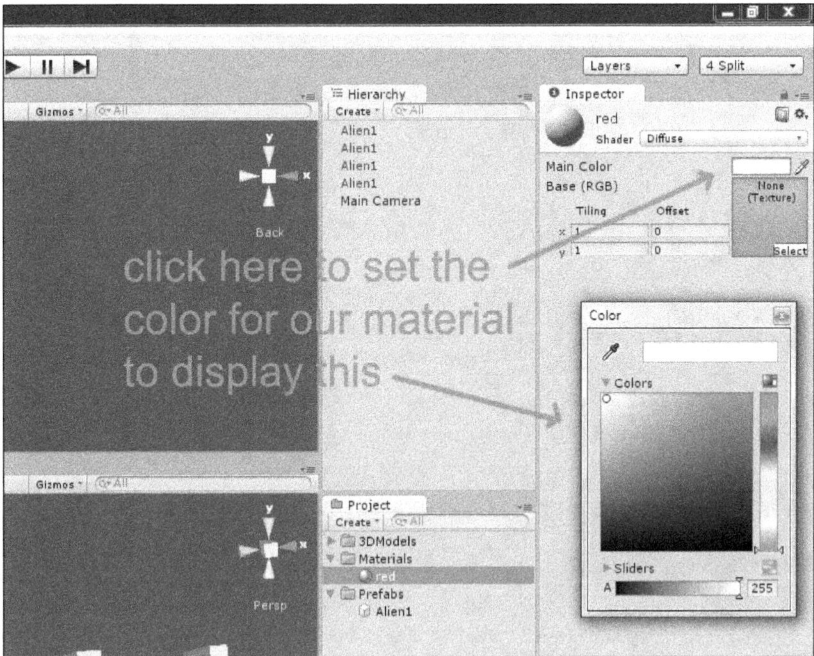

14. Pick the color you like and then, in the **Project** panel, select the `Alien1` prefab. In the **Inspector** panel you should see a **Mesh Renderer** component with a material item in it. Click on the arrow to make the **Element 0** slot appear, then drag the newly created material into that slot, as shown in the following screenshot:

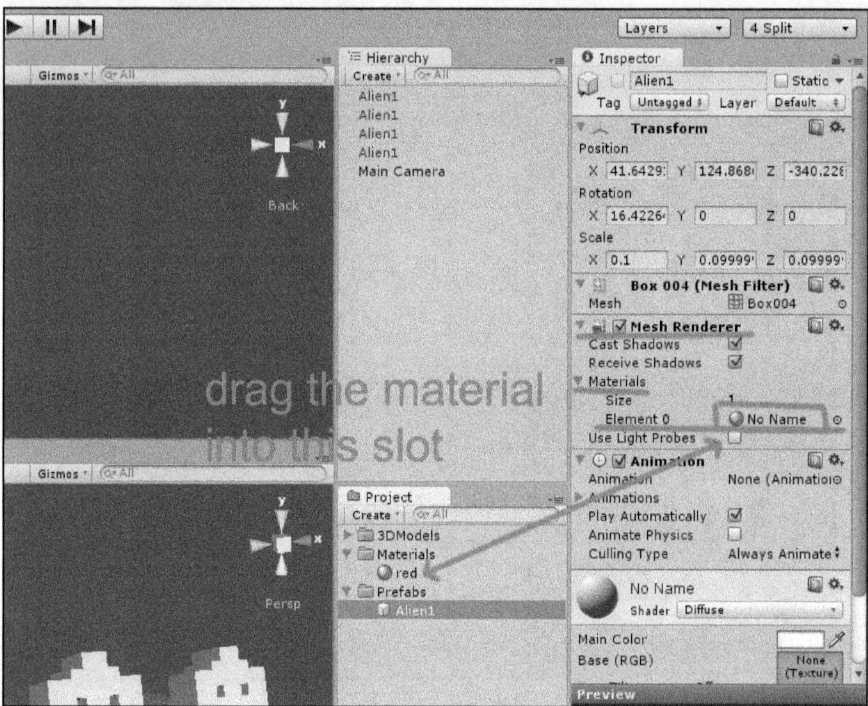

15. This is how you can quickly edit multiple game assets with a single action through Prefabs. All your aliens should now have turned red, all at once!

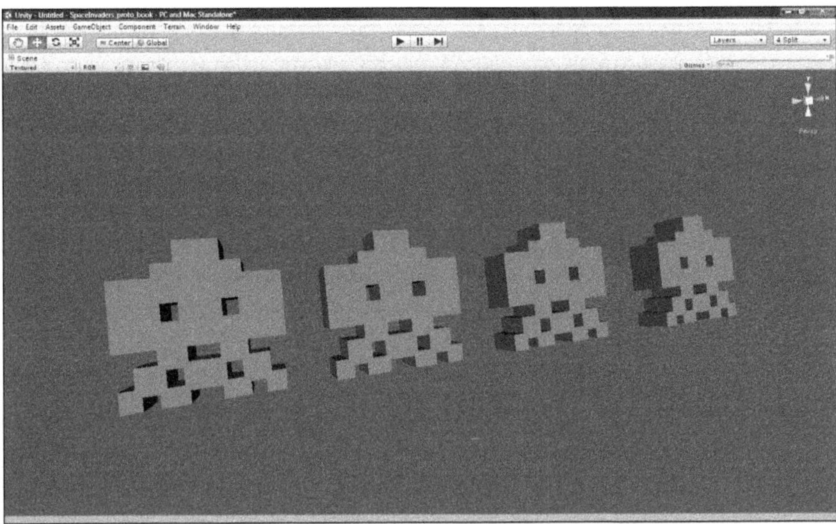

16. However, for the necessities of our project, we want the aliens to be white. So create a new white material and use it instead of red on the aliens. In the next part of the tutorial in *Chapter 9, Prototyping*, we will reference these objects.
17. Repeat the previous steps to create more Prefabs: the remaining three aliens and the player's ship. For the player ship you also need a green material.
18. Let's do a couple more assets before moving to the next section. We actually need the bullets to be fired by both the player's ship and the aliens. We will use a simple sphere for the player and a capsule for the aliens.
19. The sphere and the capsule can be created from the main menu bar, navigating to **GameObject** | **Create Other**, as shown in the following screenshot:

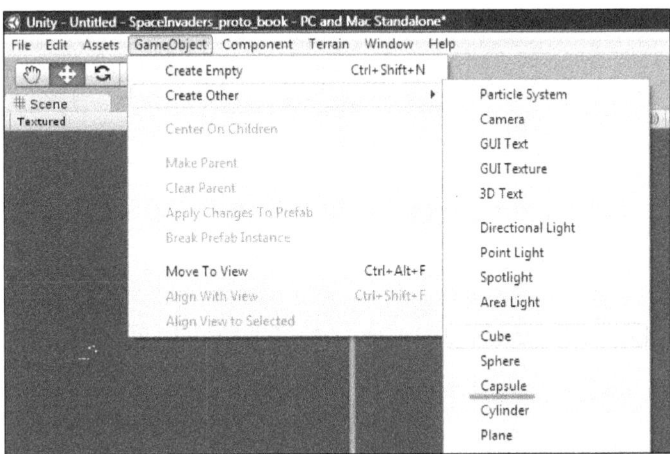

20. Size the two objects in the scene view as needed, then create two new Prefabs, name one `PLBullet` and the other `AlienBullet`, then drag the sphere and the capsule from the scene into the empty Prefabs accordingly. Remember also to make `PLBullet` green and `AlienBullet` Prefabs white.

This ends the first part of this tutorial, where we showed you how to import 3D models in Unity, how to use them to create Prefabs and the importance of using Prefabs to easily manage multiple game objects. We also showed how to create materials and how to apply them to your imported models. We finally showed how to create basic primitives which are available in the Unity main menu.

Tutorial part 1B – setting up the scene

The next step is to begin setting up the scene for our game prototype. To do that we suggest you to begin by using a screenshot of the original game as a reference layout:

1. We will use the same screenshot from Space Invaders displayed at the beginning of the tutorial, you can find one anywhere on the Internet.
2. Download a screenshot and then import it as a texture. Any `*.jpeg` or `*.png` image will do.
3. Create a `Textures` folder in the **Project** panel and then import the image as a new asset inside the folder (you can name it `InvadersTexture`).
4. Then use the image to create a new material in the `Materials` folder.
5. Create a new material, name it `InvadersMaterial` and then drag the texture into the texture slot of the material. Refer to the following screenshot for reference:

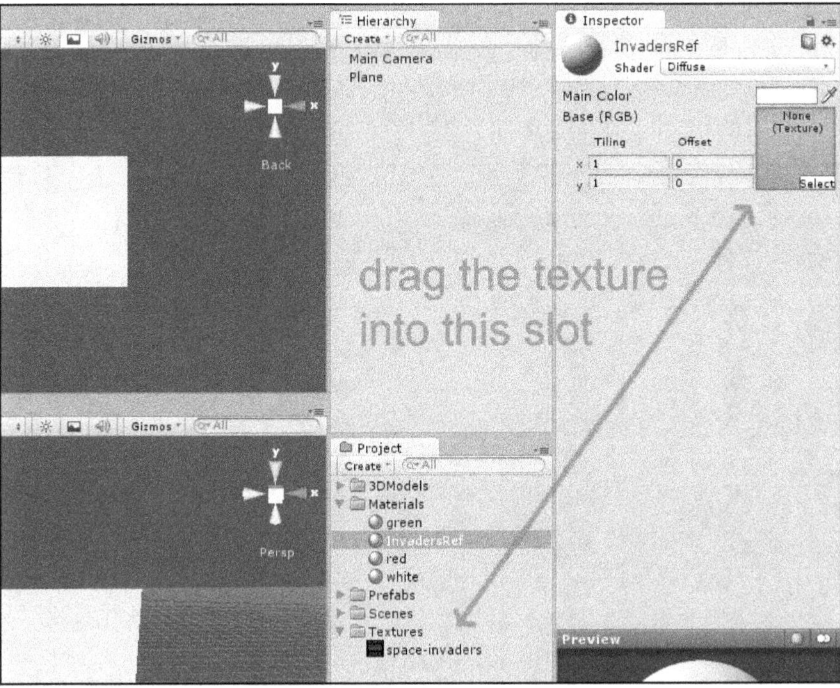

6. Now create a Plane in the scene, selecting **GameObject | Create Other | Plane** in the main menu.
7. Set the correct position for the plane, and then drag the **Invaders** material onto the plane to add it. It could happen that, once dragged onto the plane, the texture will not be displayed with the correct orientation. In such case, double-click on the texture in the **Project** panel to open it with the default image editor and rotate it as required. Then save it to have it correctly displayed in the Scene view.

8. To setup our scene, let's begin by setting the right position for our reference plane. Select the plane with `InvadersMaterial` and set its position coordinates in its **Transform** component (**Inspector** panel) to `0` for x, y and z, as shown in the following screenshot:

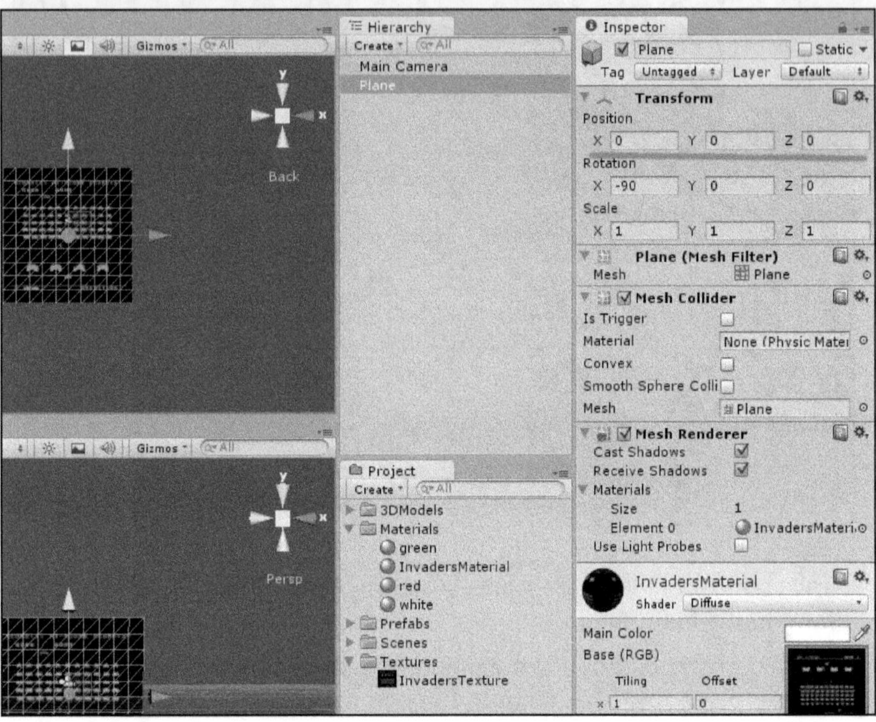

9. Now for the main camera; as you may notice, with each new scene, Unity automatically adds a default camera, named **Main Camera**. Select it in the **Hierarchy** and set its position in the scene view; you can refer to the game window to check the final result you will get.
10. To make things easier, these are the values we set the camera with:
    - Position x = 0
    - Position y = -0,05
    - Position z = -5
    - Field Of View = 81
    - Game Aspect = Standalone (1024x768)

11. To display things using 3D we also will leave the camera projection mode to **Perspective**, though our prototype will only implement 2D gameplay.
12. We also suggest adding a directional light to the scene to see things better (**GameObject** | **Create Other** | **Directional Light**).
13. Check the following screenshot to confirm what you should see on the screen:

Setting up the scene is over. In this section, we showed how to use a texture to define a material for a game object, how to set the position and rotation of a game object in the scene view by editing the values in its **Transform** component in the **Inspector** panel and how to control what is displayed by the main camera of your game, working on camera position, rotation (if needed), field of view, and projection mode.

Summary

In this chapter, we discussed what a game engine is and how it can speed up game development time. We listed several popular game engines that can handle 2D and 3D game environments.

In the next chapter, we will discuss the prototyping process and provide the second part of the tutorial, where we will define the basic game mechanics and the interface for the Space Invaders demo.

9
Prototyping

Prototyping is the process of testing various aspects of an app, usually in a quick and incomplete manner. The purpose is to find out if a good idea works as imagined. In this chapter we will cover:

- The steps in the prototyping process
- The types of prototypes
- Methods for rapid prototype development
- Prototyping tools
- A continuation of the prototyping demo

Steps in the prototyping process

The process of prototyping involves the following steps:

1. Defining it: What is your good idea supposed to do?
2. Building it: Pick a prototype type and get it done.
3. Testing it: Is it doing what it's supposed to do?
4. Fixing it: How can it better match the intended design?

Now let's look at each step in more detail.

Defining the prototype

This is the first step in designing the game. Usually a game concept starts with a good idea. Often at times it will be an activity the player will do; in general it is best to start with something the player is going to do most often.

The designer should write down, in detail, a description of the activity that the programmer will use to build the prototype. Let the team review the description to make sure everyone understands what is required.

Building the prototype

There are a number of ways to build a prototype, but the goal is to have an app that accurately reflects the design idea and that is built quickly. Leave any extraneous work such as fancy graphics and sound until later in the development process.

Testing the prototype

Now your play testers get to see how accurate the prototype is and whether it is fun. If at all possible, having new testers waiting for builds is an excellent idea. Unfamiliarity with previous builds will optimize the chances of finding overlooked bugs and/or design flaws.

Fixing the prototype

Once you have the play testing evaluations, it is time to decide what to keep in and what to cut. This can be a painful process when the team has grown attached to a project. It is imperative that the prototype is judged objectively. This can be the point at which a design dead end can be discarded to avoid a waste of time and resources.

Prototyping styles

There are two basic styles of prototypes, each of which is used at different times in the development process. These are described as horizontal (big-picture) and vertical (drill-down).

Horizontal prototype

A horizontal prototype is targeting a high-level feature list for the app; for example, a mockup of the game interface and its screens (a wireframe) is considered a horizontal prototype. It has little or no functionality; it is much like a feature laundry list that identifies necessary elements for a particular aspect of the app. Context over content!

The following diagram represents a simple wireframe mockup of a game flow:

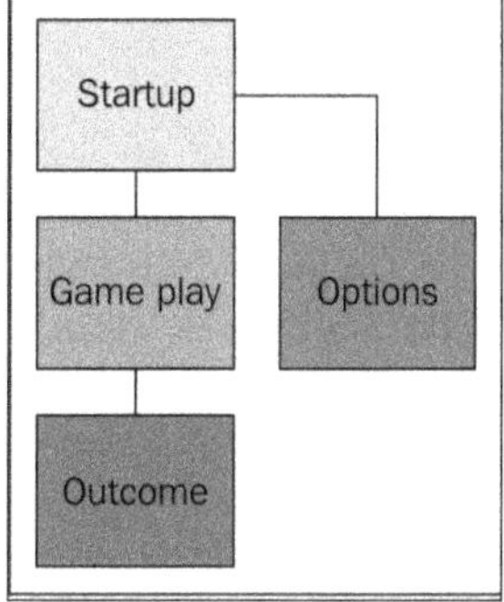

Vertical prototype

A vertical prototype is focused on a single aspect or set of aspects of the app. The goal is to explore and/or flesh out those elements to the point where it is clear whether they work or not. The emphasis is on functionality rather than presentation. Content over context!

Types of prototyping

There are two basic types of coding used in prototyping: disposable and reusable. With the first type, the goal is to get a proof-of-concept out as quickly as possible with no concern for reusability. With the second type the plan is code created for the prototype will to some degree be used in the final app.

Disposable code

Disposable code is just what it sounds like; it is meant to be tossed out after the prototyping process is complete. This type of prototyping is also called throwaway or rapid prototyping.

Disposable coding is an effective way to test out untried concepts early in the design process. Some good ideas just don't work out as planned and finding this out quickly is an important use of the prototyping process.

Mobile game development is heavily reliant on an efficient and robust development cycle. Keeping costs to a minimum can mean the difference between success and failure of a project. The ability to determine from the start of the project that a core game mechanic will be engaging and entertaining is the number one use for disposable code.

There are a number of rapid prototyping methods that range from the very simple to more complex.

Your imagination

The best place to start prototyping is at the very beginning of the design process. Take that good idea and imagine how the player will interact with it. Try to figure out what will keep the player interested with a specific activity. Are there enough options to keep the gameplay engaging? Are there other actions or gameplay aspects that will broaden the gameplay experience without unnecessarily complicating things?

Pencil and paper

Once you have a mental image of a game mechanic, work it out on paper. Do the math on a spreadsheet if possible. If appropriate, play out scenarios with other team members. The designer acts as the **game master** (**GM**) and another team member or members try different actions. The GM figures out what the result of the player actions are. This is a good way to spot weak spots in a mechanic, since the designer may not have thought of every aspect of the gameplay.

Use of game accessories: dice, playing cards, dominoes, and checkers (board and pieces) are some examples of potentially useful items. To get the creative juices flowing, try taking two or three of the accessories and coming up with a completely genre style game. For example, one of the authors used a standard card deck and a set of dominoes to prototype a simple dungeon crawl game similar to the classic "Dungeon!" (`http://en.wikipedia.org/wiki/Dungeon`).

Visual prototypes

These are usually mockups of the game screens, sometimes with limited interactivity. Also called wireframes, they contain basic information on what data is on a screen and what screens can be accessed from the target screen. Many graphics programs, such as Visio and PowerPoint allow hyperlinks between pages. Placing a link on a button mockup and then connecting it to another screen mockup is an effective tool for spotting screen navigation problems.

Interactive prototypes

The goal of an interactive prototype is to simulate the game mechanics as quickly as possible while being faithful to the designer's vision (in case you missed what a game mechanic is, you can refer to `http://en.wikipedia.org/wiki/Game_mechanics`).

This is the phase where rubber meets the pavement; stuff gets done. There may be a fair number of throwaway prototypes in this phase, possibly with multiple features in a single app.

Generally a good way to power through this stage is to define the action the player will do most during the gameplay and test it first. Once it is fun, test the second most common activity alongside the first. Continue this process of adding new actions until the gameplay feels robust; a good rule of thumb is from three to five elements and no more than seven.

Once you have a good idea of how the gameplay works, then it's time to go to the next type of prototype: reusable code.

Reusable code

Also called Evolutionary or Bread board prototyping, the goal here is to produce code that is used in the final app. The prototyping process continues, even though the goal is producing final code. Remember that in the Throwaway phase we were looking for high-level (horizontal) solutions for design problems. Now we are digging deeper, looking for low-level (vertical) solutions to the underlying, possibly unanswered gameplay details.

At this phase, it is useful to review the basic stages of the prototyping process: defining, building, testing, and fixing. These phases are critical throughout the development process, especially when the code is intended for use in the final product. Every time a feature is added, it needs to be fully evaluated in relationship to the existing features. Otherwise there is the risk of introducing a hidden, deal-breaking bug, or exploit.

The philosophy behind Evolutionary prototyping is that an app is never finished; it can always be refined, polished, and expanded. Often, a product is good enough for the current iteration and the constraints of resources. In mobile game development, this may manifest as version releases, future products or **downloadable content packages** (**DLCs**). If some cool new ideas emerge during the development cycle, but it's not possible to implement them with the available resources (time and money), write them down. Plan them for the next iteration of your game.

Why prototype?

Just in case the reasons aren't obvious yet, let's list them again.

- **It saves time and money**: This is pretty important, since changes cost less early on than later in development.
- **It promotes better overall quality of gameplay**: By giving players a chance to try out your good ideas before they are set in stone, there are more opportunities to improve the player experience, resulting in a more fun game. The more fun the game is, the better chance of more sales. And more sales are good sales!

What to avoid

These are some common mistakes that can be counterproductive.

- **Losing the big picture**: While working on individual elements of a project, don't lose sight of what the final goal is. It is fun, exciting, and very rewarding to get one thing or another up and running, which is why a secondary feature may work its way up the priority list. If this happens and it works with the overall design, great! Just remember to check that it doesn't unseat something critical to the design's original intent.
- **Feature creep**: Sometimes good ideas come along at the right time, sometimes not. Be careful not to add in something that breaks the existing app. Also the process of continually adding features means the project's milestones are constantly shifting, which makes it very difficult to hit them.
- **Feature attachment**: Just like in romance, it is easy to fall in love with the concept of a game feature. Once this happens it is difficult to see the reality that the feature (or relationship) just doesn't work as hoped. When this happens you just have to bite the bullet and toss it out, otherwise you can wind up burning yourself out trying to fix the unfixable.

- **Too much time and money**: The whole point of prototyping is to save you time and money. If you find that the prototype is costing more than you budgeted, consider paring back the features or possibly pulling the plug on the project.

Tools

Here is a partial list of tools that will assist with the prototyping process, broken down by the phase they are best suited for all phases

The following list contains the software that you are going to use throughout the entire prototyping process, as they are the basic tools for writing documents, make draws and sketches, and create diagrams and presentations.

- **Microsoft Office/Open Office**: This is essential for documentation throughout the project. MS Office is available for a price from the Microsoft website. Open Office is free and open source and includes many of the features in MS Office.
- **PowerPoint**: This is useful for wire frame mock ups and quick proof of concepts. It is included in MS Office and Open Office has an equivalent application in its bundle.
- **Visio**: This is an excellent tool for creating flow charts, placeholder graphics, screen mock ups, and wireframes. It is available for a price from the Microsoft website. Open Office contains a similar application for free tools for wireframes.

As mentioned in *Chapter 7, Interface Design for Mobile Games*, the creation of wire frames has a fundamental role in the process of designing the game flow and User Interface for a game. In the following list you will find popular tools for such tasks:

- **Pencil project**: This is designed for creating **Graphical User Interface** (**GUI**) wireframes; it's a free, open source application to mock up screen layouts. This is available at `http://pencil.evolus.vn/`.
- **Flairbuilder**: This is used to create interactive Web and mobile prototypes and wireframes. The cost is 99 dollars and up, depending on the number of licenses purchased. This is available at `http://www.flairbuilder.com/`.
- **Axure**: This is considered a top of the line prototyping tool, Axure is targeted at Web and mobile prototyping. There are trial, standard, and professional versions available at `http://www.axure.com/`.

Tools for rapid prototyping

There are many game **software development kit** (**SDKs**) available, including powerful **integrated development environment** (**IDEs**) that are free to use. We list some here for your reference.

- **Game Maker**: This is an SDK designed for 2D game development. It has a free version with reduced functionality and functional versions from 50 dollars and up. This can be found at `http://www.yoyogames.com/gamemaker/studio`.
- **Unity 3D**: This is one of the most powerful free game SDKs available. It has a very complete library as well as a robust online user community. This is why we picked Unity to build our prototype tutorial. You can check anything you may wish to know about Unity 3D at `http://unity3d.com/`.
- **Havoc Project Anarchy**: This is a recent initiative (as we write) that aims to provide users with a full featured game engine, created by the popular company Havoc. The basic license is free to use, you can check this project at `http://www.projectanarchy.com/`.

Unity3D tutorial – part 2

In the first part of our tutorial in *Chapter 8, Mobile Game Engines*, we prepared the game scene. In this second part we will show how to make things behave properly.

Let's begin thinking about the game logic we are going to implement in our game.

In Space Invaders the player controls a ship located at the bottom of the screen, which moves left and right and shoots bullets.

The goal is to destroy wave after wave of aliens approaching towards the player's ship from the top half of the screen, before they reach the bottom of the screen, while avoiding the bullets they fire.

Aliens move according to a snake-like pattern; they begin moving right and as they reach the right boundary of the screen, they invert direction and move a little bit closer to the bottom of the screen, then repeat the cycle as they move left and reach the left boundary of the screen.

Once in a while, aliens shoot bullet towards the player's ship.

Player's bullets move bottom-up, while aliens' move top-down.

The player's ship

As the player's ship is easier to implement, we'll begin with it.

1. Drag the **PLShip** prefab into the **Scene View** and set its position at coordinates **X**=`0`, **Y**=`-15`, **Z**=`15` (these are arbitrary values, but they are consistent with camera settings we defined earlier). You can edit the scale of the **PLShip** prefab in case it is not the right size by changing its scale values in the **Transform** panel in the **Inspector** panel.
2. We want the ship to move left and right and fire a bullet, to do that we create a JavaScript file and add it to the **PLShip** prefab.
3. In the **Project** panel create a new folder, name it `Scripts` and then create a JavaScript file in the folder. Name it `ControlShip` and double-click it to open in the default script editor provided with Unity, called **MonoDevelop**.
4. As you can see, any newly created JavaScript file is already provided with two main function declarations: the `Start()` function and `Update()` function.
5. The `Start()` function is useful to set default values for variables when the game starts, while the `Update()` function is a very important one, which is called by Unity engine (almost) once per frame. Basically, when you need some operation to be performed continuously, put your code inside the `Update()` function.
6. To take control of the player ship we need the following code to be added to the script. We put comments to make the operations performed clearer, as we cannot make a full explanation on game programming here.

```
#pragma strict

//this var is needed to fire bullets from the ship
var myBullet:Rigidbody;

//this is a true\false var to control player's ship fire
  //rate
static var canShoot:boolean;

function Start () {
    //we want the player to be able to shoot as the game
      //starts
   canShoot=true;
}

function Update () {
```

```
    //is the player pressing right button?
    if(Input.GetKey("right"))
    {
        //ship moves right
          transform.Translate(Vector3(2,0,0));
    }
    //is the player pressing left button?
    if(Input.GetKey("left"))
    {
        //ship moves left
          transform.Translate(Vector3(-2,0,0));
    }
    //is player pressing the fire button (spacebar)
    if(Input.GetKeyDown("space")&&canShoot)
    {
          //create the bullet
    Instantiate(myBullet,transform.position,transform.rotation);
          //player can't fire for a while
          canShoot=false;
    }
}
```

7. Save the file and go back to Unity, then, in the **Project** panel, drag the script onto the **PLShip** prefab to add it.
8. You can check in the **Inspector** panel that the script has been added to the prefab. You will also notice that the script requires a `Rigidbody` variable to be instantiated for the script to work, as defined by this line of the `ControlShip` script:

```
//this var is needed to fire bullets from the ship
var myBullet:Rigidbody;
```

9. To instantiate the variable, we first need to add the **Rigidbody** component to the bullet. To do that, select the **PLBullet** prefab in the **Project** panel, then go to the main menu and select **Component** | **Physics** | **Rigidbody**, as shown in the following screenshot:

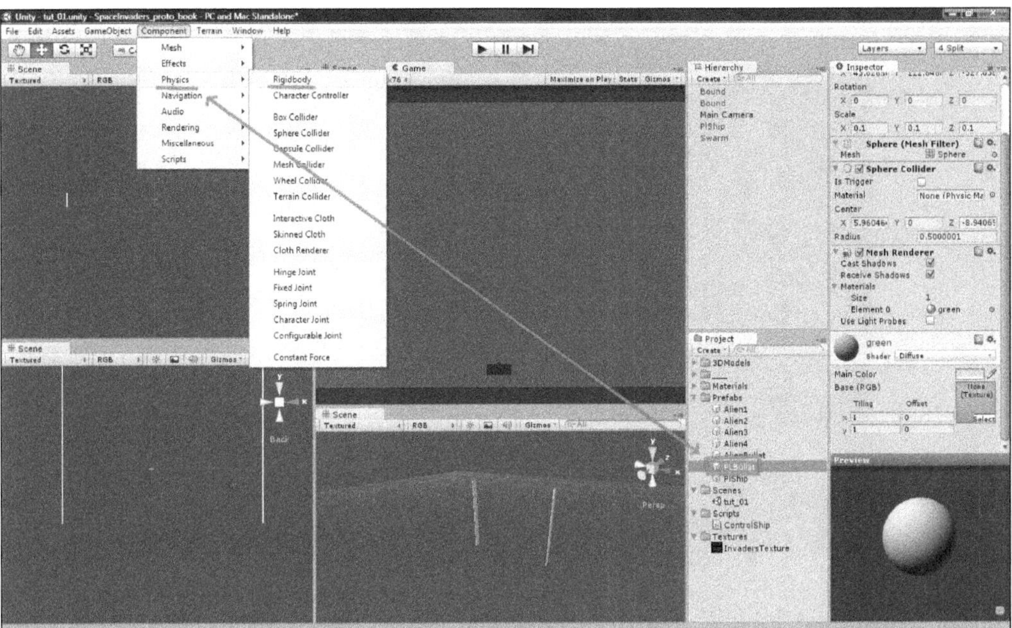

10. Select the **PLBullet** prefab and drag it into the empty slot on the script component of the **Inspector** panel.
11. Now that the **Rigidbody** component has been added to the **PLBullet** prefab, we need to edit a couple properties in the **Inspector** panel. Uncheck the **Use Gravity** option and check the **Is Kinematic** option. This way the bullet won't be affected by gravity and it will trigger collisions with other game objects. If you want to know more about **Rigidbody** and **Collision Detection**, we suggest you to refer to the Unity manual.

12. Check the following screenshot to see you did things right:

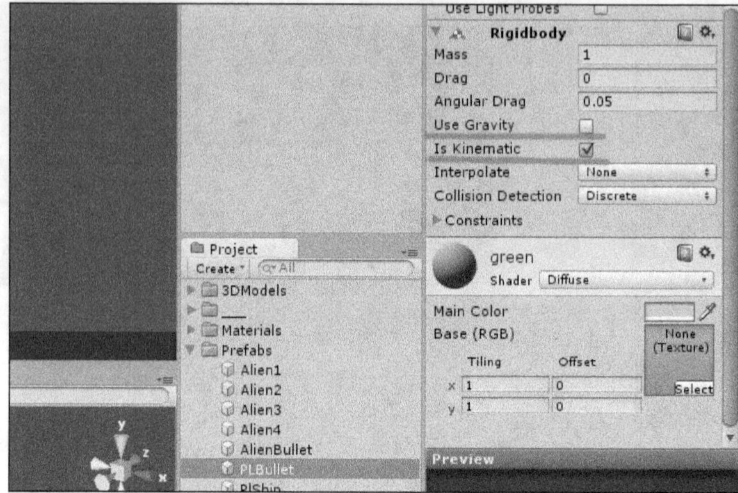

13. Now we can finally drag the **PLBullet** prefab into the **My Bullet** slot of the **Control Ship (Script)**, as shown in the following screenshot:

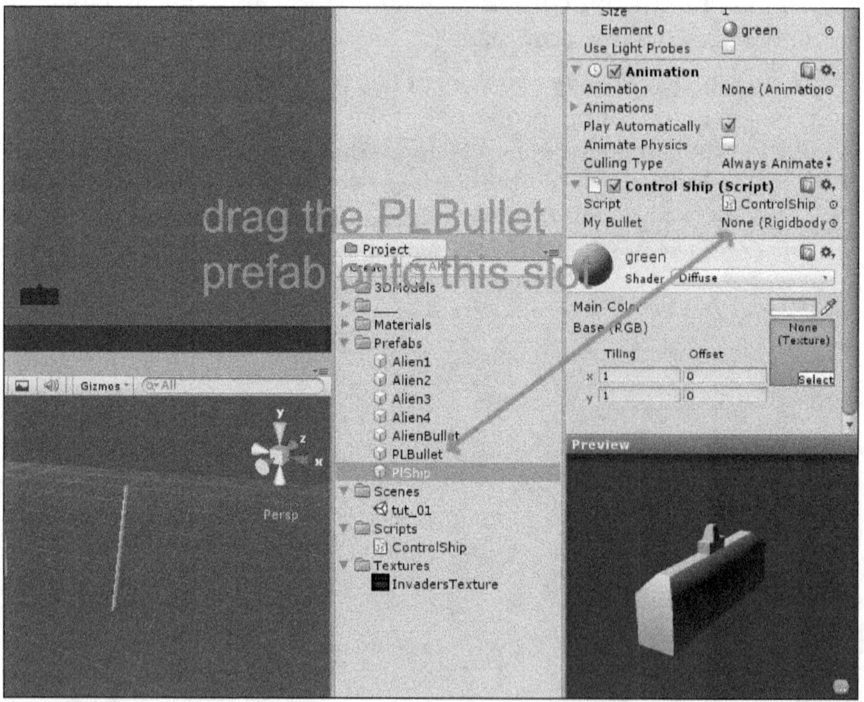

14. Next we need to take care of the **PLBullet** behavior with another script. Create one in the `Scripts` folder, name it `ControlPLBullet` and double-click on it to open.
15. With this script we are going to tell the bullet to move up once created and to check for collisions with enemy aliens and other objects such as barriers (discussed in the last part of this tutorial in *Chapter 10, Balancing, Tuning, and Polishing Mobile Games*).
16. The following code is to be put in the `ControlPLBullet` script:

```
#pragma strict

function Start () {

}

function Update () {

    //move bullet up once created
   transform.Translate(Vector3(0,2,0));

   //Y=100 defines upper screen limit
   if(transform.position.y>100)
   {
        //destroy bullet as it goes outside the upper
          //screen limit
         Destroy(gameObject);
         //once the bullet is destroyed, allow the player
           //to shoot again
         moveShip.canShoot=true;
   }
}

//this function checks for collisions
function OnTriggerEnter(other:Collider)
{
    //if bullets collides with aliens, destroy both
   if(other.gameObject.tag=="Enemies"){

         Destroy(gameObject);
         Destroy(other.gameObject);
         //once the bullet is destroyed, allow the player
           //to shoot again
         ControlShip.canShoot=true;
   }
```

```
    //if bullet collides with barriers, destroy it and a
      //piece of the barrier
    if(other.gameObject.tag=="BarrierBrick"){

          Destroy(gameObject);
          Destroy(other.gameObject);
          //once the bullet is destroyed, allow the player
            //to shoot again
            ControlShip.canShoot=true;
    }
}
```

17. The script basically controls that the bullet moves up once fired. In the `Update()` function we also check if a collision occurs and perform the desired action when this happens.
18. You will also notice that we are using **Tag** to check what the bullet collides with.
19. Tags are another very useful feature offered by Unity that allows us to give an identification name to game objects to be used to check collisions and other events. We will explain how to use tags as we go on with this tutorial.
20. It may be necessary to adjust the bullet speed, which can be done by modifying the following line in the `Update()` function:

    ```
    //move bullet up once created
       transform.Translate(Vector3(0,2,0));
    ```

21. The **Y** threshold to destroy the bullet once it goes beyond the upper screen limit could require to be changed too, by editing the following line in the `Update()` function:

    ```
    //Y=100 defines upper screen limit
       if(transform.position.y>100)
    ```

22. Now, everything should be ready to test the ship controls. Launch the application and check that the ship actually moves left and right with the arrow keys and fires when you press the spacebar.

Feel free to tweak its movement speed values according to your tastes.

The aliens

Now that the player's ship is over with, we can take care of the alien invaders.

As we want them to move as a single group, the best thing to do is to have a **GameObject**, which is not actually part of the group yet, control them.

1. Create an empty **GameObject** in the scene, name it `SwarmManager` and put it at the coordinates **X**=`-18`, **Y**=`12`, **Z**=`15`.
2. Our next step is to add a script to `SwarmManager`. We will use this script to have the `SwarmManager` game object create the alien swarm and move it in the scene.
3. Let's begin by creating the alien swarm in order to check that the position we set for `SwarmManager` is correct for the setup we defined.
4. Create a new JavaScript file in the `Scripts` folder and name it `ControlSwarm`, then double-click on it to open it in **MonoDevelop**.
5. The first part of the script takes care of creating the alien swarm. To do that we just need to declare four `GameObject` variables to store the alien prefabs and a `for {}` cycle to create four rows of aliens.

```
//we need a GameObject variable for each alien type in the
  //swarm
var Alien1:GameObject;
var Alien2:GameObject;
var Alien3:GameObject;
var Alien4:GameObject;

function Start ()
{
   //we want 11 aliens per row
   for(var i=0;i<11;i++)
   {
         //first row is created at same Y position as
           //SwarmManager
Instantiate(Alien1,Vector3(-15+(3*i),
  transform.position.y,transform.position.z),
    transform.rotation);

Instantiate(Alien2,Vector3(-15+(3*i),
  transform.position.y-3,transform.position.z),
    transform.rotation);

Instantiate(Alien3,Vector3(-15+(3*i),
```

```
    transform.position.y-6,transform.position.z),
      transform.rotation);

  Instantiate(Alien4,Vector3(-15+(3*i),
    transform.position.y-9,transform.position.z),
      transform.rotation);
      }
  }
```

6. Add the script to the `SwarmManager` game object in the scene and then drag the four aliens prefabs in the exposed `GameObject` variables, as shown in the following screenshot:

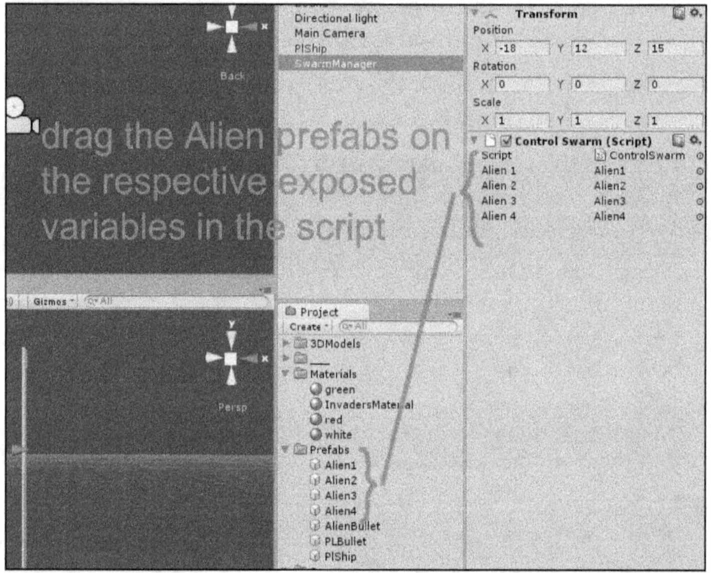

Now launch your project to check that the aliens are correctly spawned and their position is centered with respect to the player's ship and the camera. If needed, tweak the `SwarmManager` position and the numerical values inside the `for {}` cycle until you get a setup you are satisfied with.

Next we take care that the swarm moves according to the snake-like moving pattern we described at the beginning of this tutorial. Things could become a little more complex here, so stick with us. We would also like to state here that there is no single way to code things while working with videogames, though some ways are better than other. What we suggest here is the way we consider good enough for the goal of this tutorial, and those of you who are proficient with programming could find better ways to achieve the same result. We strongly recommend you to always try and find other ways that work better for you whenever it's possible.

To have the aliens change direction as they get close to the screen bounds, we will use two game objects positioned at the right and left sides of the swarm. The first alien that collides with any of the bounds will make the entire swarm change its direction and also lower their height with regards to the player's ship.

1. Create a **Cube GameObject** and name it `LeftBound`. Put it at coordinates **X**=`-20`, **Y**=`5`, **Z**=`15` and set its scale to **X**=`1`, **Y**=`100`, **Z**=`8`. Also check the **Is Trigger** option in its **Box Collider** component in the **Inspector** panel as shown in the following screenshot:

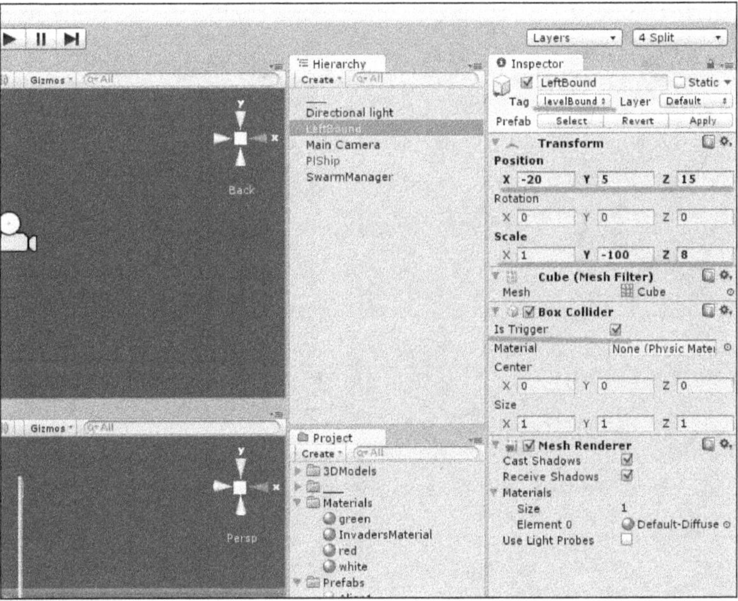

2. We also need to use a tag to check the collisions of the aliens with the bounds, so it is time to provide a brief explanation about what tags are. As usual, we suggest you to refer to the Unity documentation to delve deeper into this topic.
3. As the name suggests, tags are labels that can be attached to game objects to identify them when specific events occur. In our case, we know that the aliens will be subjected to at least two types of collisions: collisions with the player's bullets and collisions with the level bounds. Unity allows the use of tags to distinguish between these two different events.

4. To create a **Tag** click on the **Untagged** button in the top section of the **Inspector** panel as shown in the following screenshot and from the drop-down menu, select **Add Tag**.

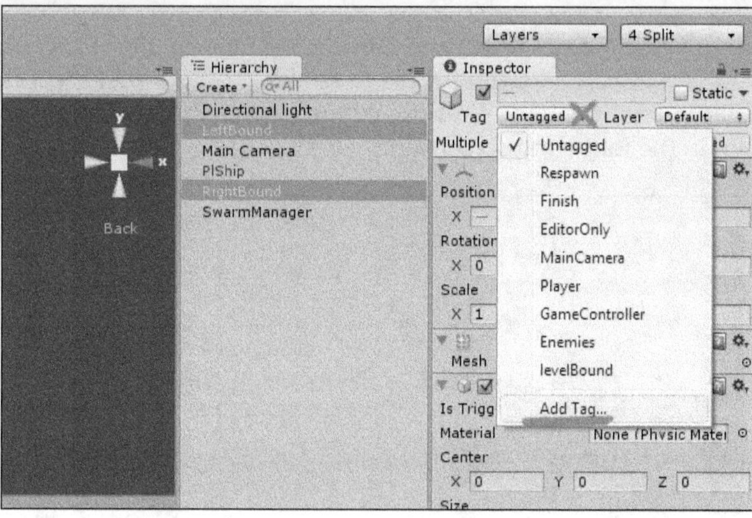

5. Find the first empty entry in the **Tag Manager** panel that opens up and name it `levelBound`.
6. Well done, you've created a tag to be used in our script files to check collisions between the aliens and the level bounds we put in the scene.

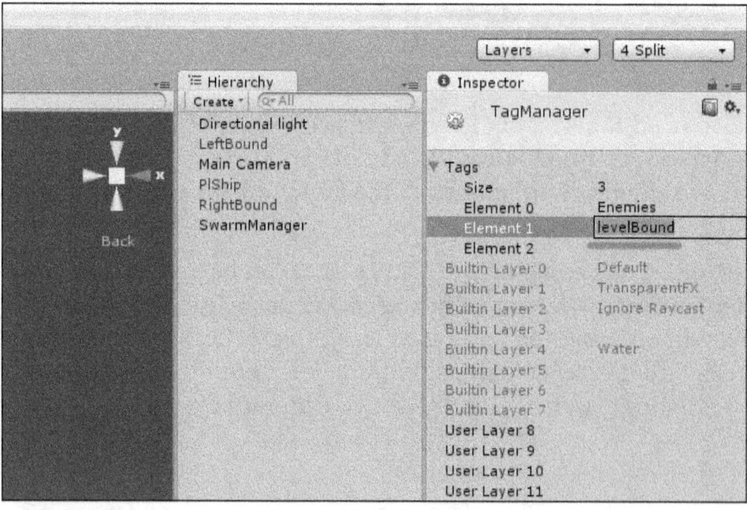

7. To add the tag to the **LeftBound** game object, select it and in the **Tag** drop-down menu, you should now be able to select the newly created `levelBound` tag.
8. To complete this part of the tutorial, we need a second bound to be added to the **Scene**. With the **LeftBound** game object selected, press *Ctrl* + *D* to duplicate it. Name the newly-created game object **RightBound** and set its **X** coordinate to `20`, then add the `levelBound` tag to **RightBound** too.

The following screenshot shows a reference of what you should have in your scene by now:

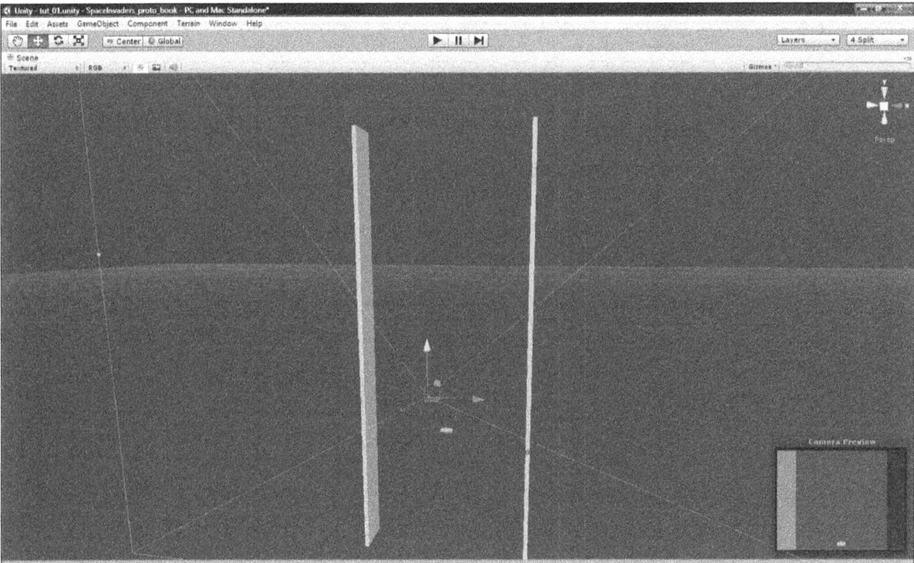

It's now time to make the swarm move. Open the `ControlSwarm` script.

1. In the upper section of the script, where we declared the alien `GameObjects`, add the following lines to create new variables:

```
//this is an array to store the instances of the aliens
  //that are part of the swarm
static var enemyList=new Array();

//we use this boolean to check the actual direction of the
  //swarm
var goRight:boolean;

//with this int value we define the horizontal speed of the
  //swarm
```

```
var vel:int;

//we use this boolean to control the collision of the
  //aliens with the Bounds
static var bCollide:boolean;
```

2. Now enter the `Start()` function and add the missing lines:

```
function Start ()
{
   //we want 11 aliens per row
   for(var i=0;i<11;i++)
   {
         //first row is created at same Y position as
           //SwarmManager
          Instantiate(Alien1,Vector3(-15+(3*i),
            transform.position.y,transform.position.z),
              transform.rotation);

Instantiate(Alien2,Vector3(-15+(3*i),
  transform.position.y-3,transform.position.z),
    transform.rotation);

Instantiate(Alien3,Vector3(-15+(3*i),
  transform.position.y-6,transform.position.z),
    transform.rotation);

Instantiate(Alien4,Vector3(-15+(3*i),
  transform.position.y-9,transform.position.z),
    transform.rotation);
   }

   //this line fills the array enemyList with aliens tagged
     //"Enemies"
   enemyList=GameObject.FindGameObjectsWithTag("Enemies");

   //the swarm starts moving right
   goRight=true;

   //tweak the swarm speed according to your tastes
   vel=4;

   //no collision when the game starts
   bCollide=false;
}
```

3. Now we take care of having the swarm move. Movement is defined by a function called `moveEnemies()`, which is called the first time in 0.5 seconds after the game starts and then every 0.25 seconds by another instruction called `InvokeRepeating()`. You can tweak these values if you like.

```
//this instruction calls the moveEnemies functions at a
  //given pace
InvokeRepeating("moveEnemies",0.5,0.25);

//we move the swarm left or right at speed defined by vel
function moveEnemies()
{
   if(goRight)
   {
         for(var myEnemy:GameObject in enemyList)
         {
                if(myEnemy)
                {
   myEnemy.transform.Translate(Vector3(vel,0,0));
                }
         }
   }

   if(!goRight)
   {
         for(var myEnemy:GameObject in enemyList)
         {
                if(myEnemy)
                {
                      myEnemy.transform.Translate(Vector3
                        (-vel,0,0));
                }
         }
   }
}
```

4. Finally, in the `Update()` function we check if a collision with the `levelBound` tag occurred to change the movement direction of the swarm and lower their height with regards to the player's ship.

```
function Update () {

   if(bCollide)
   {
         goRight=!goRight;
```

```
        for(var myEnemy:GameObject in enemyList)
        {
                if(myEnemy)
                {
    myEnemy.transform.Translate(Vector3 (0,-4,0));
                }
        }

        bCollide=false;
    }
}
```

To have the script work, we need to perform some operations.

1. First of all we need to tag the **Aliens** prefab as enemies. Add a tag named `Enemies` to the **Tag Manager** panel as we did for `levelBound` and set it for the four **Alien** prefabs.
2. Then we need to program the alien instances so that they alert the `SwarmManager` game object whenever they collide with `levelBound`. As you may remember, we created the `SwarmManager` game object as an external component of the swarm itself; therefore we now need to add another script to our `Script` folder.
3. Create a new JavaScript file, name it `BoundCollision` and open it in **MonoDevelop**. Add the following lines to the script; a variable declaration and the `OnTriggerEnter()` function to actually check the collisions between the **Aliens** and the **Bounds**:

```
//this variable is used to access the bCollide variable in
  //the ControlSwarm script
var mySwarm:GameObject;

function Start () {
}

function Update () {
}

function OnTriggerEnter(other:Collider)
{
   if(other.gameObject.tag=="levelBound")
   {
```

```
            //we access the bCollide variable in the
              //ControlSwarm script
            var scriptFile: ControlSwarm =
              mySwarm.GetComponent("ControlSwarm");
            scriptFile.bCollide=true;
    }
}
```

4. Add this script to all four **Alien** prefabs in the **Project** panel.
5. To have this script work we need to Perform a last operation, though. We need to make another Prefab out of the `SwarmManager` game object.
6. Create a new Prefab in the `Project` panel, name it `SwarmManager` and then drag the `SwarmManager` game object from the **Hierarchy** panel into the `SwarmManager` Prefab in the **Project** panel. Use the following screenshot as a reference:

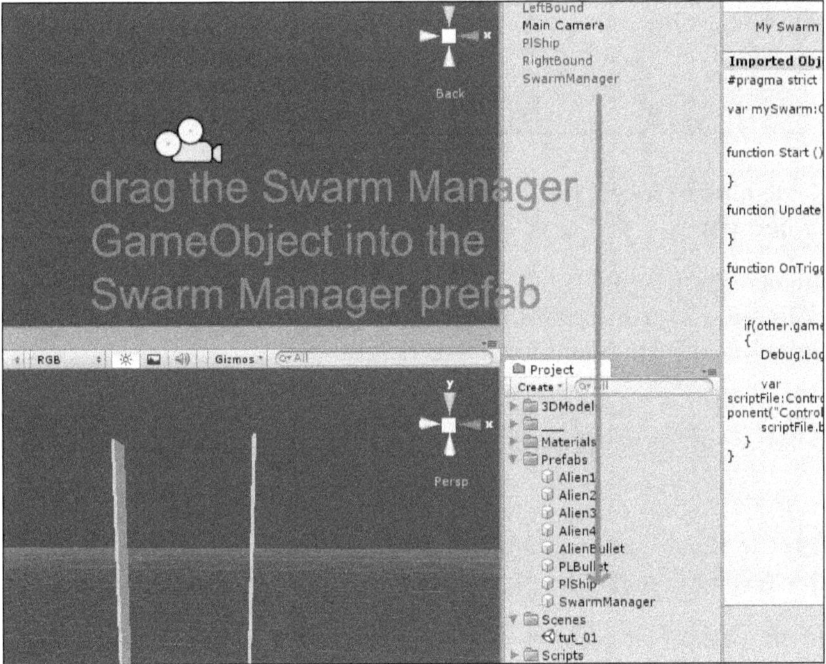

7. The last operation is to drag the `SwarmManager` prefab we just created into the `My Swarm` variable of the **Bound Collision (Script)** we added to each **Alien** prefab, as shown in the following screenshot:

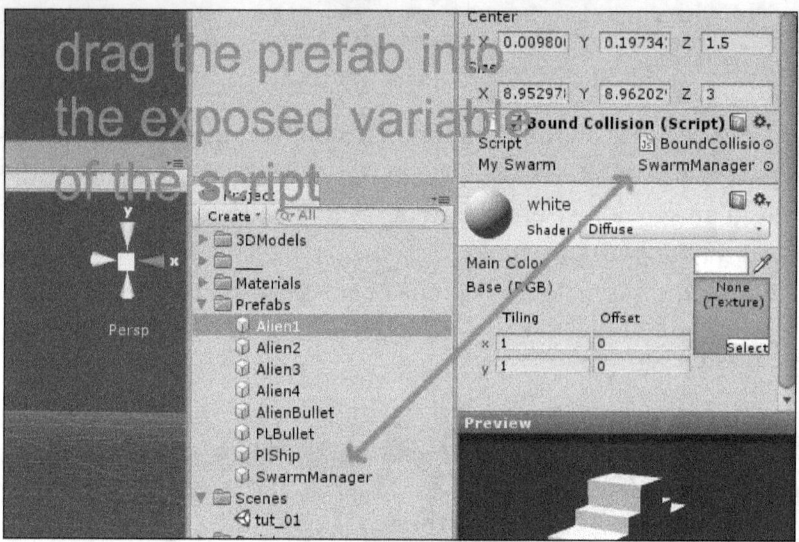

8. Remember to repeat this last operation for all **Alien** prefabs we have in the **Project** panel.

Everything is ready now to test the behavior of the alien swarm. Launch the project and check that the swarm actually starts moving right and upon colliding with the bounds, invert its direction and lowers its height.

Very well done! The fundamentals of our prototype are set now. In the next section we will take care of the firing stuff.

Firing

First of all we want to make the player's ship fire against the aliens of the swarm.

We already have a prefab representing the bullets fired by the player's ship, so we actually just need to have them spawned from the ship as the player presses the spacebar. Obviously, this action can be bound to any other key of choice.

1. Create a new JavaScript in the `Scripts` folder, name it `ControlPLBullet` and open it in **MonoDevelop**.

2. This script contains instructions for the `Update()` function and the `OnTriggerEnter()` function to check for collisions between the bullet and the aliens, their bullets and the barriers positioned between the player's ship and the swarm.

3. The `Update()` function takes care of making the bullet move up and eventually destroys it in case nothing is hit, so that the player can shoot again. The following code is to be typed into the `Update()` function:

```
function Update () {

   //move bullet up once created 2 pixels\frame
   transform.Translate(Vector3(0,2,0));

   //Y=100 defines upper screen limit
   if(transform.position.y>100)
   {
        //destroy bullet as it goes outside the upper
          //screen limit
         Destroy(gameObject);
         //once the bullet is destroyed, allow the player
           //to shoot again
             ControlShip.canShoot=true;
   }
}
```

4. In the `OnTriggerEnter()` function we check what the bullet collides with and then destroy both:

```
function OnTriggerEnter(other:Collider)
{
    //the bullet collides with aliens
   if(other.gameObject.tag=="Enemies"){

         Destroy(gameObject);
         Destroy(other.gameObject);

         //once the bullet is destroyed, allow the player
           //to shoot again
           ControlShip.canShoot=true;
   }

   //the bullet collides with barriers: destroy bullet and
     //a piece of the barrier
   if(other.gameObject.tag=="BarrierBrick"){
```

```
            Destroy(gameObject);
            Destroy(other.gameObject);

            //once the bullet is destroyed, allow the player
              //to shoot again
            ControlShip.canShoot=true;
        }
    }
```

5. Save the script and drag it onto the **PLBullet** Prefab.

If you test the project now, you should have the player's ship firing and the bullet move up, until it collides with an alien or gets out of the top boundary of the screen. You should also notice that you won't be able to shoot again until the last bullet is destroyed. In the `Update()` function you can also tweak the speed of the bullet as it goes up and the height it gets destroyed at, if it doesn't collide with anything.

Having the aliens shoot at the player's ship can be achieved in many different ways. For the sake of this tutorial we will show a very straightforward method, simply based on probabilities. We basically call a function every five seconds and with each call, we set a probability that each alien in the swarm fires a bullet against the player's ship.

The actions of the aliens' bullets, movements, and collision detection are basically handled the same way we did for the player's bullets, with a script attached to the bullet itself.

1. So create a new JavaScript in the `Scripts` folder, name it `AlienShoot` and add the following code. You should now be used to the kind of actions expressed by the instructions of the script.

```
#pragma strict

//this var instantiates the bullet prefab
var itsBullet:Rigidbody;

function Start () {

}

function Update () {

}
//repeat firing check every 5 secs
InvokeRepeating("shouldFire",3,5);
```

```
function shouldFire()
{
        //assign a random value between 0 and 1 to p
   var p:float=Random.value;

   //change p that alien fires
   if(p>0.85)
   {
         doFire();
   }
}

//this function instantiates an alien bullet
function doFire()
{
   Instantiate(itsBullet,transform.position, transform.rotation);
}
```

2. To have the `AlienBullet` prefab work properly, we first need to modify it by adding a **Rigidbody** component, so that it can detect collisions with the barriers and the player's ship. In fact we declared the bullet variable as `Rigidbody` in the script. Select it in the **Project** panel and add the **Rigidbody** component as shown in the following screenshot:

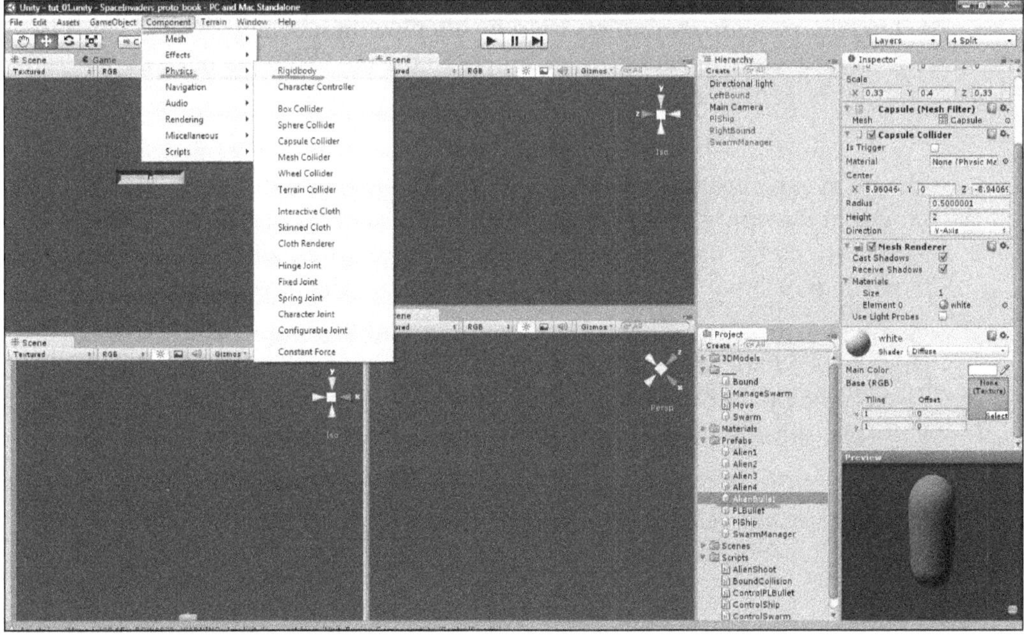

3. Then attach the script to each **Alien** prefab in the `Prefabs` folder of the **Project** panel and drag, for each **Alien** prefab, the `AlienBullet` prefab into the exposed variable of the script. Refer to the following screenshot to be sure you've done things right and check that the **Is Kinematic** option of the **Rigidbody** component is flagged, while the **Use Gravity** is not, as usual.

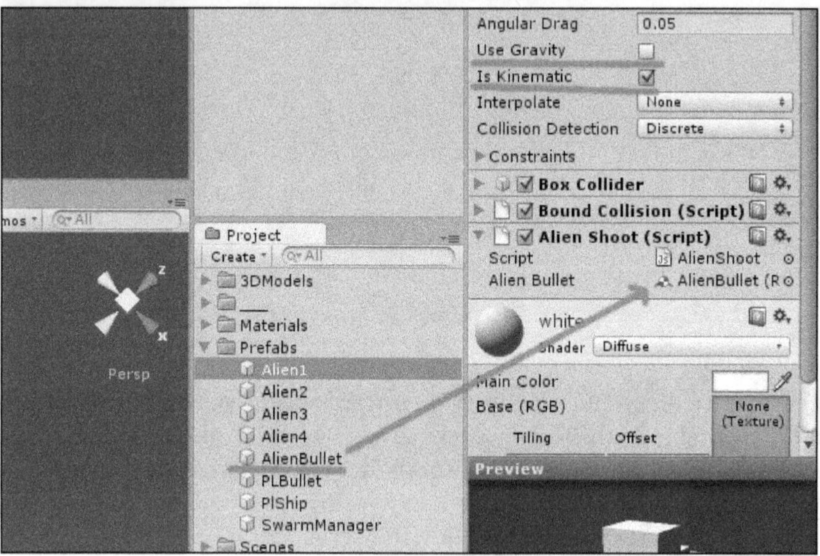

The next step is to provide the bullets fired by aliens with a behavior, since, as it is, the `AlienBullet` prefab doesn't do very much. In the next step we need to program the behavior of the bullets fired by aliens.

1. Create another script with name `ControlAlienBullet`. The script is mostly like the one controlling the `PLBullet` prefab, with the difference that it moves in the opposite way, from top to bottom of the screen. This time we also check collisions with the player's ship rather than aliens and with the barriers, which we will discuss in more detail in the next chapter.
2. Finally, we need to manage the consequence of the bullet hitting the player's ship. We will take care of this in another section of this tutorial, when we discuss the final touches to be added to the prototype. For now, we are fine with a simple log message telling that the game is over!
3. The following code is to be put in the `ControlAlienBullet` script:

```
function Start () {

}

function Update () {
```

```
    //this bullet move down
    transform.Translate(Vector3(0,-2,0));

    //destroy bullet below this height
    if(transform.position.y<-30)
    {
          Destroy(gameObject);
    }

}

function OnTriggerEnter(other:Collider)
{
    //check collision with player's ship
    if(other.gameObject.tag=="PlayerShip")
    {
          Destroy(gameObject);
          Destroy(other.gameObject);

          //we will improve this later
          Debug.Log("Game Over");
    }

    //check collisions with barriers
    if(other.gameObject.tag=="BarrierBrick"){

          Destroy(gameObject);
          Destroy(other.gameObject);
    }
}
```

4. You may notice that the collision between the alien bullet and the player's ship is dependent on the player's ship being tagged as `"PlayerShip"`. We thus need to add this tag into the **Tag Manager** panel and then add the tag to the **PLShip** prefab. You shouldn't have problems doing this by now.

5. We also need the **PLShip** Prefab to be added with a **BoxCollider** component with the **Is Trigger** flag checked in order to have the collisions with the bullet being detected. The following screenshot should help you do that:

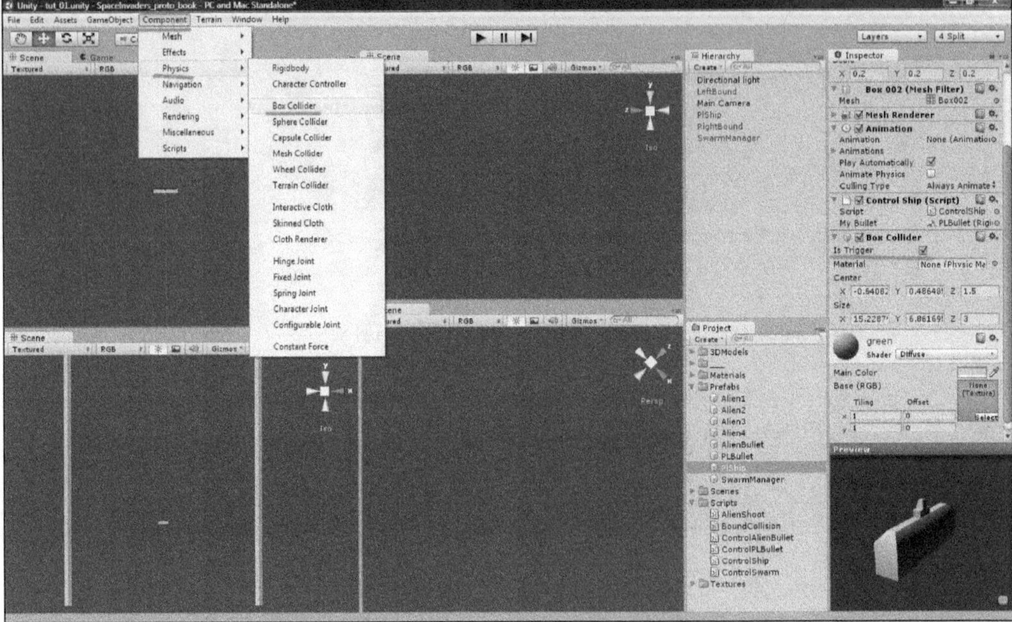

6. Add the `ControlAlienBullet` script to the **AlienBullet** Prefab and if you test the project now, you should have the aliens randomly fire at the player. Check that the player's ship is destroyed and the **Game Over** log is correctly displayed upon collision between the alien bullet and the player's ship.
7. Also remember that you can tweak the firing rate of the aliens by modifying the `InvokeRepeating` instruction or the probability that the `doFire()` function is called in the `AlienShoot` script.

This ends the second part of the tutorial, where we added the basic functionality to our Space Invaders prototype. Right now, in the `Scripts` folder of the **Project** panel you should have the following scripts:

- `AlienShoot`
    - `BoundCollision`
    - `ControlAlienBullet`
    - `ControlPLBullet`
    - `ControlShip`
    - `ControlSwarm`

The `Prefabs` folder should contain the following prefabs:

- `Alien1`
- `Alien2`
- `Alien3`
- `Alien4`
- `AlienBullet`
- `PLBullet`
- `PLShip`
- `SwarmManager`

Finally, the **Tag Manager** panel should handle the following tags:

- `Enemies`
- `levelBound`
- `PlayerShip`

Well done! In the next and final part of the tutorial we will add the final touches: GUI, the barriers, a Game Over event, and some audio.

Summary

In this chapter we covered the prototyping process, the types of prototypes, the tools for prototyping, and the dos and don'ts of prototyping. We also provided part 2 of our prototyping tutorial with Unity 3D.

In the next chapter, we discuss how to fine tune and polish up a prototype to achieve a final product, ready for publication.

10
Balancing, Tuning, and Polishing Mobile Games

When a game comes to the final steps of its development, all efforts should be directed towards adjusting the small details, which make a difference between a good game and a great one. The competition is high in this industry and no game can make its way against its competitors if it is less than perfect.

Making a game perfect can have several, and often subjective, meanings. As games are interactive media they can only be perfect inside the space defined by their interactions with the players. This means that a game can never be great by itself, but it can only be great in the perception that gamers have of it.

Basically games should meet the players' expectations at several levels; they should run smoothly, be fun to play, provide a reasonable amount of gameplay, and make players feel at ease with the game controls/interface, among others.

Each of these topics falls into a different category of actions, or set of actions that you as game developers, should perform to achieve an optimal result with your game. In this chapter we will talk about balancing, tuning, and polishing (mainly), explaining the aim of each and the best practices to perform them efficiently.

We also in this chapter finally top off the Unity tutorial, by adding the final touches to improve the gameplay provide an interface and offer better aesthetics. This will lead us to a better polished game, which is the aim of this chapter.

Balancing

Balancing has mainly to do with the longevity (longevity represents how long a game is played by a player in his life) of a title, as it affects the quality of the interaction between the player and the game he is playing.

Let's think of games as dynamic systems. As with any system, games must have some kind of equilibrium state that allows the system itself to perpetuate. In our metaphor, the longer the equilibrium is kept, the better the longevity of a game.

Now let's consider the players' actions as disturbances to the state of equilibrium the system is in at any given time. If the system of our game doesn't react properly to the players' actions, for example, it over or under reacts, the equilibrium state of the game collapses, thus ruining the gameplay experience.

In a **First Person Shooter** (**FPS**) the player usually controls a character that can sustain much more damage than the average enemy he faces, which is an example of an unbalanced condition. To balance the improved resistance of the player's character, FPSs are provided with tons of enemies for the player to kill. If a FPS had just one single weak enemy, it wouldn't be so much fun to play.

On the other hand, if the enemies were as tough as the player's character, it wouldn't be very fair for the player to have so many against him.

In a sports game where two teams compete, each team has the same number of players so it is not by chance that sending off a team member is considered a strong penalization for the team sustaining it.

In the following section we provide an explanation for all the most important techniques used in game development to balance games.

Symmetry

The competition between two teams of players in sports can help us describe the most basic technique to balance games, which is called symmetry. Symmetry means that each side (or team) starts with the exact same amount of resources. Competitive games always require some kind of symmetry, though there can be cases where total symmetry cannot be achieved, as happens with turn-based games, such as Chess and Tic-Tac-Toe, as one player will always have the advantage of the first move.

Randomization

This is another very basic technique commonly used in board and card games that consist of letting a random process be in charge of determining the initial gaming conditions. Since a random process can only lead to fairness in the long run, through several repetitions of the experience, it is good practice to use methods to overcome the initial frustration this technique can lead to. One is to make each game session short enough so that multiple attempts can be made in a single play session. Another is to give the player the possibility to set the range of random results through optimization, as is the case with building up your deck in the game Magic: The Gathering.

Feedback loops

A more advanced technique to balance a game is by making it more demanding for the successful player. **Real-time Strategy** (**RTS**) games achieve that by asking players to pay an upkeep cost for the units they control so that the largest armies require the higher cost to be paid. In Mario Kart the leading player always gets the worst power-ups and his top speed is diminished, while his opponents become a bit faster, a feature commonly known as "the rubber band effect".

In other words, feedback loops allow automatic balancing by weakening the leading player and providing small advantages to those who are losing.

Game director

An even more advanced technique is to have the game's **Artificial Intelligence** (**AI**) take control of adjusting the game difficulty based on the players' performance. The game Left4Dead by Valve offers an excellent example of such a technique, as the players advance in the game, the so called AI director gathers statistics with regards to their performance and sets enemy spawn points, enemy population, and items accordingly to keep the game optimally balanced for each player. It even controls the music scores, creating interesting, distinctive mixes for each player in the party.

Statistics

Further advice we would like to offer on the matter of game balancing is to use statistics whenever you can. The mathematical analysis of data gathered from game sessions could really help you understand what happened and identify unbalanced areas of your game, if any, to make the appropriate corrections.

As you can understand by now, game balancing is both a crucial and thorny activity, which requires several aspects to be considered at the same time. Do it wrong and your game system will be easily broken by players, as they are very smart at finding dominant strategies and dark areas that destroy the playability of your title.

Play testing is the key for optimal game balancing. While scheduling your project, allocate a proper amount of time with your testers to check that no element of your game is ineffective or undesirable and undermines the game rule set.

Tuning

Tuning a game involves a series of activities, which are related to balancing, but with a distinctive aim. Tuning has to do with making a game fun to play from beginning to its end, possibly for players at the most different skill levels (though it is true that few games specially aim towards very skilled players, sometimes).

With this last subject we enter a very dark area of games design in general and videogame design in particular because we get to the point of defining what is fun. Unfortunately, a definition of fun would require an entire book for itself, so we suggest you to refer to this very interesting Gamasutra article to begin your research into the topic of fun in Videogames found at `http://www.gamasutra.com/view/feature/173545/fun_is_boring.php`.

Sid Meyer, the founder of MicroProse and designer of several popular strategy games like the Civilization series (`http://en.wikipedia.org/wiki/Sid_Meyer`) once said that games can be described as a series of interesting choices. From such a perspective, tuning a game means that a game designer should keep the choices available to his players interesting throughout the entire game.

Let's now switch to another industry veteran, *Raph Koster*, designer of Ultima Online and author of a book *A Theory of Fun for Game Design*, by *Paraglyph Press*, we suggest you to read. In Raph Koster's opinion, play has to do with learning, which means that games keep being interesting to players as long as they keep learning while playing.

Having this in mind, we can now begin defining what tuning a game means. A well-tuned game is the one that is fun to play from beginning to end, and a game that engages players according to the improvement of their gaming skills as they play. A game that perpetuates on the delicate equilibrium between punishment and reward, if success is too easy, your players will get bored soon and quit playing. On the other hand, if the game is too hard they will curse the designer and quit playing.

Tuning strategies

Which are the key strategies we can make use of to effectively tune games?

Generalization is one. Design your games so that the core mechanics are controlled by general rules that don't change with regard to specific game entities or situations. Tuning each game mechanic separately will very likely lead you to balancing issues, while if the same game rules are consistent throughout the entire game it will be easier to make the fine adjustments required, offering the players that optimal level of engagement.

Keeping code separated from data is another strategy to help you efficiently tune a game. By putting the statistics regarding the game entities parameter in a separate file, designers and testers are able to make changes to those values during play testing without affecting the game itself or creating new bugs, thus saving coding time and coders' patience.

Now that we have described the main fine tuning strategies, we can offer some of the best practices to do it efficiently, since tuning can be a very time-consuming activity if you don't use a structured approach.

The following is the approach to user interface design:

- **One value at a time**: While editing parameters values, always change one at a time, so that you can test the effect of that specific modification and nothing else. By modifying several parameters at once you can easily lose track of what caused what, with the result that you cannot identify the very reason of the issue you desire to solve.
- **Try extreme values first**: Go for big adjustments, not small ones. By doubling or halving values you can easily verify the effects of a specific parameter, while subtle modifications may produce changes that are hard to notice. Begin with big adjustments and then progressively reduce their entity as you make reiterated tests, until you get to the ideal value you are searching for.
- **Record your actions**: Keep records of the adjustments you make. As you delve deeper into the tuning process, you can easily forget what you did in the previous step. Keeping track of your actions will help you understand what you are doing and allow you to get back to former values, if you find out that those values produced better results. This is a significant benefit of using a source code tracking app to manage your changes; they are automatically entered into the change log. A list of revision control apps can be found at `http://en.wikipedia.org/wiki/Comparison_of_revision_control_software`.

Difficulty settings

Another aspect to mention regarding game balancing and tuning concerns the difficulty settings of your game. Most games offer the opportunity to choose the degree of difficulty at which to play the game. This is a key element of any game because it has to do with the degree of gratification that your players will get from playing, and hopefully beating, your game. As personal satisfaction is a highly subjective matter, it can be pretty hard to decide which settings better fit the needs of a specific player.

It is also very important to consider that different game genres and platforms target different audiences. First Person Shooters mainly target hardcore gamers, who expect to be highly challenged by games. On the other hand, the average mobile audience is usually a casual one, so they expect the game to be pretty forgiving and rarely punishing at all.

While setting the difficulty curve of a game, always keep in mind the audience you are targeting and the time you want them to invest in your game. Have different categories of testers play it at different difficulty settings. If you succeed in adjusting your game variables to different audiences, you can exploit the advantage of addressing a broader audience for your game, increasing its potential revenues.

The following general list displays the most common parameters which affect the difficulty of a title:

- Enemy number
- Enemy accuracy
- Enemy rate of fire
- Enemy toughness
- Enemy speed
- Player's health
- Player's speed
- Weapons range
- Weapon reload time
- Frequency of power-ups
- Time limits to complete levels
- In-game hints
- Navigation directions

- Consequence of player's death
- Restart level from beginning
- Restart from last checkpoint
- Power-ups are lost/are kept

Global difficulty

Finally, once you feel you have a decent balance of the preceding list, add a master adjustment factor that allows dialing the universal difficulty up or down. This is separate from and affects the difficulty settings the player has control over.

It will also allow you as the game designer to fine tune the entire gameplay experience. Is the game too short? Crank up the difficulty a notch or two, then test again. Is it too long for a mobile game? Reduce the global difficulty and try again.

We used this method while play testing Faceball 2000 for the original **Game Boy**. At one point we had play testers falling out of their chairs, trying to get around a corner to avoid a shot. Another time one of our coders got so angry, he threw the Game Boy into a mirror. We then knew we had the perfect balance.

Unity 3D tutorial – part 3

For the final part of our tutorial, we are going to set the final touches to the Space Invaders prototype. The barriers which protect the player's ship, a game won/game lost event, the GUI, the audio, and some particle effects to improve the overall appeal of the game.

The barriers

We will create destructible barriers by assembling a number of small cubes in the shape of the barriers of the original Space Invaders.

1. Add a **Cube** to the game scene and size it as you see fit (we suggest you not to scale it too small or you may face problems with collision detection). Now create a new prefab in the `Prefab` folder and drag the cube from the scene into the newly created prefab. Name it `Brick` and make it green like the player's ship.

2. Now we need to create several instances of this prefab to shape the barrier. You can do that by selecting the `Brick` in the **Hierarchy** panel and pressing *Ctrl* + *D* to duplicate it. Then position each duplicated `Brick` to create a shape like the one shown in the following screenshot:

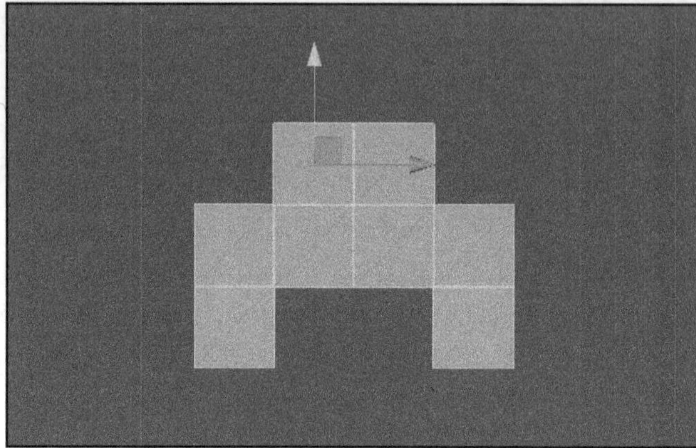

3. The next step is to create a prefab for the complete barrier too. First add an empty **GameObject** to the scene by selecting **GameObject** | **Create Empty** from the main menu bar as shown in the following screenshot. The newly created empty **GameObject** will be added to the **Hierarchy** panel.

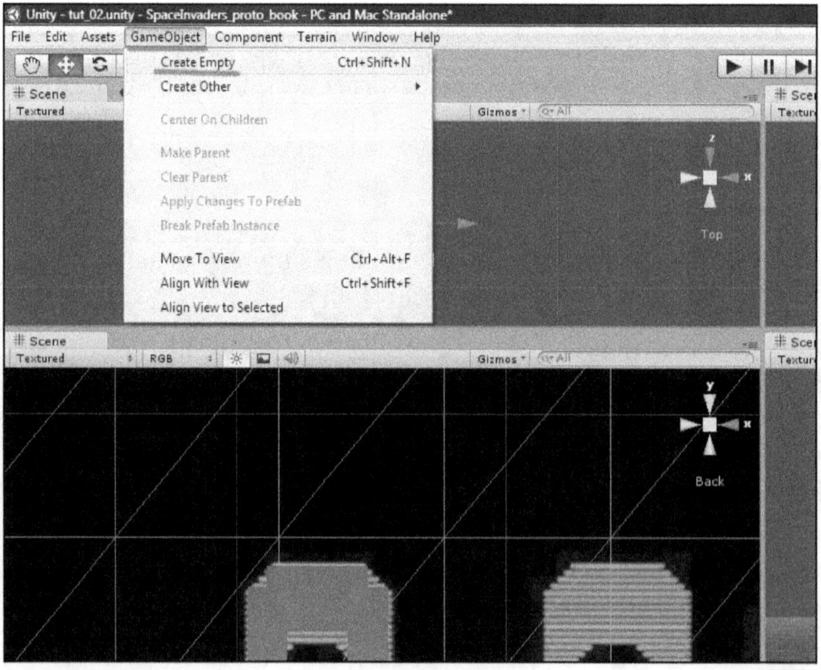

4. Select all the `Brick` instances in the **Hierarchy** panel and drag them into the **GameObject** from the **Hierarchy** panel. Refer to the following screenshot to be sure you are doing the right thing:

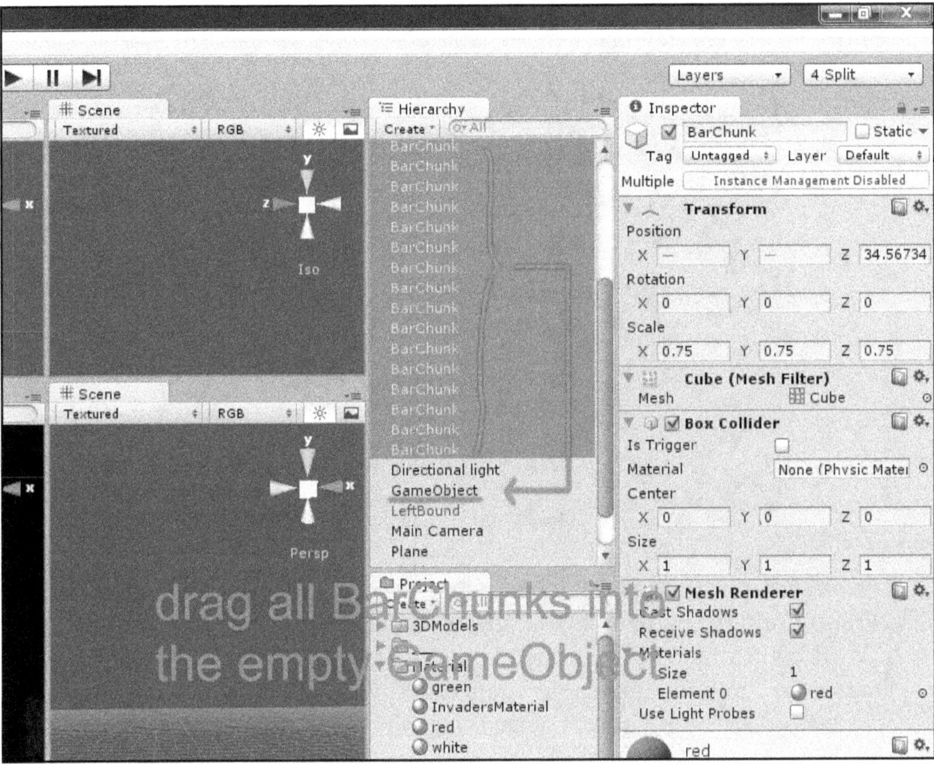

5. Now create a new prefab in the `Prefab` folder of the **Project** panel and name it `Barrier`, then drag the **GameObject** containing the `Brick` instances into it.

6. You can now delete the **GameObject** with the `Brick` instances from the scene and put the `Barrier` prefab in its place. You actually need four barriers on top of the player's ship, as shown in the following screenshot. Please ensure that the barriers are positioned at the same **Z** value of both the player's ship and the aliens in the swarm.

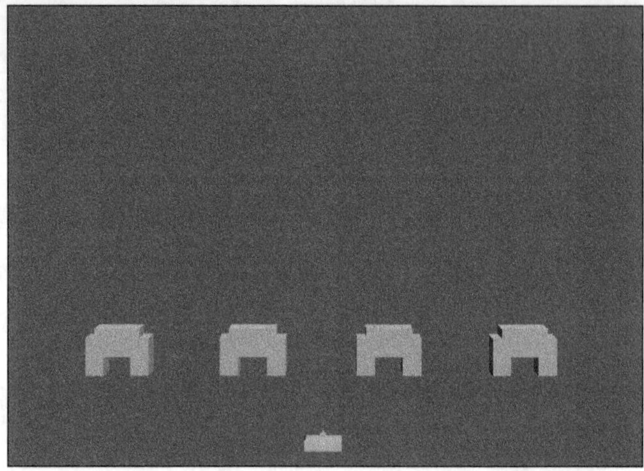

7. The last step is to tag the `Brick` instances as `BarrierBrick` and to flag the **Is Trigger** option on their **Box Collider** component so that they can be affected by the collisions with both the player's and aliens' bullets. You should remember how to create a new tag and how to assign it to a prefab, but in case you don't remember, please refer the following screenshot:

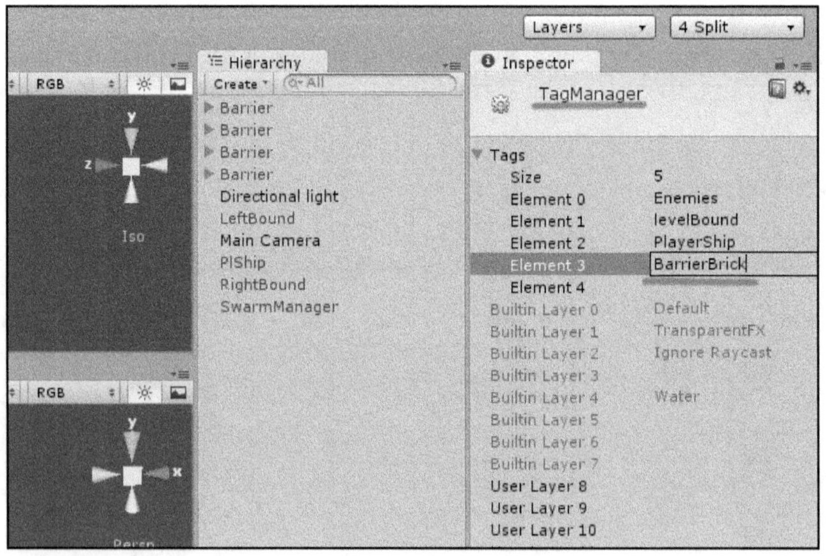

Now test your game. Both the player's and aliens' bullets should destroy a piece of the barriers upon collision.

The player's ship reprise

We need to go back to the player's ship to prevent it from moving outside of the game area boundaries. This is easy to achieve. We simply add an **X** coordinate position check of the ship itself before allowing the player to move left or right.

Modify the `Update()` function in the `ControlShip` script as shown in the following code:

```
function Update () {

    //is the player pressing right button and the ship can move
      //right
    //tweak the x reference value as needed
    if(Input.GetKey("right") && transform.position.x<25)
    {
         //ship move right
          transform.Translate(Vector3(1,0,0));
    }

    //is the player pressing left button and the ship can move left
    //tweak the x reference value as needed
    if(Input.GetKey("left") && transform.position.x>-25)
    {
         //ship move left
          transform.Translate(Vector3(-1,0,0));
    }

    //is player pressing the fire button (spacebar)
    if(Input.GetKeyDown("space") && canShoot)
    {
          //create the bullet
    Instantiate(myBullet,transform.position,transform.rotation);
          //player can't fire for a while
          canShoot=false;
    }
}
```

Refining the details

In this section we are going to add some fine details to the prototype to make it more appealing. We just cover here a few examples of things that can be done to improve our project and many more you can think of yourself. We strongly encourage you to do so! You may prefer the level boundaries not to be displayed in the game area while the game plays. This can be done by adding a **NotToRender** layer in the **Layer Manager** panel, putting the left and right game boundaries on such layer and forcing the **Main Camera** not to render that layer.

1. First we add the new **Layer**. With any of the bounds selected in the **Hierarchy**, click on the **Layer** button and select **Add Layer**, as shown in the following screenshot, where we have selected **LeftBound**:

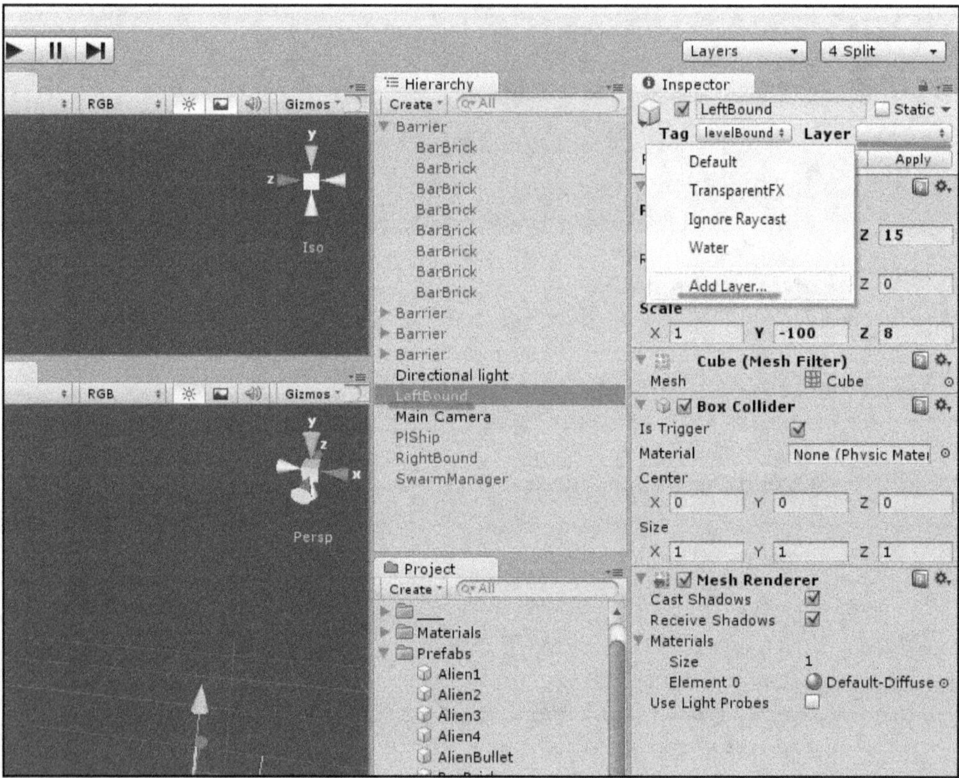

2. To begin with, name the first free **User Layer** slot available in the list, which opens as `NotToRender` as shown in the following screenshot:

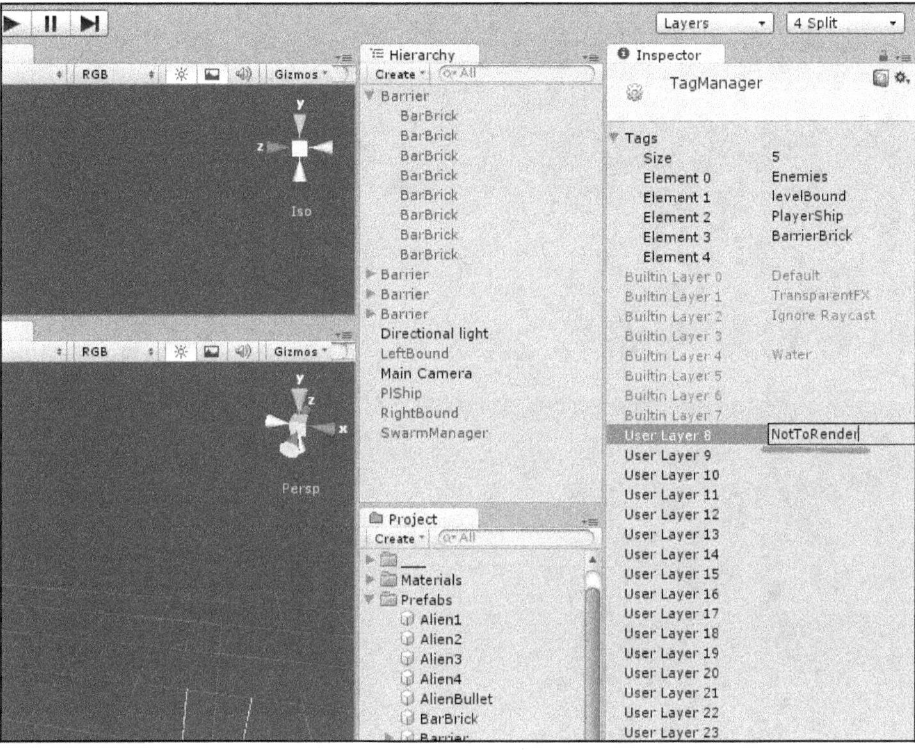

3. Next put both **LeftBound** and **RightBound** on the newly created layer, as shown in the following screenshot:

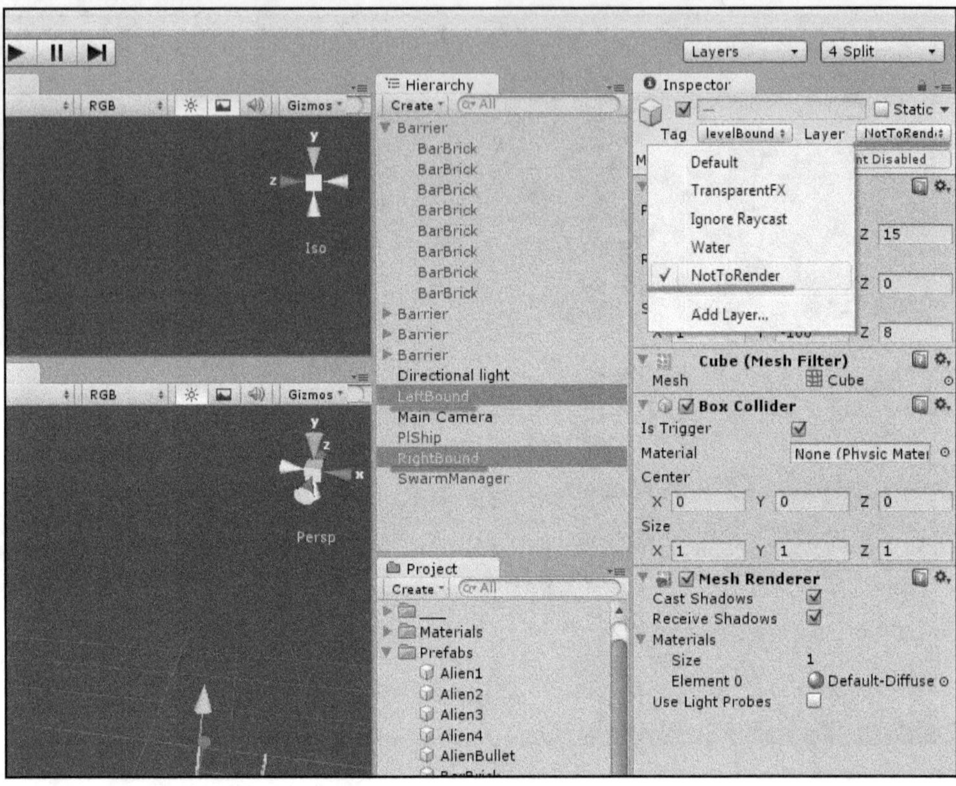

4. The last step is to select the **Main Camera** in the **Hierarchy** panel, access its **Camera** properties in the **Inspector** panel, click on the **Culling Mask** menu and de-flag the **NotToRender** layer, which appears in the window that opens. Use the following screenshot for reference:

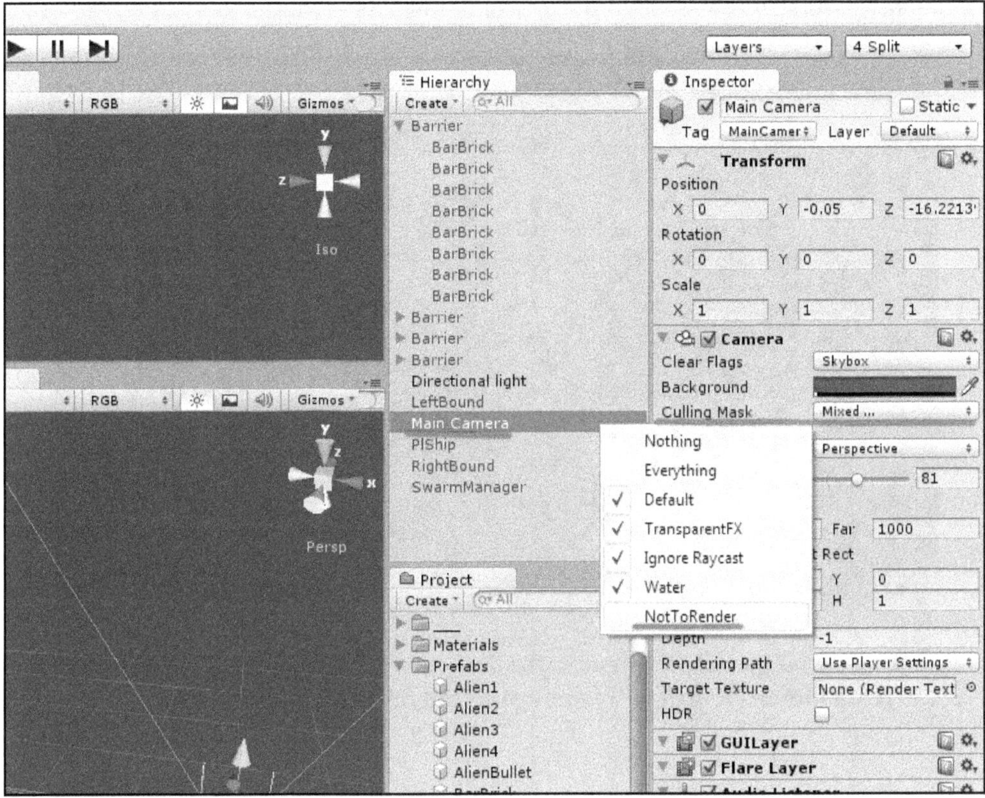

This way we told the game camera not to render anything we put on the **NotToRender** layer. Since we put the left and right bounds on this layer, they won't be displayed on screen. Launch your game now and check that these last modifications we made work as expected.

Our prototype also needs a better deep-space background. We will make it with a plane and a particle effect.

1. Add a **Plane** to the **Scene**, name it `Background`, paint it black with a material (create one if you haven't already), scale it as needed and put it right behind the game scene, as shown in the following screenshot:

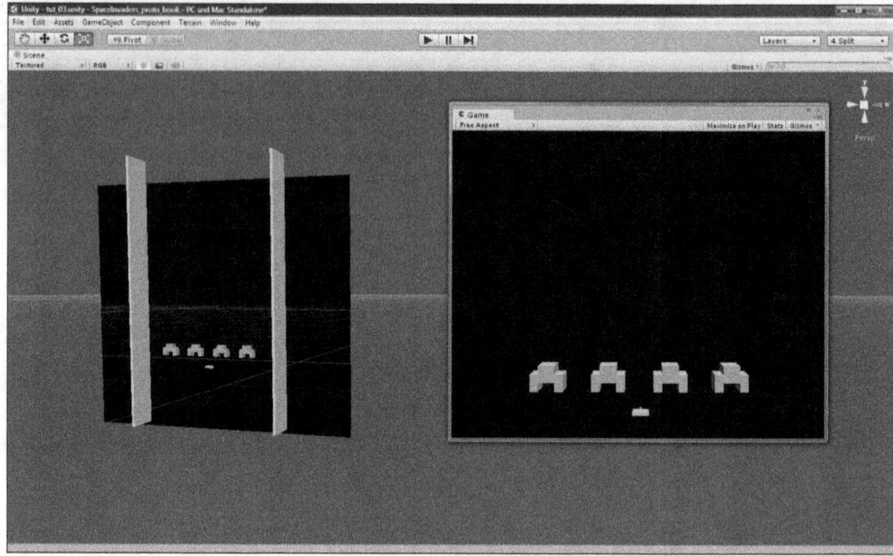

2. Now add a **Particle System** to the scene by navigating to **GameObject** | **Create Other** | **Particle System** from the main menu bar.

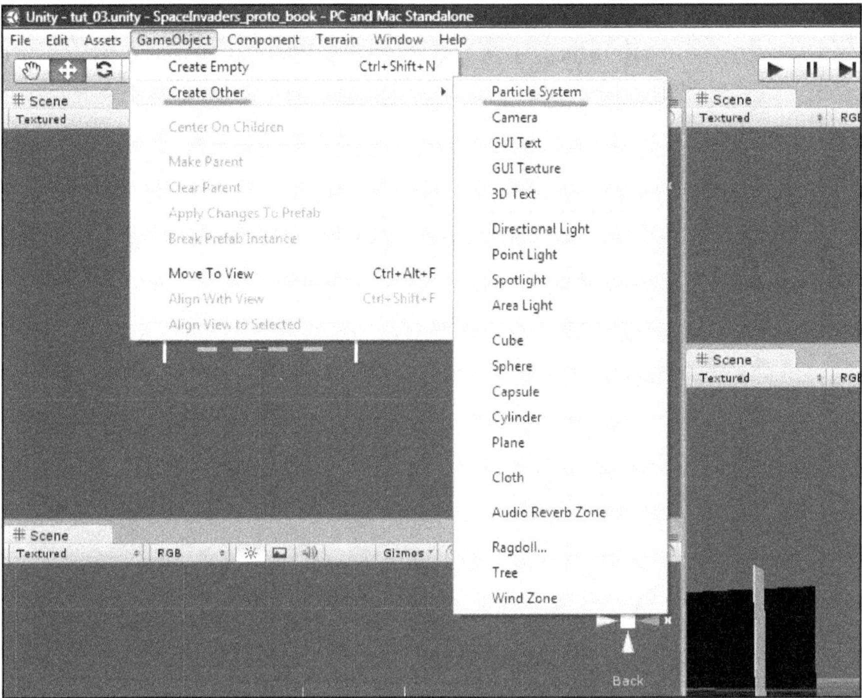

3. We begin by naming the **Particle System** as `BackStars`. Then we need to set its properties according to our needs. Though we cannot provide a thorough tutorial about particle system here, we will only tell you how to edit it with regard to our Space Invaders prototype needs. Take the following suggestions for what they are; you can obviously use different values if you like so.

4. For this prototype we will put the particle system at the bottom of the game scene, as we want particles to move bottom up. In our reference setup the particle system is located at coordinates **X**=`0`, **Y**=`-50`, **Z**=`15`.

5. Then we need to change the shape of the particle system from a **Cone** to a **Box** by accessing its **Shape** properties in the **Inspector** panel. Refer to the following screenshot:

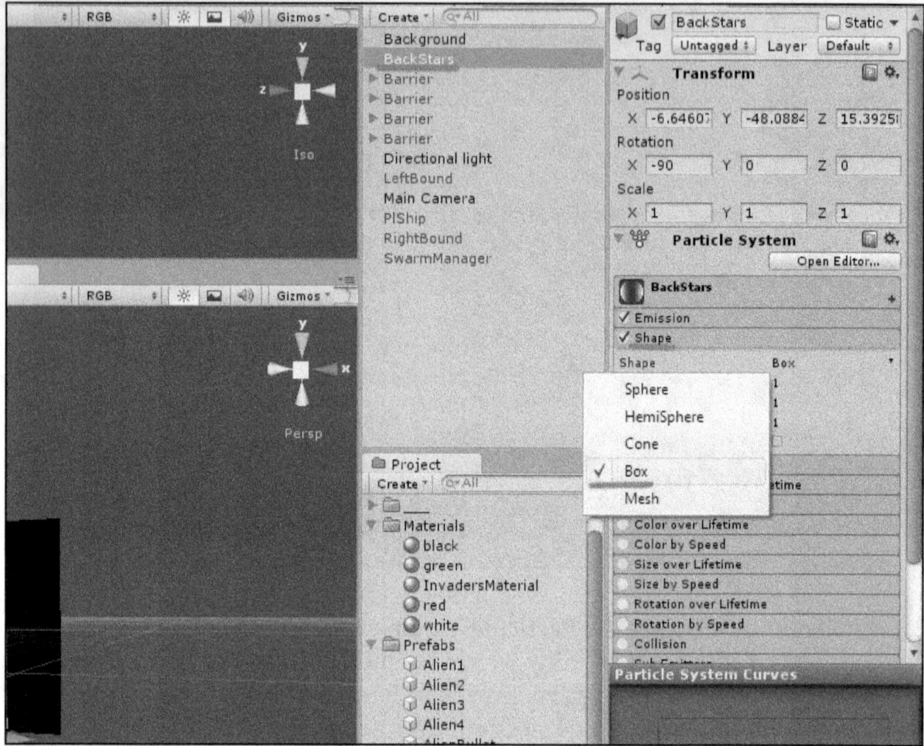

6. We also need to set the **Box** dimension according to the game scene. The following screenshot shows the dimensions we set for the particle system in our game scene:

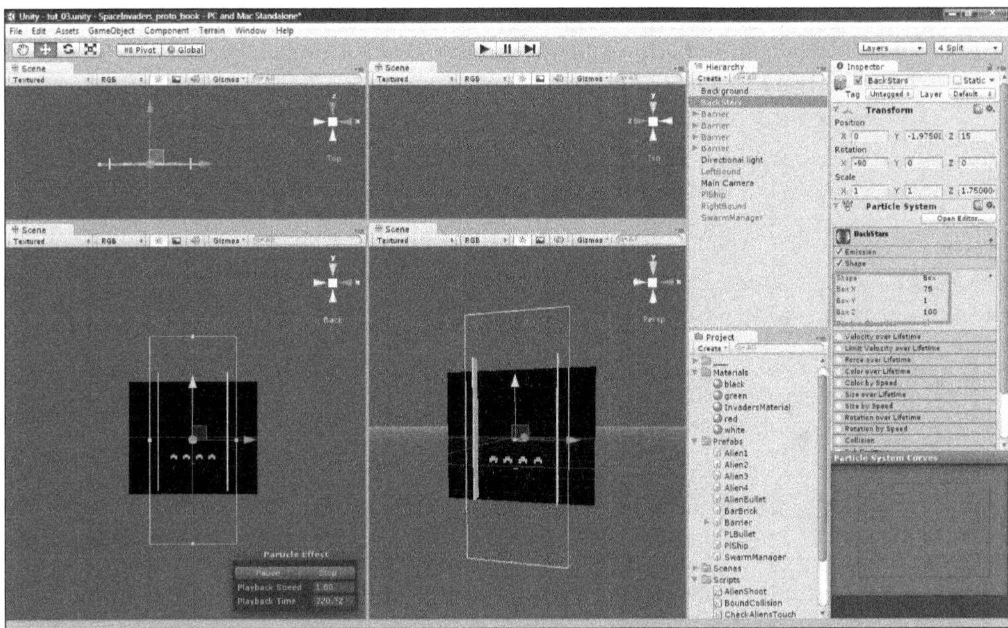

7. Now access the **Emission** panel in the **Inspector** panel to increase the number of particles created to `20`, as shown in the following screenshot:

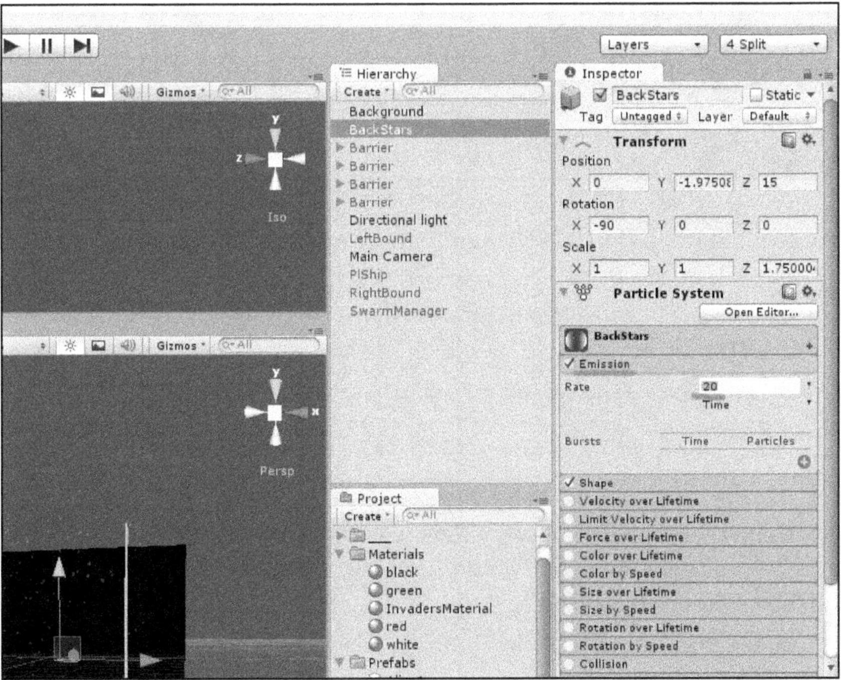

8. Next we want to change the direction in which the particles move, let's say, a little bit to the left. You can achieve this by accessing the **Velocity over Lifetime** property and editing its **X** value to `-2`, as shown in the following screenshot:

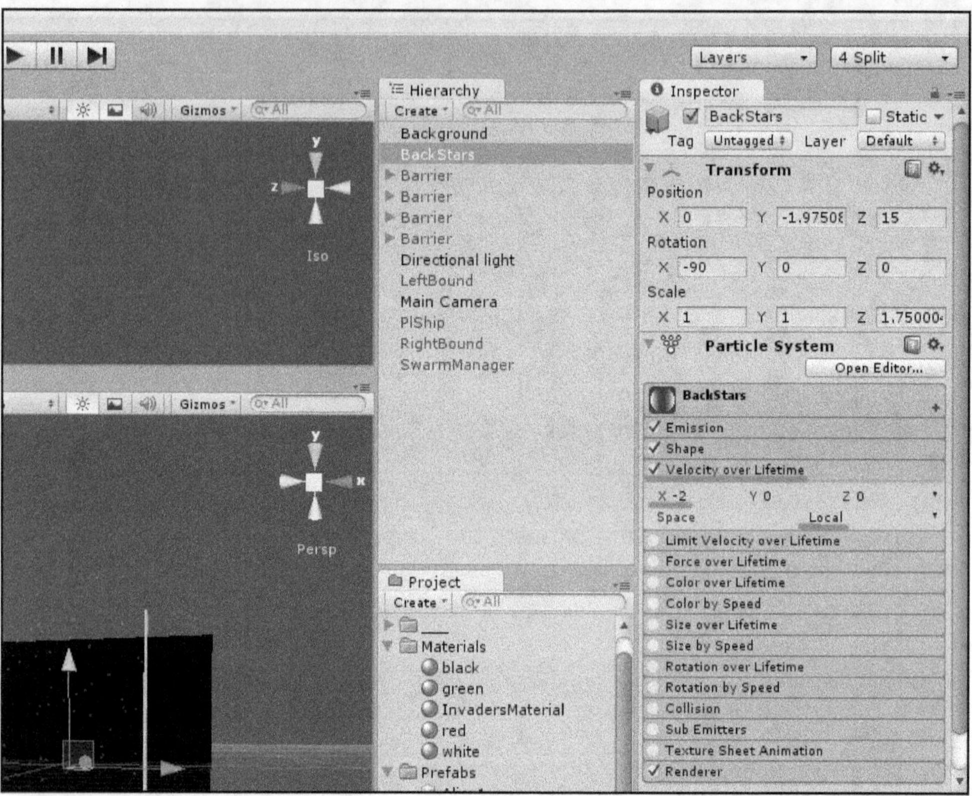

Finally we edit the main **Particle System** panel and set the following values:

- **Duration**=`10.0`
- **Start Lifetime**=`10`
- **Start Speed**=`3`
- **Start Size**=`0.5`
- **Max Particles**=`1500`

Remember that you can tweak these values as you prefer according to your tastes, we strongly encourage you to do so, to understand how to manage particle systems in Unity by experimenting with the values.

Refer to the following screenshot to check what we did:

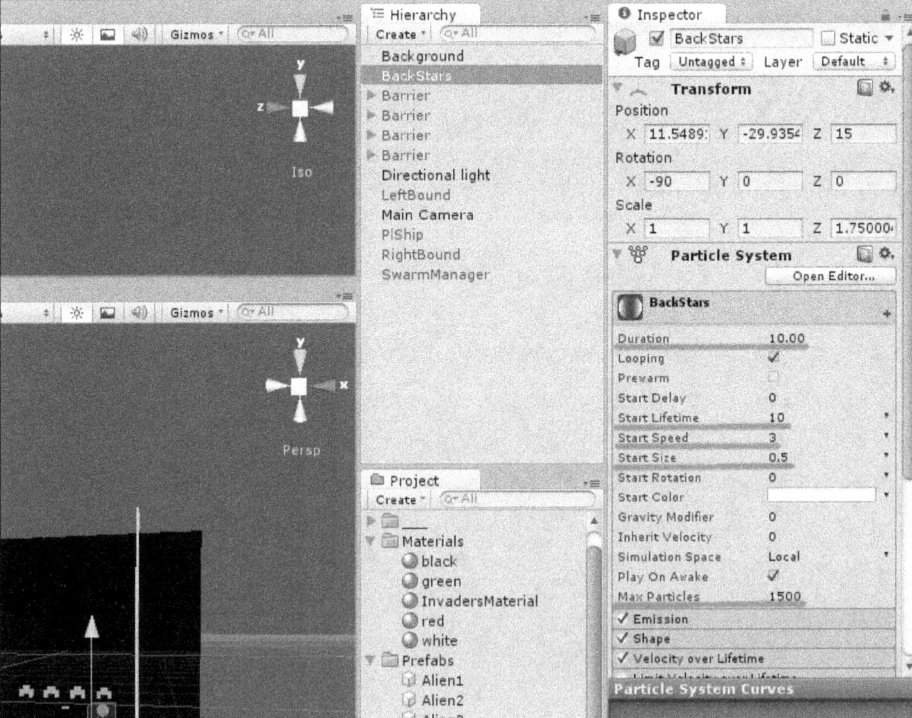

We now have a nice animated background for our prototype representing deep space and stars. Test your game and check if you like it!

Adding a GUI

No game can be considered polished without some kind of **Graphical User Interface** (**GUI**). For our Space Invaders prototype we just need few things like the actual score, the hi-score, and messages to be displayed for game over/game won events.

1. First we need a font to be used to display information on screen that will be put into a **GUI Skin**, which is the entity that defines how a GUI looks and behaves. We also need a single script file.
2. Create a `Fonts` folder in the **Project** panel and import a font of choice from your standard fonts folder (for Windows users it is located in the directory `C:\Windows\Fonts`); for our prototype we used the **consola** font.

3. To add the font you can right-click on the `Fonts` folder in the **Project** panel, select **Import New Asset...** and then browse in your directories to pick the font you chose, as shown in the following screenshot:

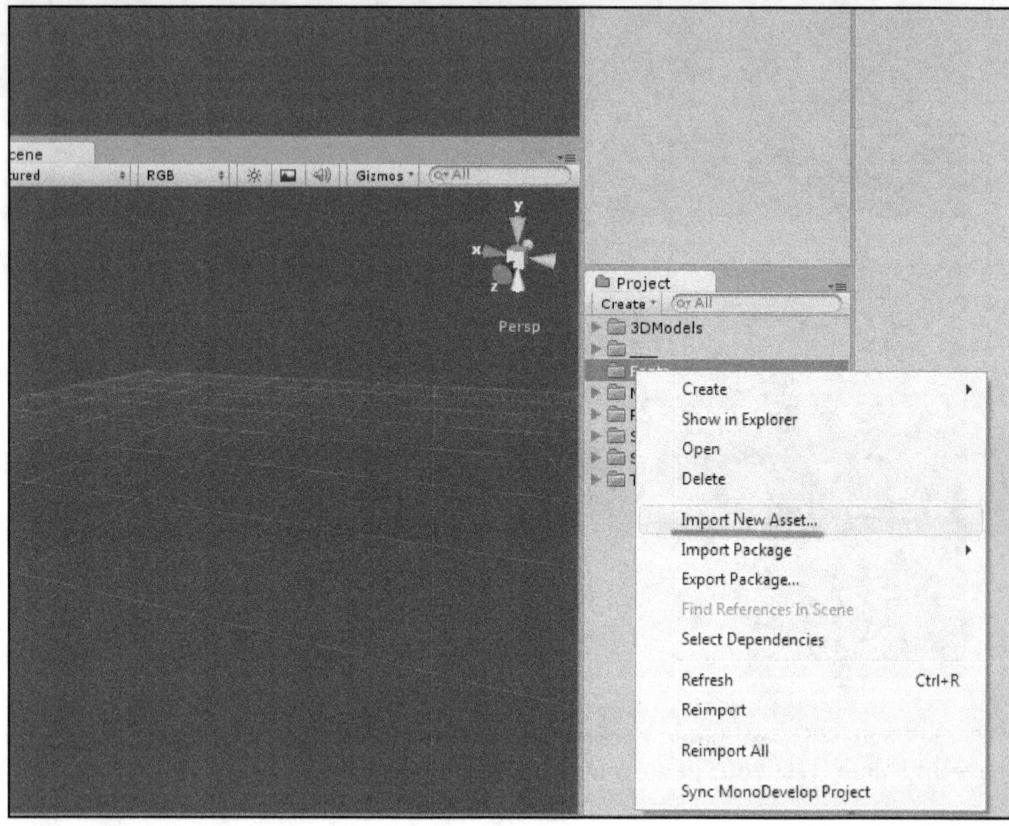

4. Now create another folder in the **Project** panel and name it `GUI`. Select the folder and create a new **GUI Skin** inside it, as shown in the following screenshot:

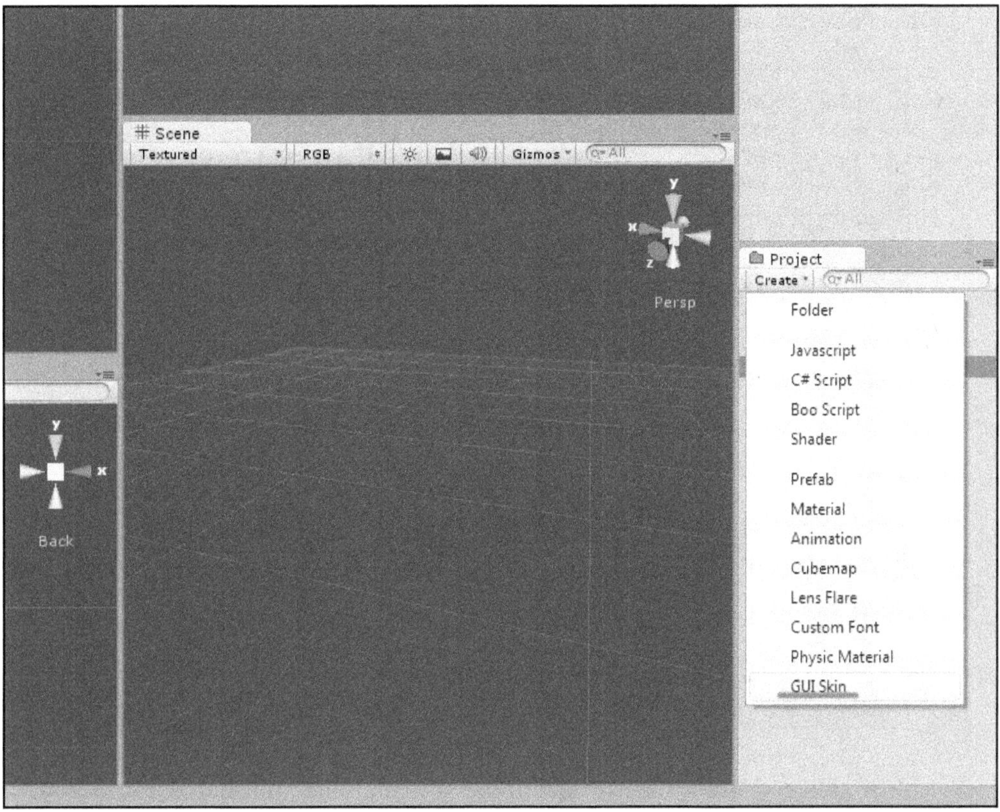

5. Name the newly created **GUI Skin** as `myGUI` and select it in the **Project** panel.

6. In the **Inspector** panel you should see a **Font** entry set to the default **Arial** value. Click on the small button on the right to open a window that displays the available fonts for your project. Here you should find the font we added before, **consola** in our case. Select it. You can refer to the following screenshot to check if you are doing it right:

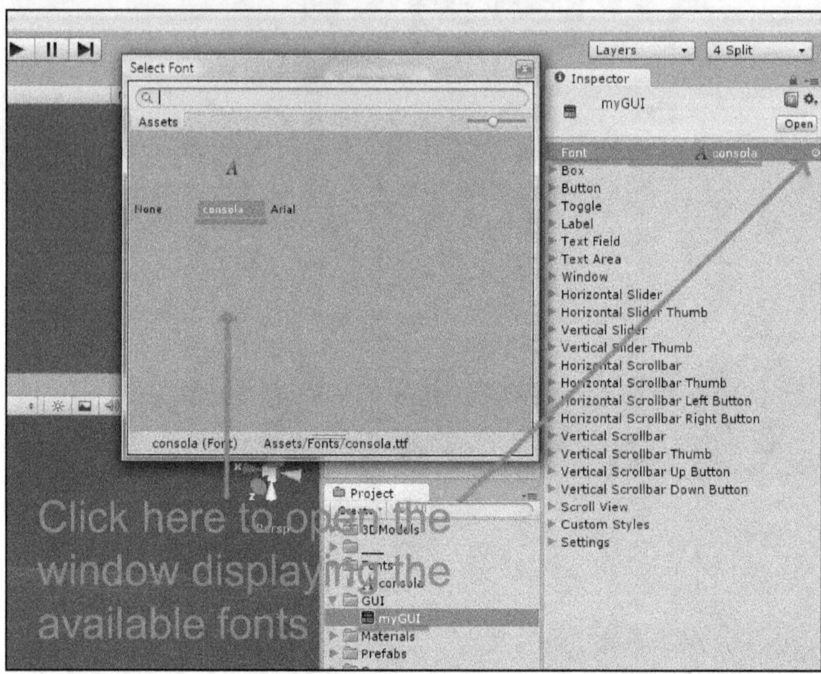

7. Now create a new JavaScript file in the `Script` folder and name it `DisplayGUI`.
8. Inside the script we need to define a `GUISkin` variable for the project; add the following lines to the top of the newly created script:

```
var myGUISkin : GUISkin;
```

9. Save this script for now, we will add more lines later.
10. The next step is to add a **GameObject** to the scene to attach the `GUI` script to. Create an empty **GameObject** into the scene, name it `GameMaster` and add the `DisplayGUI` script to it.

11. Now drag the **myGUI** asset from the **Project** panel into the `myGUI` variable inside the script, as shown in the following screenshot:

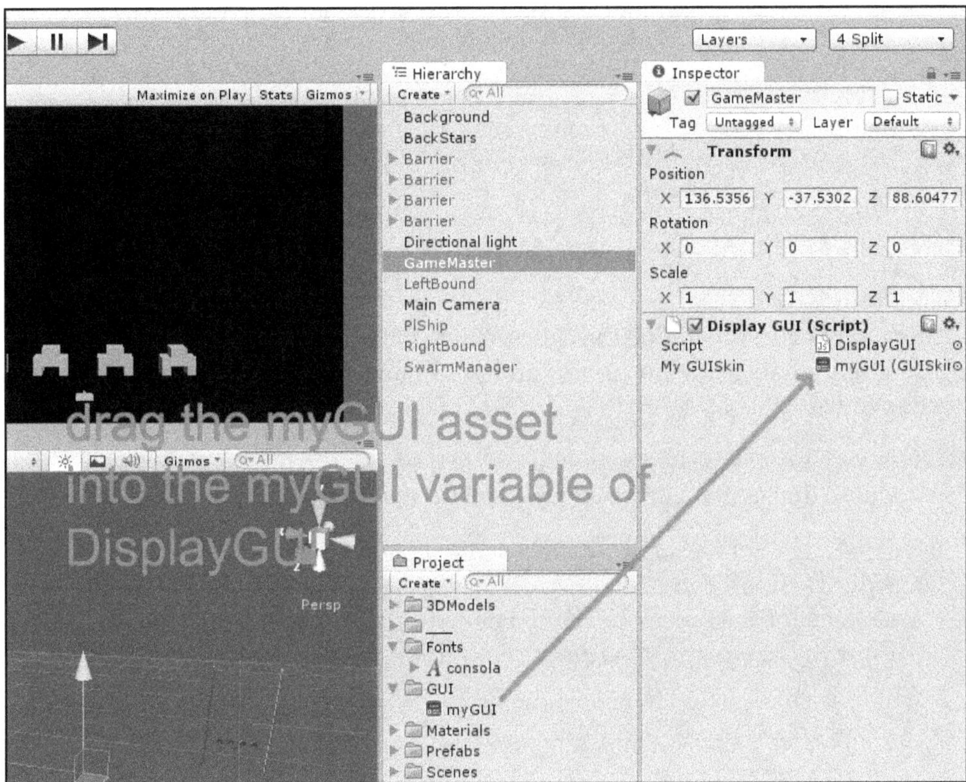

12. Go back to the `DisplayGUI` script in **MonoDevelop** script editor. We need to define the `OnGUI` function to put the code for our game interface. Add the following lines to the script:

```
function OnGUI () {

   GUI.skin=myGUISkin;

   GUI.color = Color.white;

   //pl1 score
   GUI.Label (Rect (0, 5, 200, 40), "SCORE <1>");
         GUI.Label (Rect (0, 20, 200, 40),
           DisplayScore.Score.ToString());
```

```
        //pl2 score, not implemented
        GUI.Label (Rect (Screen.width-200, 5, 200, 40),
          "SCORE <2>");
        GUI.Label (Rect (Screen.width-200, 20, 200, 40),
          "0");

        //hiscore
        GUI.Label (Rect ((Screen.width/2)-100, 5, 200,
          40), "HI-SCORE");
        GUI.Label (Rect ((Screen.width/2)-100, 20, 200,
          40),  DisplayScore.HiScore.ToString());
}
```

The numerical values to define the coordinates for the text to be displayed may vary according to the setup of your project and your game window dimensions, so tweak them as needed.

Now that we have correctly positioned our text on the screen it is time to have the score updated during the gameplay; we will do that with a dedicated script.

1. Create a new JavaScript file and name it `ManageScore`. Open it with **MonoDevelop** and create two static variables: one for the actual `PL1` score and one for the `HiScore`. The reason we declare these variables as static is to allow the `DisplayGUI` script to access their values.
2. In the `Start()` function, add the following lines to set the initial values of `Score` and `HiScore` variables:

```
#pragma strict

static var Score:int;
static var HiScore:int;

function Start () {

   Score=0;
   HiScore=1000;
}

function Update () {

}
```

3. Attach this file to the **GameMaster** game object to have the `Score` and `HiScore` variables displayed on screen. Since we don't have a two player feature, we will keep the `PL2` score as a mere string placeholder. You can add such feature as an exercise, if you want to.
4. The next step is to have the score increase as the player destroys enemy aliens. We can do that inside the `ControlPLBullet` script.
5. Open it in **MonoDevelop**, get to the `OnTriggerEnter()` function and add the following line:

```
//add 50 points to score for each alien destroyed
DisplayScore.Score+=50;
```

6. For the sake of clarity here is the updated `OnTriggerEnter()` function of the `ControlPLBullet` script:

```
//this function checks for collisions
function OnTriggerEnter(other:Collider)
{
    //if bullets collides with aliens, destroy both
   if(other.gameObject.tag=="Enemies"){

         Destroy(gameObject);
         Destroy(other.gameObject);

         //add 50 points to score for each alien destroyed
         DisplayScore.Score+=50;

         //once the bullet is destroyed, allow the player
           //to shoot again
         ControlShip.canShoot=true;
   }

   //if bullet collides with barriers, destroy it and a
     //piece of the barrier
   if(other.gameObject.tag=="BarrierBrick"){

         Destroy(gameObject);
         Destroy(other.gameObject);
         //once the bullet is destroyed, allow the player
           //to shoot again
         ControlShip.canShoot=true;
   }
}
```

If you want to, you can improve the prototype by defining different amounts of points for different enemy types, as it is with the original Space Invaders; you can achieve that by adding more tags and assigning them to different enemy types.

1. The last thing we want to do with the score is to update the `HiScore` variable when the match ends, whether the player or the aliens win. We can achieve it with the following simple line of code:

   ```
   //update the Hiscore
   if(DisplayScore.Score>DisplayScore.HiScore){

      DisplayScore.HiScore=DisplayScore.Score;
   }
   ```

2. We need to add this line into two scripts. First in the `OnTriggerEnter()` function of the `ControlAlienBullet` script, which handles the event of an enemy bullet hitting the player and second in the `Update()` function of the `ControlSwarm` script, which handles the case of the entire swarm destroyed.
3. This is the updated `OnTriggerEnter()` function of the `ControlAlienBullet` script:

   ```
   function OnTriggerEnter(other:Collider)
   {
      //check collision with player's ship
      if(other.gameObject.tag=="PlayerShip")
      {
            Destroy(gameObject);
            Destroy(other.gameObject);

            //player's ship destroyed, pause the game
            Time.timeScale = 0;
            Debug.Log("Game Over");

            //update the hiscore
            if(DisplayScore.Score>DisplayScore.HiScore){
                  DisplayScore.HiScore=DisplayScore.Score;
            }
      }

      //check collisions with barriers
      if(other.gameObject.tag=="BarrierBrick"){

            Destroy(gameObject);
            Destroy(other.gameObject);
      }
   }
   ```

4. This is the updated `Update()` function of the `ControlSwarm` script:

```
function Update () {

   if(bCollide)
   {
         goRight=!goRight;

         for(var myEnemy:GameObject in enemyList)
         {
                if(myEnemy!=null)
                {
   myEnemy.transform.Translate(Vector3(0,-3,0));
                }
         }

         bCollide=false;
   }

   //update the enemyList count
   enemyList=GameObject.FindGameObjectsWithTag("Enemies");

   //check when the count of aliens gets to 0
   if(enemyList.length==0)
   {
         //all aliens destroyed, pause the game and display
           //a message
         Time.timeScale = 0;
         Debug.Log("You Won!");

         //update the hiscore
         if(DisplayScore.Score>DisplayScore.HiScore){
                DisplayScore.HiScore=DisplayScore.Score;
         }
   }
}
```

We also want to display a message when the player destroys the alien swarm or the player's ship is destroyed.

1. To do that we need to create a new `GUISkin` in the `GUI` folder and name it something like `GameEndGUI`.
2. Then we define a font for this `GUI`; we suggest to choose something which fits a large text size, like 48 points, for we want to display a message almost screen-sized.

3. Now access the `DisplayGUI` script and add two variable declarations: a `GUISkin` variable and `String`. This is the code we added at the top of the script:

   ```
   //new GUI Skin
   var gameEndGUI: GUISkin;
   //a static variable string to be accessed from another
     //script
   static var GameEnd:String="";
   ```

4. We also need to add the following lines at the bottom of the `OnGUI()` function in the `DisplayGUI` script:

   ```
   //set the second GUI and make it yellow
   GUI.skin=gameEndGUI;
   GUI.color=Color.yellow;

   //game end message
   GUI.Label (Rect ((Screen.width/2)-400, 200, 800, 100),
     GameEnd);
   ```

5. Now access the `ControlSwarm` script and add the following line inside the `Update()` function:

   ```
   //Display a "you won" message
   DisplayGUI.GameEnd="YOU DESTROYED THE ALIENS!";
   ```

6. This is the updated `Update()` function of the `ControlSwarm` script:

   ```
   function Update () {

      if(bCollide)
      {
            goRight=!goRight;

            for(var myEnemy:GameObject in enemyList)
            {
                  if(myEnemy!=null)
                  {
      myEnemy.transform.Translate(Vector3(0,-3,0));
                  }
            }

            bCollide=false;
      }

      //update the enemyList count
      enemyList=GameObject.FindGameObjectsWithTag("Enemies");
   ```

```
    //check when the count of aliens gets to 0
    if(enemyList.length==0)
    {
          //all aliens destroyed, pause the game and display
            //a message
          Time.timeScale = 0;

         //we also want the ship to stop and prevent it
           //shooting
          ControlShip.canShoot=false;
          ControlShip.shipSpeed=0;

          //Display a "you won" message
          DisplayGUI.GameEnd="YOU DESTROYED THE ALIENS!";

          //update the hiscore
          if(DisplayScore.Score>DisplayScore.HiScore){
                DisplayScore.HiScore=DisplayScore.Score;
          }
    }
}
```

7. To display a message for the player's ship being destroyed we put the same command line into the `OnTriggerEnter()` function of the `ControlAlienBullet` script, with a different message. This is the updated `OnTriggerEnter()` function of the `ControlAlienBullet` script:

```
function OnTriggerEnter(other:Collider)
{
   //check collision with player's ship
   if(other.gameObject.tag=="PlayerShip")
   {
         Destroy(gameObject);
         Destroy(other.gameObject);

         //player's ship destroyed, pause the game
         Time.timeScale = 0;

         //display a "You lose" message
         DisplayGUI.GameEnd="THE ALIENS DESTROYED YOU!";

         //update the hiscore
         if(DisplayScore.Score>DisplayScore.HiScore){
               DisplayScore.HiScore=DisplayScore.Score;
         }
   }
```

```
    //check collisions with barriers
    if(other.gameObject.tag=="BarrierBrick"){

        Destroy(gameObject);
        Destroy(other.gameObject);
    }
}
```

8. The player also loses if the aliens reach the bottom of the game area and touch his ship. To keep things nice and clean, we create a new script to be attached to the four alien prefabs, which we also use to destroy the barriers, should they be touched by the aliens.
9. Create a new script in the `Script` folder, name it `CheckAliensTouch` and add the following command lines:

```
#pragma strict

function Start () {

}

function Update () {

}

function OnTriggerEnter(other:Collider)
{
    if(other.gameObject.tag=="PlayerShip")
    {
        //player's ship touched by aliens, pause the game
          //and display a message
        Time.timeScale = 0;
        //display a "You lose" message
        DisplayGUI.GameEnd="THE ALIENS DESTROYED YOU!";

        //update the hiscore
        if(DisplayScore.Score>DisplayScore.HiScore){
              DisplayScore.HiScore=DisplayScore.Score;
        }
    }

    if(other.gameObject.tag=="BarrierBrick")
    {
        Destroy(other.gameObject);
    }
}
```

This ends our section about the basics on developing GUIs using Unity. The next step is to add some audio effects to our prototype.

Adding audio effects

For our prototype we will use only four audio effects (fx):

- One for the player's ship firing
- One for the aliens moving
- One for the when the aliens are destroyed, one for when the player's ship is destroyed

Let's begin with the player's ship firing.

1. The first thing to do is to import our audio files into the project. Create a new `Audio` folder in the **Project** panel and import your audio files of choice as **New Assets**. For this prototype, we used audio clips taken from the site `http://www.classicgaming.cc/classics/spaceinvaders/sounds.php`.
2. Next we need to add an **AudioSource** component to the **PLShip** prefab. Select it from the **Project** panel and from the main menu, select **Component** | **Audio** | **Audio Source**. The **Audio Source** component will be added to the **PLShip** prefab.

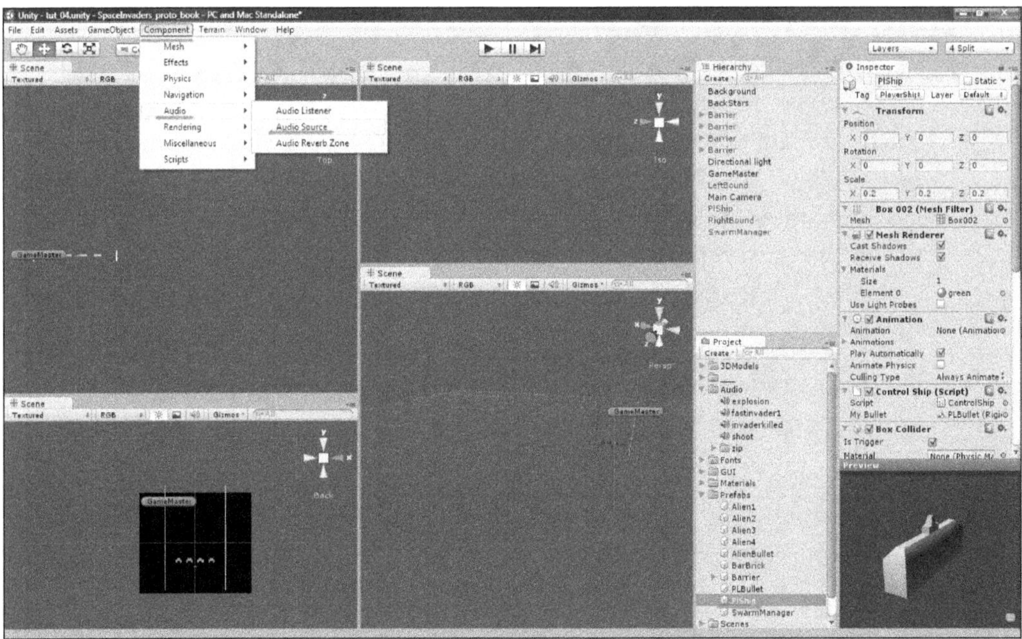

3. Now drag the desired audio file into the **Audio Clip** slot of the **Audio Source** component you added, in the **Inspector** panel. Refer to the following screenshot for clues:

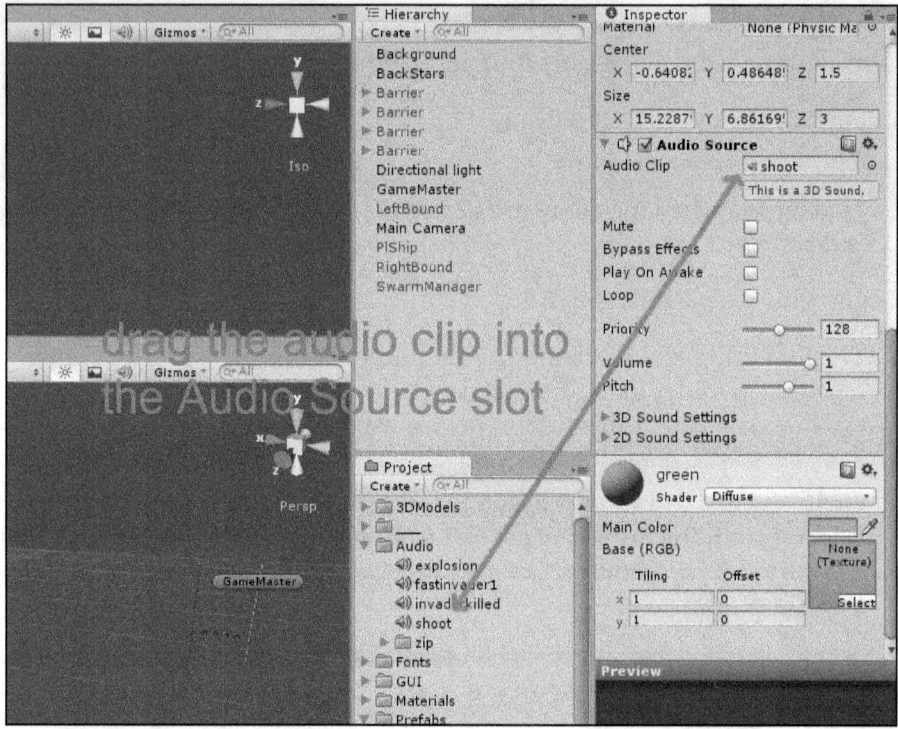

4. Since we want this clip to be played when the player's ship shoots, we will add the requested code to play this audio file in the `ControlShip` script.

5. Add the following line into the `Update()` function, inside the press spacebar event:

```
//play shooting audio fx
audio.Play();
```

6. This is the updated `Update()` function of the `ControlShip` script:

```
function Update () {
   //is the player pressing right button?
   if(Input.GetKey("right") && transform.position.x<25)
   {
         //ship move right
           transform.Translate(Vector3(shipSpeed,0,0));
   }
```

```
    //is the player pressing left button?
    if(Input.GetKey("left") && transform.position.x>-25)
    {
         //ship move left
          transform.Translate(Vector3(-shipSpeed,0,0));
    }
    //is player pressing the fire button (spacebar)
    if(Input.GetKeyDown("space")&&canShoot)
    {
          //create the bullet
    Instantiate(myBullet,transform.position, transform.rotation);
          //player can't fire for a while
          canShoot=false;
          //play shooting audio fx
          audio.Play();
    }
}
```

7. The same process applies to the other three audio clips we chose for this project. Add an **Audio Source** component to a prefab and drag the desired audio file into its **Audio Source** slot.
8. For the aliens moving fx, we added the `Audio Source` component to the `SwarmManager` prefab. Since all aliens move as a whole, we can simply play the audio once for each step from the `SwarmManager` prefab.
9. Add `audio.Play()` line into the `MoveEnemies()` function of the `ControlSwarm` script. What follows is the updated `MoveEnemies()` function:

```
//we move the swarm left or right at speed defined by vel
function moveEnemies()
{

    if(goRight)
    {
           for(var myEnemy:GameObject in enemyList)
           {
                  if(myEnemy)
                  {
     myEnemy.transform.Translate(Vector3(vel,0,0));
                  }
           }
    }
```

```
    if(!goRight)
    {
        for(var myEnemy:GameObject in enemyList)
        {
            if(myEnemy!=null)
            {
                myEnemy.transform.Translate(Vector3(-vel,0,0));
            }
        }
    }

    //play the aliens moving audio
    audio.Play();
}
```

Adding sound fx to be played when the aliens and the player's ship are destroyed poses a problem, which is interesting to discuss. The idea is to attach the audio clip to the player's bullet so that we can play the clip when the bullet hits an alien.

The problem is that since we destroy both the bullet and the alien upon collision, we need to delay the destruction of the bullet until the audio clip is played; otherwise no sound will be played because the bullets gets destroyed before the audio clip is actually played.

There are many ways to avoid this problem, here is our solution.

1. Once you have attached the **Audio Source** component to the **PLBullet** prefab and dragged the audio clip into the **Audio Source** slot, we can then make some modifications to the `ControlPLBullet` script. This is the logic we implemented.
2. When the bullet collides with an alien, we play the enemy destroyed audio clip and destroy the alien enemy. We also disable the **Collider** component attached to the bullet and put the bullet itself on the layer of assets not to be rendered by the camera, so that the bullet disappears from the scene.
3. Finally, we set a Boolean variable to `true`, so that in the `Update()` function we can check at every frame the value of the Boolean variable. If the Boolean variable is set to `true` and the audio component attached to the bullet is not playing, it means we can finally destroy the bullet.

4. This is the updated code lines of the `ControlPLBullet` script:

```
#pragma strict

//var used if the bullet must be destroyed in the Update()
  //function
var bMustDestroy:boolean;

function Start () {

   //set the initial boolean value to false
   bMustDestroy=false;
}

function Update () {

   //move bullet up once created 2 pixels\frame
   transform.Translate(Vector3(0,2,0));

   //Y=140 defines upper screen limit
   if(transform.position.y>100)
   {
        //destroy bullet as it goes outside the upper
          //screen limit
         Destroy(gameObject);
         //once the bullet is destroyed, allow the player
           //to shoot again
         ControlShip.canShoot=true;
   }

   //destroy bullet after audio is played
   if(bMustDestroy && !audio.isPlaying)
   {
         Destroy(gameObject);
   }
}

//this function checks for collisions
function OnTriggerEnter(other:Collider)
{
    //if bullets collides with aliens, destroy both
   if(other.gameObject.tag=="Enemies"){
```

```
            //play the fx
            audio.Play();

            //destroy the alien
            Destroy(other.gameObject);

            //add 50 points to score for each alien destroyed
            DisplayScore.Score+=50;

            //once the bullet is destroyed, allow the player
              //to shoot again
            ControlShip.canShoot=true;

            //disable collider and put the bullet on
              //NotToRender layer
             collider.enabled=false;
             gameObject.layer=8;

            //we destroy it once the fx is over in Update()
            bMustDestroy=true;
        }

        //if bullet collides with barriers, destroy it and a
          //piece of the barrier
        if(other.gameObject.tag=="BarrierBrick"){

            Destroy(gameObject);
            Destroy(other.gameObject);
            //once the bullet is destroyed, allow the player
              //to shoot again
            ControlShip.canShoot=true;
        }
    }
```

You can apply a similar solution to the audio clip to be played when the player's ship is destroyed, attaching the audio source to the **AlienBullet** prefab. Also, remember to address the aliens themselves hitting the player's ship. Try to find a solution yourself!

Particle system effects

The last touch is to add some particle system effects to be played when the aliens and the player's ship get destroyed.

As we already showed how to create a particle system to our scene, we will just provide here the values to be set within and the coding required for the particle effect to be played.

1. Add a **Particle System** to the scene and edit it with the following reference values:
    - General:
    - Duration: 0.5
    - Start Lifetime: 0.5
    - Start Speed: 3
    - Start Size: 1
    - Looping: unflagged
    - Play on Awake: flagged
    - Emission:
    - Rate:15
    - Shape:
    - Shape: Sphere
    - Radius: 0.5
    - Emit from Shell: flagged
2. We don't need much more than that for a prototype. Now create a new prefab in the `Prefab` folder, name it `AlienPS` and drag the particle system from the scene into this prefab, then delete the particle system from the scene.
3. In the `ControlPLBullet` script we need to declare a new variable to hold our `AlienPS` prefab. Add the following line at the top of the script:

    ```
    //var used to store the alien destroyed PS
    var AlienPS:Transform;
    ```

4. Then in the `OnTriggerEnter()` function add the following line beneath the `audio.Play()` instruction:

    ```
    //create ps here
    Instantiat(AlienPS, other.transform.position,
    other.transform.rotation);
    ```

5. To complete the process, we add a very simple script to the `AlienPS` prefab so that after the particle effects have been played, we can destroy it.

6. Create a new JavaScript file in the `Script` folder, name it `DestroyPS` and add the following lines into it:

```
#pragma strict

var myPS:ParticleSystem;

function Start () {

}

function Update () {

   if(!myPS.isPlaying )
   {
         //wait for the PS to finishing playing before
           //destroying the PS
         Destroy(gameObject);
   }
}
```

7. The last step is to add the script to the `AlienPS` prefab and drag the `AlienPS` prefab into the `myPS` variable of the script.

The same approach applies to the particle effect to be added to the player's ship, in case it is destroyed. Now, you should be able to figure it out by yourself.

Unity 3D tutorial summary

This ends our tutorial about using Unity to develop games. In the first part of *Chapter 8, Mobile Game Engines*, we set up a scene, in the second part of *Chapter 9, Prototyping*, we defined the basic behaviors and put some coding into the pot, while in this last part we added some details to make the game more appealing to play.

Still, there is much you can add to turn this prototype into a complete game. Here is a list of things you could implement as an exercise:

- A main screen to open the game with
- Add a number of player's lives; the original Space Invaders had three
- Add a two-player option
- Add a boss ship to appear once in a while for extra score
- Have the aliens get faster as time passes
- Make extra levels for the game

Summary

In this chapter we covered balancing techniques including symmetry, randomization, feedback loops, a game director, and statistical analysis. We also covered tuning strategies and difficulty settings. We then finished up the Unity tutorial; adding audio, visual effects, win/lose conditions, enemy and player shots, destructible enemies, and other features. Next we will review four existing games and give our analysis of them.

11
Mobile Game Design

As we get to the end of our journey, it is time to channel all the info we have given you so far into what the main goal of this book is—to provide you, the readers, with the knowledge it takes to approach the practice of game design for today's mobile phones.

Game design can be daunting for a first timer but there is a methodology that breaks this scary process into palatable pieces. Remember, the best way to eat an elephant is one bite at a time!

We begin with a brief summary of the general game design process and then we will delve into the details of mobile game design, with its good practices and lists of dos and don'ts.

The last part of the chapter is dedicated to the theory of fun in games by Nicole Lazzaro, a popular researcher who studied how fun can help us designers to create better and more compelling games.

In this chapter we will cover:

- The basic game design process
- The dos and don'ts of game design
- The distinctive aspects of mobile game design
- Hardware limitations
- Mobile design constraints
- The mobile market

The basic game design process

The game design process shares many stages with any type of software design; identify what you want the game to do, define how it does it, find someone to program it, then test/fix the hell out of it until it does what you expect it to do. Let's discuss these stages in a bit more detail. Find an idea.

Unless you are one of the lucky few who start with an idea, sitting there staring at a blank piece of paper trying to force an idea out of your blank slate of a brain, may feel like trying to give birth when you're not pregnant: lots of effort with no payoff.

Getting the right idea can be the hardest part of the entire design process and it usually takes several brainstorming sessions to achieve a good gameplay idea. In case you get stuck and feel like you're pondering too much, we suggest you to stop trying to be creative; go for a walk, watch a movie, read a book, or play a (gasp!) video game! Give the subconscious mind some space to percolate something cool up to the surface.

- **Rough concept document**: Once you have an idea for a game firmly embedded in your consciousness, it's time to write it down. This sounds simple and at this stage it should be. Write down the highlights of your idea; what is/are the fun parts, how does one win, what gets in the way of winning, how the player overcomes their obstacles to winning, and who you imagine would like to play this game.
- **Storyboarding**: The best way to test an idea is, well, to test it! Use pen and paper to create storyboards of your game and try to play it out on paper. These can save a lot of (expensive) programming time by eliminating unsuccessful ideas early and by working through interface organization on the cheap.

The goal of storyboarding is to get something on paper that at least somewhat resembles the game you imagine in your head and it can go from very basic sketches, also called wire-frames, to detail schematics in **Azure**. Either way you should try to capture as many elements in the sketch as possible. The following figure represents the sketch of the double jump mechanic for a mobile platform made by one of the authors:

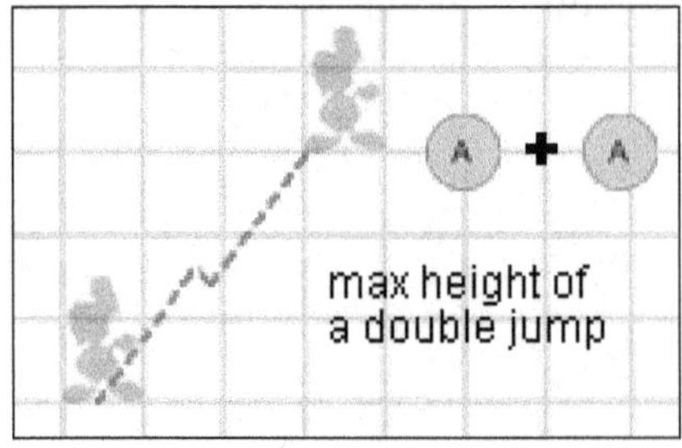

We discussed this process in depth in *Chapter 9, Prototyping*. Once you have concrete proof that your idea is good, invest some time and resources to create a playable demo that focuses on the action(s) the player will do most during the gameplay. It should have nothing extra such as fancy graphics and sound effects. It should include any pertinent actions that rely on the action in question and vice versa, for example if a previous action contributes to the action being tested, include it in the prototype. The question the prototype should answer is: do I still like my initial idea?

While prototyping, it is acceptable to use existing assets scavenged from the net, other projects, and so on. Just be aware of the subtle risks of having the project become inadvertently associated with those assets, especially if they are high quality.

For example, one of the authors was working on a simple (but clever!) real-time strategy game for Game Boy Advance. It was decided to add on a storyline to support the gameplay, which included a cast of characters. Instead of immediately creating original art for these characters, the team used the art from a defunct epic RPG project. The problem was that the quality of this placeholder art was so high (done by a world class fantasy/sci-fi artist) that when it was time to do final art for the game, the art the in-house artist did just wasn't up to the team's expectations. And the project didn't have enough money in the budget to hire the world-renowned artist to do the art for it. So both the team and the client (Nintendo) felt like the art was second rate, even though it was appropriate for the game being made. The project was later cancelled, but not necessarily due to the art.

The following screenshot shows an adventure title prototype made by one of the authors with GameMaker studio by using assets taken from the Zelda saga:

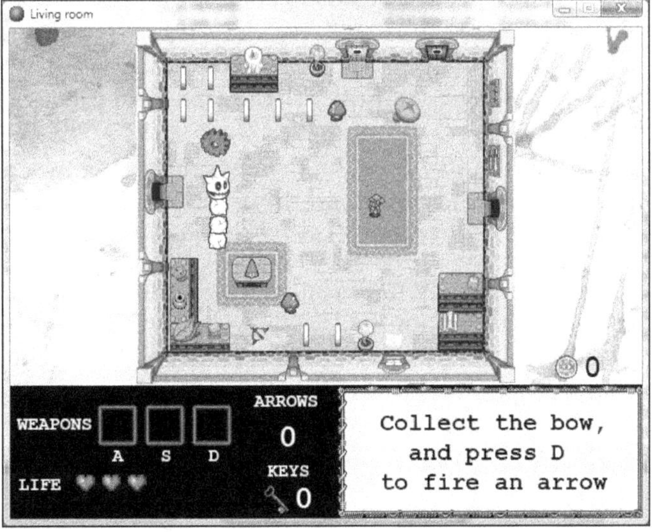

Test it once you have a working prototype, it is time to submit your idea to the public. Get a variety of people in to test your game like crazy. Include team members, former testers (if any), and fresh testers. Have people play often and get initial reactions as well as studied responses and collect all the data you can.

Fix the issues that emerge from those testing sessions and be ready to discard anything that doesn't really fit the gameplay experience you had in mind. This can be a tough decision, especially for an element that the designer/design team have grown attached to. A good rule of thumb is if this element is on its third go around on being fixed; cut it if it doesn't pass. By then it is taking up too much of the project's resources.

Refine the design document as implemented features pass the tests and the test, fix, or discard cycle is repeated on all the main features of your games, take the changes that were implemented during prototyping and update the design document to reflect them.

By the end of this process, you will have a design document, a document that will be what you built for your final product. You can read an interesting article on Gamasutra about the layout of one such document, intended for a mobile team of developers at `http://www.gamasutra.com/blogs/JasonBakker/20090604/84211/A_GDD_Template_for_the_Indie_Developer.php`.

Please note that this does not mean there won't be more changes! Hopefully it means there won't be any major changes, but be prepared for plenty of minor ones.

End the preproduction once you have a clear idea of what your gameplay will be and a detailed document about what needs to be done, it is time to approach game production by creating the programming, graphics, audio, and interface of your game. As one works towards realization of the final product, continue using the evaluation procedures implemented during the prototyping process. Continually ask "is this fun for my target audience?" and don't fall into the trap of "well that's how I've always done that". Constantly question the design, and/or its implementation. If it's fun, leave it alone. If not, change it, no matter how late it is in the development process. Remember, you only have one chance to make a good first impression.

When is the design really done? By now you have reached the realization that a project is never complete, you're simply done with it. No doubt you have many things you'd like to change, remove, or add but you've run out of time, money, or both. Make sure all those good ideas are recorded somewhere. It is a good idea to gather the team after release, and over snacks and refreshments capture what the team members would change. This is good for team morale as well as a good practice to follow.

The dos and don'ts of game design

We would like to end this section about game design with a list of good practices and things to avoid while designing games, regardless of the genre or the platform you are designing for. They will provide a solid background to approach the opportunities and constraints inherent to designing games for today's smartphones.

Dos

The following are the dos of game design:

- The designer's role is to lose gracefully. If the player wins having been challenged, the designer wins.
- Provide enough hints to guide the player to a solution of a puzzle.
- Reward the player's efforts appropriately; the higher the challenge, the higher the payoff, and vice versa.
- Make creative use of the features the game has; avoid the underuse of the game's unique/cool elements.
- If a situation can have only one outcome, make it a cutscene. Don't give the player the illusion of control when they don't have it; this breaks the player/designer trust.

Don'ts

The following are the don'ts of game design:

- Don't allow the player to miss essential content.
- Don't cheat; play by the same rules the player has to follow.
- Avoid mindless repetition; it's not fun in real life so skip it in your game too.
- Don't allow the player to be lost; if they need a map, provide one. Same goes for clues.
- Don't break the game's illusion by introducing story-inappropriate elements.
- Avoid randomness for the sake of same. Being weird for weird's sake is not fun; it's lazy design.
- Avoid obscure solutions to obstacles; if it doesn't make sense in the real world, it won't make sense in the game.

- Put players in the conditions to understand what is expected from them and provide clues to overcome obstacles. There is nothing worse than quitting playing because you don't understand how to proceed in a game.
- Unless it is a trivia game, you don't require knowledge from outside the game to proceed (unless you provide the answer within the game, before the player needs it).

Designing mobile games

So far we have discussed game design in general. In this section we will cover design specifically aimed to the mobile platforms. Designing for the mobile platform has its own unique drawbacks and advantages and only by overcoming its traps and exploiting its features will you be able to create a product that can emerge from the competition and make money.

The differences between mobile and other platforms such as **Personal Computer** (**PC**) and console are significant, ranging from hardware capabilities to control schemes, to fruition, business models, and pricing policies. Let's delve into each of such categories.

Hardware limitations

Though the advancement of mobile technology allows high-end devices to have the same capabilities of the former generations of consoles, an average mobile user possesses an average mobile device with limited capabilities, especially with regards to memory and processing power. As the mobile market is a mass market, it is a good practice to target the broadest audience possible, which means it is mandatory to design games that run smoothly on less than edgy smartphones and are fun to play on small screens.

Hardware variability also matters here. The one thing you can be sure of when you plan to design a mobile game, especially if you target the Android market, is that the game will have to run on several different device configurations. Screen size and resolution, CPU speed, touch screen responsiveness may vary, and so on.

Let's see how these factors pose a completely new set of challenges for the game designer.

Screen size

Let's face it, except for the pad style devices; the screen on most of the mobile platforms is tiny. This presents two problems: how to show enough information for the gameplay to be meaningful and how to make that information identifiable.

In *Chapter 3, Graphics for Mobile*, we described the most common techniques to design nice graphics for mobile games; we will reiterate them here.

First of all, pick two/three reference mobile phone models to design your game graphics and interface around and make separate assets for each main screen resolution. We know now that simply shrinking icons up and down won't work. The following figure displays a comparison between different smartphone screens:

Use smart color schemes to make the main character, its enemies/obstacles, and the background environment well recognizable. Also spend some time on character design to be sure that game characters are appealing and meaningful.

It may seem trivial, but if your game relies on large gameplay areas, display less of the play field at a time and allow the window of the visible gameplay to scroll over the total play field.

Game controls

While designing the user interface, be aware of the fact that virtual buttons encumber the gameplay area, so try to find a good balance between game mechanics and the number of controls required to manage them.

The following screenshot represents a mobile platform game with virtual buttons made by one of the authors:

The touch screen scheme seems really cool at a glance. But as a game designer, one quickly realizes that we are now sharing screen real estate with the game graphics and the game controls. In general, you don't want to use up the screen space with virtual buttons. The controllers need to be integrated with the game graphics and mobile phones have sensors (accelerometer above all). They can help in implementing controls that don't affect the gameplay area.

Most of all, remember that mobile games shouldn't require complex controls, anyway.

On the other hand, touch screens offer distinct ways to interact with games and perform game actions, such as tapping and dragging. As a smart mobile game designer, you will exploit them to make the most out of your mobile user experience and user interface!

Audio output

We know that most mobile devices can't feature stereo sound, as they are provided with a single speaker. No need then to say that audio for mobile games should be treated as a "secondary feature" and that it's better not to design games that strongly rely on audio for the gameplay or for involving the player in the action.

Moreover, as mobile games are frequently played outdoors, if game audio is noisy or annoying, it is quite likely to be rejected by the player himself, because he might not want to bother others around him or let them know he's playing. We strongly recommend you to design game sounds that are appealing but can also be excluded without affecting the general gameplay experience.

File size

Since mobile games are downloaded from sites, it is mandatory that all game contents are included in a small sized file, for example, though the max size for an iOS application is 2 GB, the limit for over the air downloads is only 50 MB! As you create assets and contents for your game, you will find out how easily that threshold can be overrun.

Optimization is the key word to deal with that. Have your programmers engineer your project so that memory requirements are kept at minimum. Invest some time and resources to find solutions to the technical issues posed by mobile devices memory limits. The internet is full of sites, offering technical support to those facing problems with mobile devices limitations. Android developers can, for example, refer to `http://developer.android.com/index.html`.

Processing power

We mentioned it several times, we restate it here: don't expect the majority of users to possess phones equipped with the latest Qualcomm Snapdragon CPU. Half Bricks' Jetpack Joyride slows down on 800 MHz CPU speed devices. Unless you aim to make a tech demo to show the capabilities of a specific high-end hardware, keep your system requirements as low as possible to have the opportunity to target the broader audience. At 99 cents per download, it takes thousands of downloads to make a game to recoup its development costs and eventually make a profit!

Mobile design constraints

There are a few less obvious design considerations, based on the player's play behavior with a mobile device. What are the circumstances that players use mobile devices to play games? Usually they are waiting for something else to happen: waiting to board the bus, waiting to get off the bus, waiting in line, waiting in the waiting room, and so on. This affects several aspects of game design, as we will show in the following sections.

Play time

The most obvious design limitation is play time. The player should have a satisfying play experience in three minutes or less. A satisfying play experience usually means accomplishing a goal within the context of the game. A good point of reference is reaching a save game point. If save game points are placed about two and a half minutes of an average game player's ability apart, the average game player will never lose more than a couple of minutes of progress.

For example, let's say an average player is waiting for a bus. She plays for three minutes and hits a save game point. The bus comes one minute later so the player stops playing and loses one minute of game progress (assuming there is no pause feature).

Game depth

Generally speaking, mobile games tend not to have much longevity, when compared to titles, such as Dragon Age or Fallout 3. There are several reasons for this, the most obvious one being the (usually) simple mechanics mobile games are built around.

We don't mean that players cannot play Fruit Ninja or Angry Birds for a total of 60 hours or so, but it's not very likely that the average casual player will spend even 10 hours to unfold the story that may be told in a mobile game. At five hours of total gameplay, the player must in fact complete 120 two and a half minute save games. At 50 hours of the total gameplay, the player must complete 1200 two and a half minute save games. Are you sure your gameplay is sustainable over 1200 save game points?

Mobile environment

Mobile games are frequently played outdoors, in crowded, noisy, and even "shifting" or "scuffling" environments. Such factors must be considered while designing a mobile game.

Does direct sunlight prevent players from understanding what's happening on the screen? Does a barking dog prevent the players from listening to important game instructions? Does the gameplay require control finesse and pixel precision to perform actions?

If the answer to any of these questions is yes, you should iterate a little more around your design because these are all factors which could sink the success of your product.

Smartphones

Smartphones are still phones, after all. It is thus necessary that mobile games can handle unexpected events, which may occur while playing on your phone: incoming calls and messages, automatic updates, automatic power management utilities that activate alarms.

You surely don't want your players to lose their progress due to an incoming call. Pause and auto-save features are thus mandatory design requirements of any successful mobile game.

Single player versus multiplayer

Multiplayer is generally much more fun than single player, no question. But how can you set up a multiplayer game in a two and half minute window? For popular multiplayer titles it is possible. Thanks to a turn-based, asynchronous play model where one player submits a move in the two and half minute window and then responds to the player's move. Very popular titles like Ruzzle, Hero Academy, or Skulls of the Shogun game system do that, but keep in mind that to support asynchronous gameplay it requires servers, which cost money and complex networking routines to be programmed. Are these extra difficulties worth their costs?

The mobile market

The success of any commercial project cannot arise with disregard to its reference market, and mobile games don't make exception.

We the authors, believe that if you are reading this book, you are aware that the mobile market is evolving rapidly. The Newzoo market research for the games industry trends report for 2012 states that there are more than 500 million mobile gamers in the world and around 175 million gamers pay for games and that the mobile market was worth 9 billion dollars in 2012 (source: `http://www.newzoo.com/insights/placing-mobile-games-in-perspective-of-the-total-games-market-free-mobile-trend-report/`).

The following screenshot represents the numbers of the mobile gaming market 2012 reported by Newzoo:

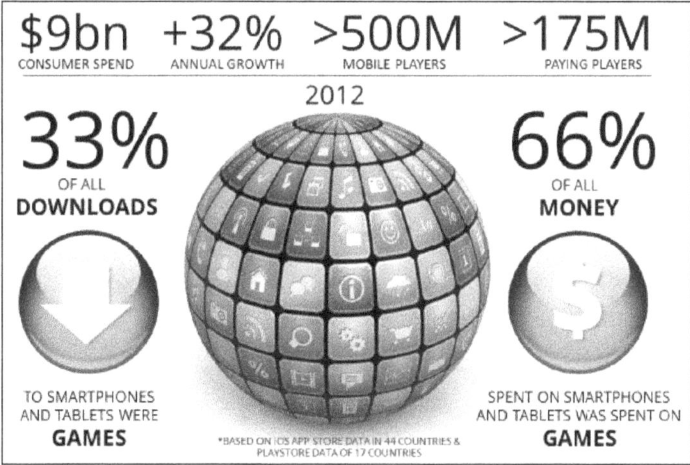

As Juniper Research, a market intelligence firm, states, "smartphones and tablets are going to be primary devices for gamers to make in-app purchases in the future. Juniper projects 64.1 billion downloads of game apps to mobile devices in 2017, compared to the 21 billion downloaded in 2012." (source: `http://www.gamesindustry.biz/articles/2013-04-30-mobile-to-be-primary-hardware-for-gaming-by-2016`). Even handheld consoles, such as the 3DS by Nintendo or the PSVita by PlayStation are suffering from the competition of mobile phones and tablets, thanks to the improvements on mobile hardware and the quality of games.

With regard to market share, a study by Strategy Analytics (source: `http://www.strategyanalytics.com/default.aspx?mod=reportabstractviewer&a0=8437`) shows that Android is the leading platform in Q1 2013, with 64 percent of all handheld sales. Japan being the only market where iOS is on the lead; though, as Apple is fond of pointing out, iOS users generally spend more money, when compared to Android estimators.

All the data tell us that the positive trend in mobile devices growth will continue for several years and that with almost one billion mobile devices in the world, the mobile market cannot be ignored by game developers. Android is growing faster than Apple, but Apple is still the most lucrative market for mobile apps and games. Microsoft phones and tablets, on the other hand, didn't show positive trends as to be compared with iOS and Android growth.

So the question is how can an indie team enter this market and have a chance of success?

Mobile gamers

A crucial aspect while planning to make a mobile game is to think about your target audience. We know that mobile games generally aim towards a casual audience. Statistics tell us that there is a relation between gender, age, and game genre, with women preferring Solitaire, social turn-based and management games, while men are more oriented towards action, strategy and betting games (source: `http://blog.flurry.com/bid/92377/The-Gamification-of-Mobile-Games`).

The same study tells us, with regard to monetization, that Solitaire, Endless, and social turn-based games have a high retention value upon gamers, while Strategy games is the most often accessed game category.

We also know that, though in some western countries there is a 50/50 split between male and female mobile gamers, men still tend to spend more, as we know that in the US, 61 percent of paying gamers are men.

But there is more information that we know about mobile gamers. We know that as a casual audience (mainly), they prefer polished games with well-tested mechanics, clear goals, and cute graphics. We know that they don't like being frustrated while playing and expect forgiving difficulty levels. We know that they prefer to play the titles their friends play and that "word of mouth" is a powerful medium for popularity in the mobile market. Finally, we know that as they are not used to paying much, if at all for games, and we cannot expect too much investment from them in learning and mastering your game's mechanics. The first impression for a mobile game is very important, as it is far too easy to download another title if you don't immediately like the one you are playing. This doesn't usually happen if you spent 60 dollars on a traditional console or PC game!

Business models

So you have an idea, you know the platform to develop it for, and you know the genre and target audience of your mobile game. The next step is to decide how you will make money out of it!

When releasing a game on the mobile market, there are several options available to make it profitable. Deciding which business model to use is an important, and is a tough decision that will affect the commercial success of your product. Let's invest time in describing each of them and their pros and cons.

Premium

Premium was the predominant business model in the beginning years after Apple launched its App Store. It means that users are charged an amount of money, usually 99 cents, to download a game. It is used by some of the most popular mobile games, such as Angry Birds, Doodle Jump, or Cut the Rope.

Today, premium games tend to perform worse in terms of sales than games that are offered for free or with in-game advertising. On February 2013, Minecraft was the only paid app among the most downloaded 20 apps on the App Store. We suggest you refer to such a business model only if you can provide some kind of unique, differentiated contents, such as a game based on a popular license of some sort, for example, a sports game or if your average gameplay session is generally so short that you can't get advertising to work.

Freemium

Freemium means that you give away your game for free, planning to make money through **In-App Purchases (IAP)** of virtual goods. It is the dominant business model today, if you consider that of those 20 most profitable apps on the App Store, 15 are Freemium games, including Clash of Clans, Zynga's Poker, and Bejeweled Blitz.

Freemium works best when your game delivers value over time or has the characteristics of a viral product, which encourages free users to attract paid customers.

In-App Purchases consist of stocks of consumable items that allow players to obtain currencies to be spent in the game to perform actions. It can be time to quickly build structures, currency to spend in gambling in a game, or mana to cast spells in a RPG title.

While using IAP it is very important to gather as many statistics as possible about your daily and monthly users, such as how many they are, how much time they spend playing, how many times they play each day/each month, how much virtual and real currency they spend every day/every month, and how much are they willing to spend on a single purchase. You will use this data to constantly adjust prizes and craft targeted offers to maximize revenue and players' engagement.

If you'd like to have your jaw drop as you read the revenues, Freemium games can make it happen. We suggest you to read the following Forbes' article about Supercell's Clash of Clans at `http://www.forbes.com/sites/karstenstrauss/2013/04/18/the-2-4-million-per-day-company-supercell/`.

Ad supported

Ad supported games include several kinds of in-game advertising to be displayed in the game. They range from banners constantly displayed on screen, right outside of the gameplay area to interstitial videos of 15 to 30 seconds in length displayed during breaks of the game (careful with these, they can have a strong detrimental effect on users' retention!), to offer walls, which provide users with free contents in exchange of taking actions, such as signing for a free trial of a different app or linking the game to Facebook or Twitter.

Imangi Studios' Temple Run is an Ad supported game of success, though this business model is generally used by utilities that are so essential that people need to open them every day or which promote long session times.

Ad Supported business models work as they offer a way to monetize the majority of users who usually don't pay, giving the opportunity to non-paying users to earn free game contents and allow to cross-promote third parties' apps.

It's not uncommon that games feature advertising as part of a hybrid business model, such as Freemium plus in-game Ads.

Hybrid

As each title has a story of its own, and for the sake of completeness, we also mention the most popular hybrid forms of mobile business models: the Freemium plus Ads supported which we already mentioned and the Premium plus in-app purchase.

The possibility to download a game for free (Freemium), which display banners (Ads supported) but offers the option to pay to remove those banners (IAP) is an example of a very smart, very hybrid, mobile business model!

Choosing the right business model

We would like to close this section about the mobile market and its business models with useful hints to help you choose the correct business model for your next mobile game.

To begin with, we are happy to tell you that after so many cold numbers and analysis, we finally go back to the pulsing heart of what we love to do. In fact our first piece of advice is that although we make games for money (and obviously because we love them!) never put the monetization policy interests ahead of your game interests! If the business model you choose doesn't fit the characteristics of your game, take a step back and change it. The fact that the Freemium model is the most popular and (sometimes) profitable one today doesn't mean that you must implement it at all costs. Sometimes the old way (read: premium) is still the best way. Consider that the industry giants, such as EA, Popcap, Zynga, and Gameloft invest a lot of money on the games they make and part of that money is spent to support their business models. You are not likely to be able to compete with them on their field! Our second bit of advice is to consider the decision about the business model to adopt as part of the game design process itself. The earlier you think of your game in terms of its monetization policy, the better you can embody the business model into the game mechanics.

A game well-designed around its business model offers more chances for players to spend money on it, as you can read in an article about Supercell's Clash of Clans monetization policy at `http://www.salon.com/2013/04/17/this_is_how_you_win_the_internet_economy/singleton/`.

The following screenshot shows Clash of Clans, courtesy of Supercell:

If the game cannot make money directly through IAP, still it can produce indirect income for you through viral activities. Exploit the potential of your game to create viral loops by allowing to easily post scores on Facebook, Twitter, and other social networks. Let your free users do the marketing for you!

Since it is known that some users will never pay to download a game, no matter what its cost, a viable option is to make two versions of the game: one for free and one paid. The paid version of the game could offer extra (meaningful!) contents, such as extra game levels, customizable characters, customizable UI, or you can have a free version of the game with in-game Ads and a paid version without banners.

If you decide to have IAP in your game, consider that they require a lot of balancing, analysis and corrections to costs over time to produce income. Such results cannot be achieved if you don't have a clear understanding of the criteria why a given item is available at a given cost at a given time. Metrics are important for understanding your audience. Several services provide data mining and game analytics about mobile players; use them or you will miss the revenue opportunities your game may offer.

Finally, be prepared to spend money to acquire users. Less than five percent of Freemium players pay for game contents and the average cost to acquire users is around 1.50 dollars per user. It means that you need thousands of free users to have dozens of paying players, and the more they get, the more it will cost to acquire them.

What makes games fun

We desire to end this chapter with a section about a very popular theory of what fun is, and what makes games fun, by XeoDesign: a research firm founded by Nicole Lazzaro that helps organizations increase player engagement in their products by eliminating barriers to having fun.

Ms. Lazzaro is a world-renowned researcher in **Player Experience** (**PX**) who has been acknowledged as one of the top women working in high tech and one of the top 20 women in video games.

The following description is a breakdown of Xeo/Nicole's examination of what is fun in games. These are purely emotional responses that arise from specific game situations rather than from storyline.

This section is meant as a starting point for your research on the many theories on the subject.

The four keys to fun – the game mechanics that drive play

Lazzaro's theory is based around four types of fun, as different people play games for different reasons. Some people search for a challenge to test their skills, some people search for progression for the sake of having something growing in their hands, while others play games to spend time with friends.

In the following sections we will examine each category of fun described by Lazzaro's theory.

Hard fun – emotions from meaningful challenges, strategies, and puzzles

For many players overcoming obstacles is the reason why they play. Hard fun creates emotion by structuring experience towards the pursuit of a goal. The challenge focuses attention and rewards progress to create emotions, such as frustration and Fiero (an Italian word for personal triumph). It inspires creativity in the development and application of strategies. It rewards the player with feedback on progress and success. Players use this key play to test their skills and feel accomplished. In their study players who enjoy the hard fun of challenge say they like:

- Playing to see how good I really am
- Playing to beat the game

- Having multiple objectives
- Requiring strategy rather than luck

Games with this key offer compelling challenges with a choice of strategies. They balance the game difficulty with player skill through levels, player progress, or player controls. In Mario Kart, the difficulty of the challenge matches the skill of novice and advanced players (if you can't drive, you can at least throw stuff); plus it offers emotional opportunities from cooperative and competitive gameplay. Games with this key include Civilization, Halo, Top Spin Tennis, Crosswords, Hearts, Tetris, and Collapse. Some games offer a choice of winning conditions such as EverQuest and The Sims.

Easy fun – grab attention with ambiguity, incompleteness, and detail

Other players focus on the sheer enjoyment of experiencing the game activities. Easy fun maintains focus with player attention rather than a winning condition. The immersion key awakens a sense of curiosity in the player. It entices the player to consider options and find out more. Ambiguity, incompleteness, and detail combine to create a living world. The sensations of awe, wonder, and mystery can be very intense. Players use this key play to fill attention with something new. In their study players who enjoy the easy fun of immersion say they like:

- Exploring new worlds with intriguing people
- Excitement and adventure
- Wanting to figure it out
- Seeing what happens in the story, even if I have to use a walk through
- Feeling like me and my character are one
- Liking the sound of cards shuffling
- Growing dragons

Games with this key entice the player to linger, not necessarily in a 3D world but to become immersed in the experience. Rich stimuli and ambiguity as well as detail cause the player to pause with wonder and curiosity. Repetition and rhythm can be hypnotic. In Mario Kart the visual display, cart technology, and zany game obstacles inspire curiosity and immersion. Other games with easy fun mentioned by players include Myst, Splinter Cell, EverQuest, GTA III, Max Payne, Halo, Civilization, Collapse, Tetris, Dark Age of Camelot, and Hearts.

Altered states - generate emotion with perception, thought, behavior, and other people

Players report that how a game makes them feel inside is one of the major reasons why they play or consider games as therapy. They describe enjoying changes in their internal state during and after play. The internal experience key focuses on how aspects of the game external to the player create emotions inside the player. This aspect of the player's experience is the way in which perception, thought, and behavior combine in a social context to produce emotions and other internal sensations most frequently those of excitement and relief. Players using this key play to move from one mental state to another or to think or feel something different. In our study the players whose enjoyment focuses on their internal state say they like:

- Clearing my mind by clearing a level
- Feeling better about myself
- Avoiding boredom
- Being better at something that matters

Games with this key stimulate the player's senses and starts with emotion from compelling interaction, for example, Mario Kart combines rich visceral graphic and audio stimuli, intriguing concepts, and behaviors to create wildly fun emotions in the player. Games listed in this key include: Collapse, Crosswords, Halo, GTA, Civilization, Tetris, and EverQuest.

The people factor – create opportunities for player competition, cooperation, performance, and spectacle

Many player comments center on the enjoyment from playing with others inside or outside the game. In addition to buying multiplayer games, players structure game experiences to enhance player to player interaction. Participants play the games they don't like so they can spend time with their friends. Wisecracks and rivalries run hot as players compete. Teamwork and camaraderie flourish when they pursue shared goals. Dominant emotions include amusement, schadenfreude (the joy at others' misfortune), and naches (Yiddish word for pleasure). Players using this key see games as mechanisms for social interaction. In their study XeoDesign found that players whose enjoyment came from interaction with other people say that:

- It's the people that are addictive not the game
- I want an excuse to invite my friends over
- I don't like playing games, but it's a fun way to spend time with my friends
- I don't play, but it's fun to watch

Multiplayer games are best at using this key, although many games support some social interactions through chat and online boards. Games that offer both cooperative and competitive modes offer a wider variety of emotional experiences. For example Mario Kart's multiplayer mode allows two to four players to sit and play together providing performance opportunities and plenty of spectacle for anyone watching. Other games with this key include EverQuest, Dark Age of Camelot, Soul Calibur II, Halo, and GTA (it is fun to watch). You can refer the article at `http://xeodesign.com/xeodesign_whyweplaygames.pdf`.

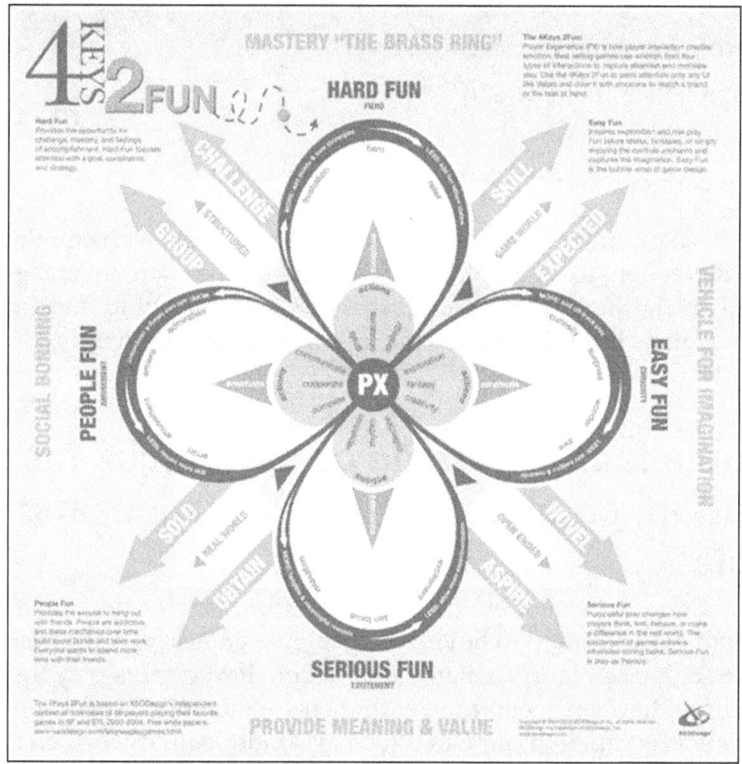

Source: http://xeodesign.com/whyweplaygames.html

Raph Koster and Roger Caillois

There are two other very popular theories about fun that are commonly mentioned as reference theories of fun in videogame community, which we would like you to have a look at.

One theory of fun is nicely described in the book *A Theory of Fun for Game Design*, by *Raph Koster*, designer of Ultima Online, *Paraglyph Press* available at `http://www.amazon.com/A-Theory-Fun-Game-Design/dp/1932111972`.

The other theory is expressed in the book *Man, Play and Games*, by *Roger Caillois*, a French sociologist, *University of Illinois Press* available at `http://www.amazon.com/Man-Play-Games-Roger-Caillois/dp/025207033X`. It is based on the contents of the popular book *Homo Ludens*, by *Johan Huizinga*, *Beacon Press* available at `http://www.amazon.com/Homo-Ludens-Study-Play-Element-Culture/dp/0807046817`.

We strongly suggest you review the material presented here and then start your own explorations on the field of research.

Summary

In this chapter we discussed the best practices for designing mobile games that can have chances to emerge in the highly competitive mobile market. We reviewed the agreed upon dos and don'ts of game design and discussed the factors that come into play while designing games for the mobile platform, with regards to hardware and design limitations to the mobile market characteristics and the most successful mobile business models.

Finally, we looked at what some authorities in the field think in making games fun, and how to create compelling game mechanics.

In the next chapter we will create a game document based on popular concepts of successful, classic games.

12
Pitching a Mobile Game

As the aim of this book has been to provide a practical guide to mobile game development, we the authors, desire to end this work with a pitch document example that may serve as a reference template to approach the design of your own mobile games. A pitch is targeted at potential investors and/or publishers who will fund your project to publication.

A pitch document should provide the information required to understand what kind of game you have in mind, how it will look and play like, what is its intended audience, target platform, and business model, and some technical aspects such as the number of graphics and audio assets required, the development schedule, and the cost. In other words, anything in the decision-making process that affects how and whether to invest time and money into developing the game.

You are now ready to confront the task of thinking about games from the perspective of how you are going to actually develop them!

In this chapter, we will cover the following topics:

- The characteristics of a pitch document
- Lilypads pitch
- The game concept
- Game mechanics
- Interface and graphics
- Business plan

The pitch document

Though there is no universal standard in the video game industry, the pitch document is the tool used to present a game idea to a potential publisher or to a team, with the purpose of getting the go-ahead for its development.

It is both an advertising tool and a brief manual of the game, as it is usually made up of different sections that address different aspects of game development.

The pitch document must capture the attention of its audience with catchy phrases, nice images, and clear concepts. It must provide detailed information about the gameplay of the title and explain why the game is fun to play. It must declare what the target audience of the title is, its competitors and references, and what puts this game above them.

Finally, the pitch document estimates the number of assets required to develop the game and the people required to make them, it provides the expected cost for the production, and explains its marketing strategy.

Based on our personal experience, we the authors consider that a pitch document should contain at least three main sections. As for the content of each section, we provide some references here, and then we suggest you to be wise and try to describe your game in the way it flows most naturally!

The first section is what we call **The concept** and answers the questions such as what is this game? Where does its idea come from?

The second section we call **Game mechanics** and should answer the questions such as how does this game work? How is it played?

The third and the last section is called **Tech** and answers the questions such as what do you need to make this game? How much will it cost?

Importance of pitching

Pitching a game does not only have to do with convincing a potential investor that you can make the game and that the game is worth making.

The practice of pitching is also a fundamental step for any game designer to learn to think about games from a true development perspective. By answering the questions posed by the pitch document, a designer leaves the field of "I have a nice idea for a game" and enters that of "I will spend the coming months developing a game like this, and with the collaboration of my team, we will produce a product that will meet or beat our expectations".

Game concept

The first section of the pitch generally addresses the concept of the game and the idea behind it. The concept should be described in a few sentences that allow anyone to quickly grasp the basic mechanics of the game and communicate its look and feel, using little, if any, technical jargon.

When describing the concept, include anything that is necessary to explain the basic gameplay of your title but leave out what relates to special cases, additional contents, and information that may confuse the reader.

If your concept is not brief or very clear and it cannot be grasped with a single reading, it means that you still haven't got a good concept to begin with.

Work on it until you can provide a single, short sentence, usually called high concept, which communicates what the game is all about. It should be a catchy phrase, put in the heading of the document to catch the reader's attention and make him willing to continue reading.

In game design courses, students are asked to provide high concepts of three to five words in total, things such as *Pac Man – eat 'em all.*

This is an excellent exercise to learn to think of games from the perspective of the central gameplay element they are built around.

There is this interesting article by *James Mardsen* of FutureLab about the development of Velocity that we suggest you to read. It offers great insight on the process of developing a gameplay idea (what *James Mardsen* calls "the toys" of gameplay) with a commercial purpose in mind:

This is the opening screenshot for the pitch document of the game Velocity. You can find the entire document online at `http://www.gamasutra.com/blogs/JamesMarsden/20130629/195334/Designing_An_Awesome_Videogame.php?utm_source=feedburner&utm_medium=feed&utm_campaign=Feed%3A+GamasutraNews+%28Gamasutra+News%29`.

References

When thinking about a concept for a game, look for references. Are there any games which make use of the same or similar mechanics? How do they work? What would you change in those games? Such questions will help you find a clear direction for your game. By examining what worked and didn't work for other titles is the best way to avoid common errors and to save the time and money needed to reinvent the wheel.

Be aware that your references need not to be video games at all. Any kind of game or human activity in general can be a reference for a video game mechanics. Always try to keep your mind and eyes as open as possible.

You don't need a large number of references, two or three should be enough to give your reader the feeling of how your game will work. Remember that popular games are usually those that take a well-known game mechanics and change just what it takes to make it feel fresh again! If you take too many references into consideration, it will be harder to focus around that one central element which adds fun to your title.

Prototypes

As you try to focus around an idea and search for references, it is very important that you begin to test that idea immediately with pen and paper prototypes. Does your idea work in practice? Testing is the only way to quickly understand if an idea actually works and it also can help you spot special cases which could lead to minor (or even major, sometimes!) changes to the mechanics you are sketching.

Stuck?

Should you find yourself stuck on a dead end, we suggest you to get some distractions and move away from your desk for a while. It is very likely that once you go back to work, you will be able to come out from the impasse you found yourself stuck in and move on with your design.

Genre

Once you decide that your idea is actually a good one, it is time to ask yourself if the game is worth making from a commercial perspective.

Defining the genre of your game is a good starting point because having a clear idea of the genre allows you to identify the market in which it will compete.

Target audience

No game can become popular if you don't design it with a specific target audience in mind. Any attempt to create a game that is enjoyed by everyone is a chimera that usually leads to failure.

The clearer your idea of who's going to play your game and why, the easier to focus on those features that are really important for your target players.

We know now from analysts that different populations of gamers play different genres of games with distinctive features. You must take advantage of this knowledge!

Key features

Describing key game features is a very important section of your pitch document, especially if you plan to submit your idea to a potential investor. By declaring a list of interesting and innovative key features you can get the investors' attention and persuade them to give you the money to develop your title.

If your game lacks the elements which give it the chance to emerge from the competition, well, easily put, you won't likely make it!

Remember that commercial successes, which just changed one or few aspects of other successful games, succeeded because they targeted a specific audience, offering what they expected and encouraging them to play and spend money on the game.

Unfortunately, there is no universal recipe for this. Market analysis and extensive examination of other games' gameplay is required to spot which are the key features that can predict the commercial success of your game.

Target platform and competitors

Along with the audience, the decision about which platform to target is important for the commercial success of any title.

The best scenario would be to have your mobile game available and running smooth on all three main mobile platforms: iOS, Android, and Windows Phone, especially if you plan to make a Freemium game.

On the other hand, to develop a game version for each individual platform requires time and money.

If you plan to make a Premium game, which is downloaded for a cost, we suggest that you target the iOS platform, as Android is known for being considered an open source platform preferred by those who aren't likely to pay for contents in general, and Windows Phone is not yet popular enough to propel exclusive development for this platform alone.

Also look for competitors when deciding the platform for a game. Are there other games similar to yours already available, or will there be at the time you plan to ship? Which are the key features of such titles?

The idea is to find a niche for your title where it can profit!

Game mechanics

Now that you have a description of the game concept and its market, it is time to explain how your game works and how it is actually played.

Any game mechanics should be described with clear text and nice images. The goal is to make the reader feel like he played the game, even if he actually didn't.

Work on this section until you have proof that anyone can read it and understand it without you providing any extra explanation. Avoid technical words and use examples. Examples taken from other popular, successful titles can do a fine job, as they are references that can be immediately grasped by your readers.

An image is worth a thousand words. Use all the pictures you need when describing the mechanics of your game, to be sure they are super clear.

But also remember this is just a pitch document, so you don't need to explain absolutely everything about your game. There is the Detailed Design Document for that! Only include the most important mechanics, those that are required to understand the gameplay and the potential of the game, and those that are distinctive, key features that can make it successful.

Once you have described the main mechanics, you can mention how you will improve the gameplay as the game progresses by unlocking new game elements such as additional character abilities, new types of enemies, obstacles and game surfaces, bonuses, and so on. Include one or two unlocks in detail and two or three additional unlocks in general terms.

Control scheme and interface

Obviously, to explain how a game works requires that you describe in detail its control scheme and explain how the player performs the main game actions.

This is mobile gaming, remember to keep controls simple, try to avoid virtual buttons (since they take up precious screen space), and make use of sensors, if they suit your gameplay idea!

Also explain here how the player interacts with the game and how he moves between game screens.

Scoring system and achievements

Take some time at this point to describe how the player earns points and credits, and how they are used to provide incentives to the player to keep playing. If you have an In-App Purchase system in your game, explain here how it is integrated into gameplay and how the player can take advantage of the purchased items to progress in the game.

A gameplay example

Now that you have showed how the game is played and what it should look like, this is a perfect moment to offer your readers a gameplay example of the game.

Describe an in-game situation or a problem and explain how and by which operations the player gets to the solution step-by-step. A picture is worth a thousand words, especially if you cannot be present when others read your document.

If you have a game with levels, provide a small number of them as examples.

Designing levels for your games early on is another activity which brings the collateral benefit of forcing you, the designer, to deal with potential problems that could arise from your game mechanics, before true development begins.

Screen flow and screens relationship

At this point you've said enough about the gameplay of your title and it is time to look at the game from an app perspective. This part of the pitch document should describe how the player experiences your application; which screens are available and how does he move between them, how he can access one screen from another, and which options are available (at least the most important) in each screen.

This task is usually done through one or more diagrams. The screen flow shows the layout of the screens available in the game and their connections. Individual diagrams can be provided as required for any main game operation, such as starting a new game, resume a previously saved game, create a player profile, access or modify the game options, and so on.

Microsoft Visio is the industry standard for such tasks, but there are several freeware software packages that can do the job as well. For example, one of the authors found that Freemind by *Joerg Mueller* is a good tool to make diagrams and it is a freeware software. You can download it from `http://freemind.sourceforge.net/wiki/index.php/Download`.

Game flow

The game flow is a different diagram which describes how a typical match unfolds to the player.

The diagram should display the number and sequence of operations required by the player to start a match, the basic actions performed by the player during a match, and what happens when the match ends.

Tech

Now that we have covered everything that is important to explain how your game works, the last step is to provide numbers and evaluations about what is needed to make this game (resources, time, and money) and how this game will make a profit, once shipped.

In this section are enlisted the technical aspects related to the development of the game.

You put here the information regarding the resolution of the application, the estimated parameters for graphics and audio assets, the number of assets for graphics (2D and 3D) and audio, animations, and so on.

It is here that you declare the resources required for development (people and software), the estimated time required for development, and its cost.

You also explain here how you plan to make money out of your game, by detailing its business model and the marketing strategy.

Expect to fill this section with charts and diagrams, as it is the clearer way to make people quickly grasp numbers and trends.

Parts of this section are the budget and schedule. In order to create reasonably accurate predictions of cost (budget) and the project's timetable (schedule), you must have a relatively complete list of assets (art, sound, screens) and tasks (programming modules, play testing, project management, and other things people get paid to do). One of the author's favorite programs to handle budget and scheduling is Microsoft Project. It is very robust and covers almost all of the features for project management. It is also expensive, especially if you use the full-featured server version. That said, there are also a large number of open source project management applications; Wikipedia has an extensive list of them and their capabilities, for more information visit `http://en.wikipedia.org/wiki/Comparison_of_project_management_software`.

Screenshot

Provide a screenshot of your game. What do you imagine your game to look like?

Approach this task from a conceptual point of view. You don't need to put actual graphics into this screenshot if you cannot afford an artist. Loot the Internet and use image editing tools to assemble something that resembles and conveys the idea of the look you want for your game.

On the other hand, the nicer the graphics of your designs and screenshots, the more appealing your pitch document will be for your readers. If you are pitching for a potential investor, find the best artist you can afford. Having a document with professional layout and top quality graphics says a lot about your team's abilities. Remember, there is no second chance to make a first impression!

Team/Designer resume

At the end of the document it is a nice touch to attach the resume of the team or the designer who made the document.

Especially, if your team has shipped or otherwise released other products, it is the best proof that the team is professional and reliable.

Otherwise, it is still a good way for the readers to get an idea of who the person behind the game idea and the pitch document is.

We are done with this discussion on the pitch document and can now begin working with the design of Lilypads!

Lilypads pitch document

The following is a sample pitch document for the fictional game Lilypads. It contains all the sections necessary to produce an effective pitch document.

Concept

Lilypads is a puzzle game for the iPhone, inspired by the games such as Peg Solitaire and Draughts. The player is asked to help a small frog named Grof, to get back to his home. Unfortunately, Grof got lost in the swamp of the endless ponds and now he must go through all of them to exit the swamp and hug his worried parents!

High Concept: Jump, eat, and get out of the pond!

Lilypad is 2D game played from a top-down view. The display shows the game level, represented by the pond Grof must escape from.

Each pond hosts a number of lilypads, scattered according to a given configuration:

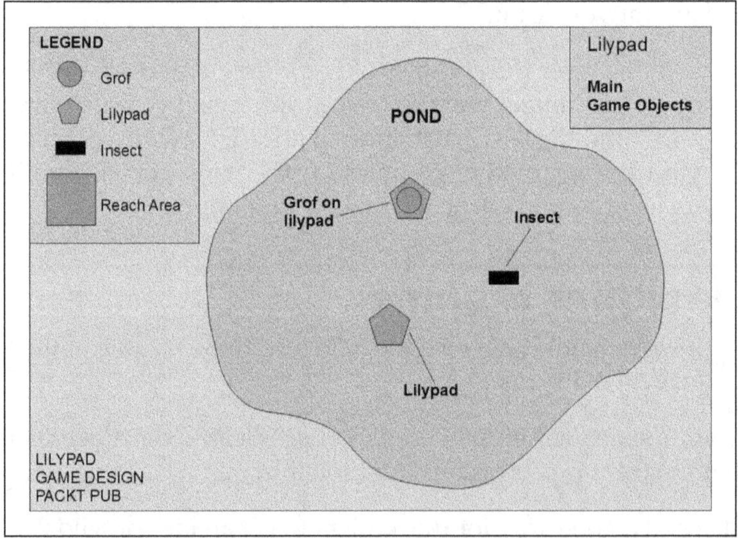

To get out of each pond, Grof must clear all lilypads by jumping on them.

Once all the lilypads in the pond have been removed, the player moves to the next pond (game level).

Game levels unlock as the player progresses in the game.

As the game progresses, the schemes presented with each pond get more complex and harder to solve.

The player has an unlimited number of tries and any unlocked game level can be replayed at will to aim for the highest score.

Score is obtained depending on the time taken to clear each game level according to the criteria that the lower the time, the better the score.

The player can also earn and/or buy (IAP) virtual currency to be used to get additional game levels and scenarios, customizable character skins, and other special features.

Genre

Lilypads is a single player puzzle game, which can be played in small chunks. It is divided into levels and the player is asked to find the solution to each game level.

The game will be made in two versions:

- **Freemium**: It is downloadable for free, it displays advertising banners, has reduced number of game levels, and only allows a single redo for the last move in a level.
- **Gold**: It is a Freemium version that can be upgraded for a price. It removes the advertising banners, unlocks extra contents such as skins and sound effects, provides additional game levels and unlocks the advanced redo feature, which allows the player to go back any number of moves in a level.

References

What follows is a list of games that we took inspiration from when designing the mechanics for Lilypads:

- **Peg Solitaire/Draughts**: These board games need no presentation, as popular as they are. One is a classic solo game where the player is asked to remove all elements from a grid according to one single moving rule. The Wikipedia page which you may want to check is available at `http://en.wikipedia.org/wiki/Peg_solitaire`.
- The other is a two player game on a checkerboard. We readapted its mechanics to fit into the concept of Lilypad. You can learn about it at `http://en.wikipedia.org/wiki/Draughts`.

- **Frog Bog (Intellivision)**: It is a classic game from the early '80s where up to two players eat the highest number of flying insects. The frogs controlled by players could only jump back and forth between two pads and players were only required to make their frog jump with correct timing (at simple difficulty settings).

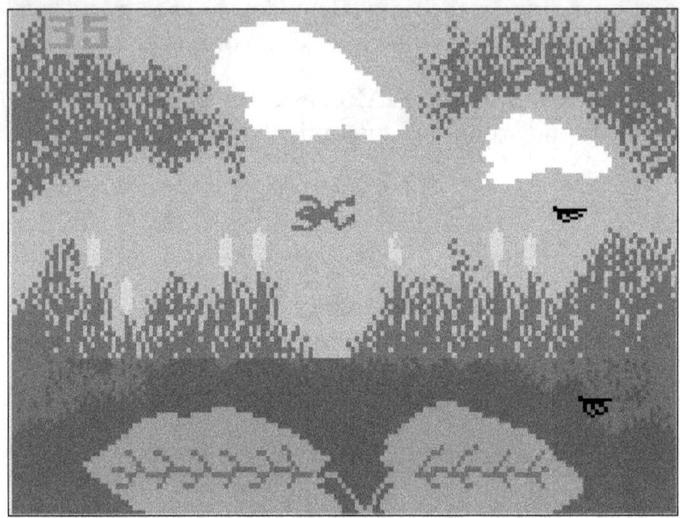

- **Diamond Dash (Wooga)**: It is one of the most popular Facebook games where the player is required to simplify sequences of game elements by quickly clicking on them. This game was the inspiration for the scoring system based on time taken to tap on an element to simplify it.

Target

Casual players who enjoy puzzle games with cute graphics and touch controls:

- Kids 4-13
- Women above 30

The theme, graphics, and game characteristics aim for the goal of having kids play the game with their mothers and friends.

Platform

Lilypads is designed for the iPhone (reference model, the iPhone 4), but can be easily converted for any touch device running iOS, Android, or Windows Phone, depending on its commercial success. The developing environment is Unity 4.

Competitors

We leave you with the task of filling in this section. The scenario of competitors as we write these words could change by the time you read them.

Get on the Internet and search yourself for which games, if any, can be considered competitors of Lilypads. This is the kind of exercise you should get used to doing often!

Key features

What follows here is a sample list of key features for Lilypads.

We strongly encourage you to think accurately about this potential game and come out with a reasonable and effective list of key features to improve this document:

- Easy to grasp gameplay, based on the mechanics of popular board games
- Crisp graphics that shine on the iPhone display
- Game theme is family-friendly and ideal for the targeted audience of young children
- IAP system to buy extra game levels, skins for the character and customizable audio
- Players can upload their score on public leaderboards and on most popular social networks

Character design

We add here a few considerations about the character design for Lilypads. For this game we need a cute character, which immediately attracts kids and women with its likeness, and we the authors agreed that the eyes could be the most expressive characteristic in Grof's appearance.

We tried several options and finally came up with the following reference of a nice frog with large and expressive eyes:

By working on the eyes of such a model, a good artist can provide Grof with a full set of facial expressions to be called according to in-game situations and thus improve the appeal of the main character of the game for its target audience.

If you are an artist yourself or have an artist in your team, we suggest you to create a sketch based on this reference model and exercise by working on a set of facial expressions for it.

We also encourage you to make a study of the other game characters too, starting from the insects.

Game mechanics

To explain the mechanics of Lilypads, let's begin by showing a concept image with the main game objects.

Each game level in Lilypad is represented by a pond from a top view where a number of lilypads lie. Grof can jump from one lilypad to an adjacent one.

Insects may be scattered between lilypads, so that Grof can eat them as he jumps from one lilypad to the other:

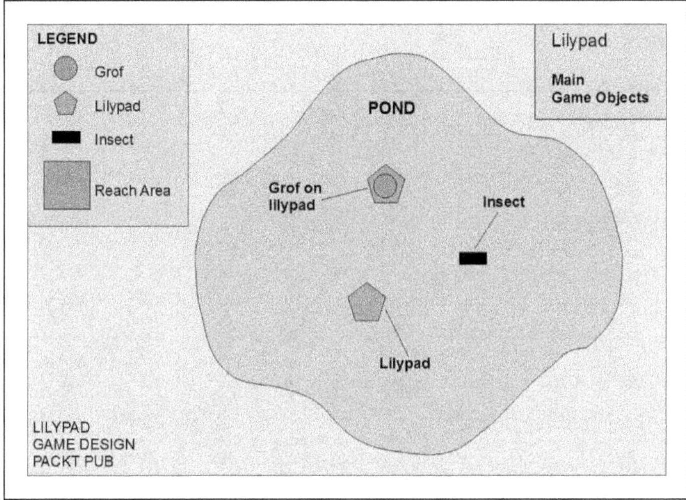

Lilypad is played by tapping on the lilypad the player wants Grof to jump to. The following screenshot represents the player tapping on a lilypad to have Grof jump on it:

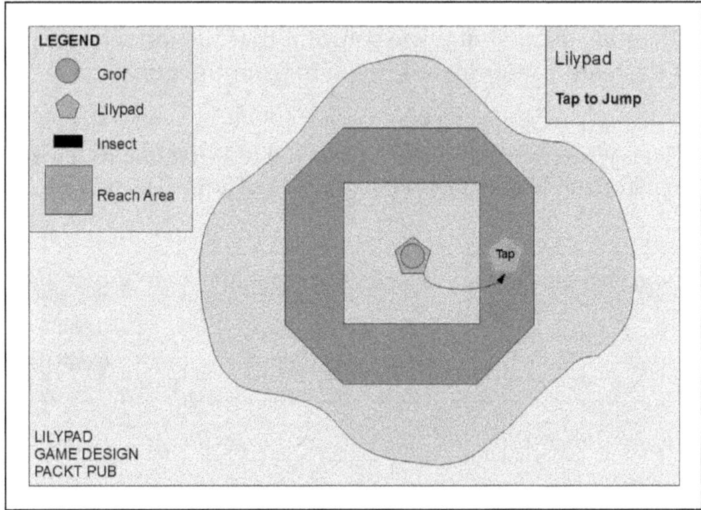

Each pond is a game level that challenges the player with a given configuration of a given number of lilypads.

Grof can jump to any adjacent lilypad in the eight cardinal directions, as shown in the following figure:

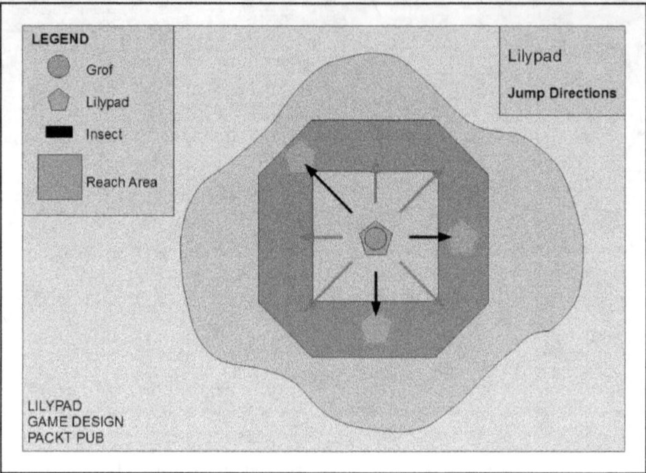

Lilypads sink after Grof has jumped on them, so that the player must resolve each scheme by jumping on each lilypad only once.

To clear a level the player must find the solution that fits the scheme given by the configuration of lilypads, removing all lilypads from the pond.

> The last lilypad of the level is assumed to be cleared as it is reached by Grof, while the others sink when Grof jumps away from them.

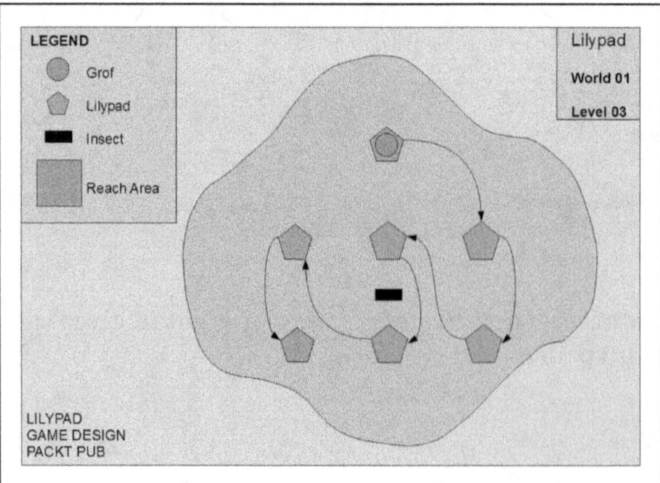

New game levels unlock as the player progresses in the game, as shown by the following figure, which represents a collection of the first game levels:

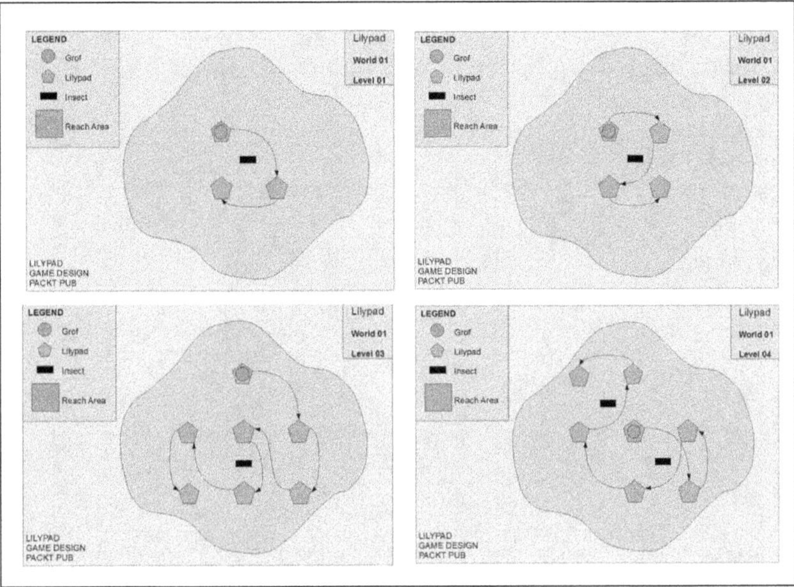

Score

The score is given to the player based on the time criteria in the following way.

As long as the player doesn't tap on the first lilypad of a level, time is not considered.

From the moment the player taps the first lilypad to make Grof jump, the counter starts and it stops when the player taps the last lilypad of the sequence.

This way the time clock actually records the time it took by the player to produce the correct sequence, but not the time required to come out with the sequence itself.

Each game level has a `par` parameter (for example, the game of golf), which defines the optimal time interval suggested for that level. The closer to (or even better than) the time par the player gets, the better his score in that level.

This is the criteria in the opinion of the authors that fits the characteristics of a mobile puzzle game because it leaves the player all the time he wants to think about the solution of each level, without forcing him, and only requires some skill when the correct sequence must be performed.

We encourage you to push this analysis further and provide Lilypad with alternative options for the scoring system.

Virtual currency

Ponds don't only host lilypads. In each pond a number of insects are scattered according to a predefined configuration between two adjacent lilypads.

When Grof jumps through an insect, he automatically eats it.

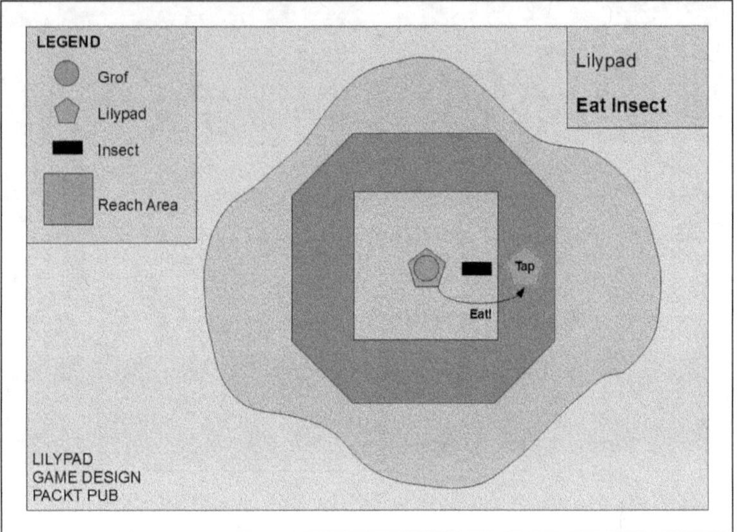

By eating insects the player gets stars (up to three per level), which can be converted into virtual currency to buy game extras.

Stars are earned according to the percentage of insects eaten, where three stars are granted after eating 100 percent of total number of insects available in the level.

IAP (In-App Purchase)

Additional levels and scenarios can be bought by spending virtual currency earned by eating insects.

This mechanics is meant to push players towards replaying levels to collect the maximum number of insects.

Virtual currency can also be bought by spending real money, so that lazy players can still get additional contents by paying a small price.

Other contents that could be considered are as follows:

- Additional skins for Grof
- Additional sound fx to customize Grof
- Advanced redo feature to go back any number of moves in a level

We ask you to invent more as an exercise on this section. Think in particular about contents that allow players to quickly progress in the game. Any ideas?

Achievements and leaderboards

Through the connection to social networks such as Facebook and Twitter, it is possible to send a message to the users' networks of friends whenever an achievement is reached.

It could be a particular high score in a game level, having completed a game world by beating all its levels or having purchased something with the IAP system. Spreading messages via social networks is a proven, powerful way to achieve viral popularity.

As an exercise we suggest you to develop the flow of this game feature.

Additional game elements

A main character (Grof), one surface type (the lilypads that sink), and one collectible (the insects) don't make a game, yet. More elements are needed to make the gameplay more interesting and articulate.

For example, there could be lilypads that don't sink. Or there could be swarms of insects which require more than one jump through to be eaten, or insects which move according to a pattern that the player must take into consideration when searching for the solution to a game level.

How do such elements integrate, improve, or ruin the basic set of mechanics?

We leave you, the readers, to answer these questions; find more game elements to improve the basic set we suggested here and add more mechanics to this title.

Also think about the possibility of offering virtual gadgets to progress in the game and their effect on keeping players' involvement with the game high.

Screen flow

The following figure represents a basic screen flow for Lilypads. From the main screen the player can access any other screen, and from there, again get back to the main screen.

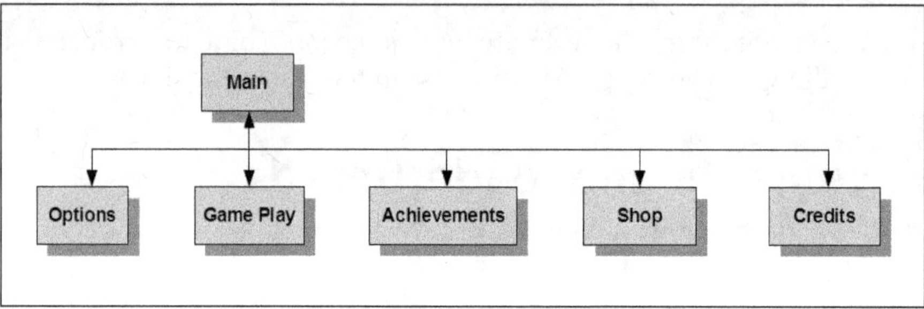

The next figure shows the main actions available for the player in each screen:

Main		
	•	Play
	•	Go To Shop
	•	Access Options
	•	Check Leaderboards and Achievements
	•	Watch Credits
	•	Quit Game
Game Play		
	•	Pause\Resume
	•	Redo Last Move
	•	Show Suggested Move
	•	Restart Level
	•	Quit Current Level
Options		
	•	Toggle SFX
	•	Toggle Music
	•	Change Difficulty Settings
	•	Back
Achievements		
	•	Sign In
		• Facebook
		• Twitter
	•	Upload Score
	•	Challenge Friends
	•	Back
Shop		
	•	Buy Contents
		• Categories
	•	Buy Virtual Credits
	•	Back
Credits		
	•	Back

Game flow

The following figure represents the game flow for Lilypads, with particular regard to its gameplay, and the connection between the score in a match and the **Achievement** screen:

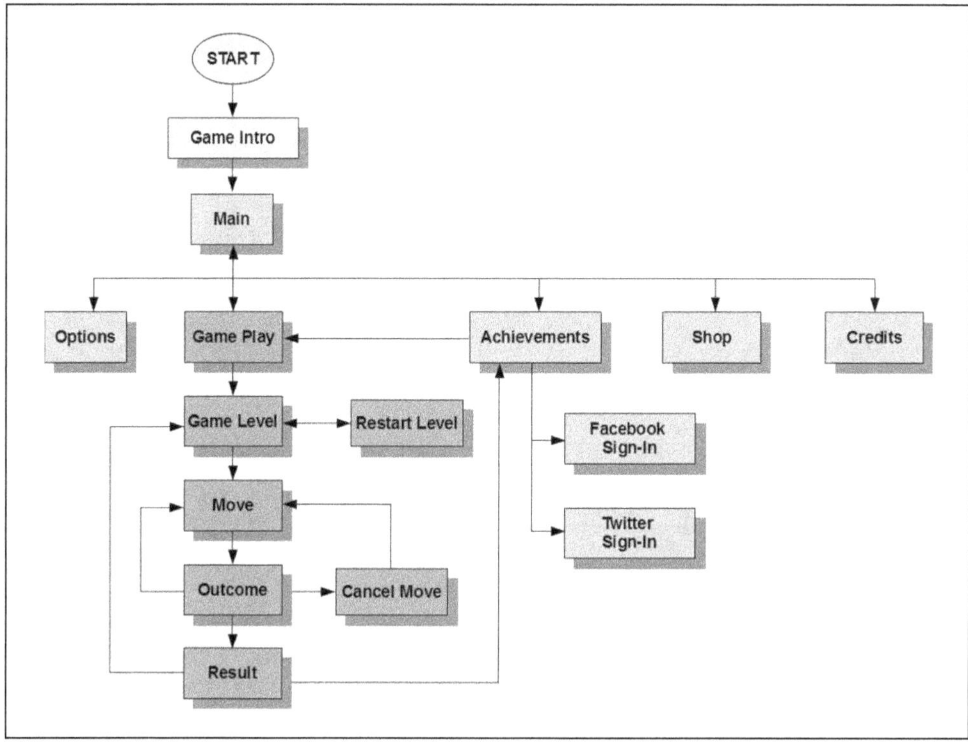

It is useful for your artists and programmers to have one such diagram for each game screen, to better address development. We encourage you to make the others as an exercise to get used to such practice.

Tech

And now the last part of the pitch document; let's provide our potential investor with numbers to help him understand whether this game idea is profitable. What and how much is needed to make this game? How long will it take before it can make money?

Game features

Let's begin by stating the main characteristics of the game, starting from the assumption that, given the genre (puzzle game) and basic mechanics (tapping on screen), we believe that 2D is the right choice for Lilypads. Since there is no gameplay-related reason to go 3D for this concept, by choosing 2D graphics the development time, costs, and difficulties can be kept low, in favor of level design and additional game elements to add depth to the gameplay.

- Graphics
    - 2D backgrounds
    - 2D sprites
    - Reference sprite size for game objects: 64 px
- Camera
    - Fixed
    - Top-down
- Control interface
    - Touch

Platform

Next, we list the tech-specs of the platform we are addressing. This is a necessary step to provide guidelines for designing the game graphics and interface.

The following tech data are related to developing the game for iPhone 4, which we picked as our target device. We encourage you, as an exercise, to adapt graphic template we suggest here to the iPad (res: 2048 x 1536 px) and iPad mini (res: 1024 x 768).

The iPhone 4

- Screen resolution: 960*640 pixels at 326 pixel per inch
- Display size: 3, 5 inches
- Audio output: Mono

Game screen study

The following figure represents the suggested subdivision of the total display area among the main functions that it is supposed to host (with regard to the Freemium version of the game, which hosts advertising banners): the gameplay area, the higher screen portion for displaying info related to gameplay, and the lower section, left for banners and advertising:

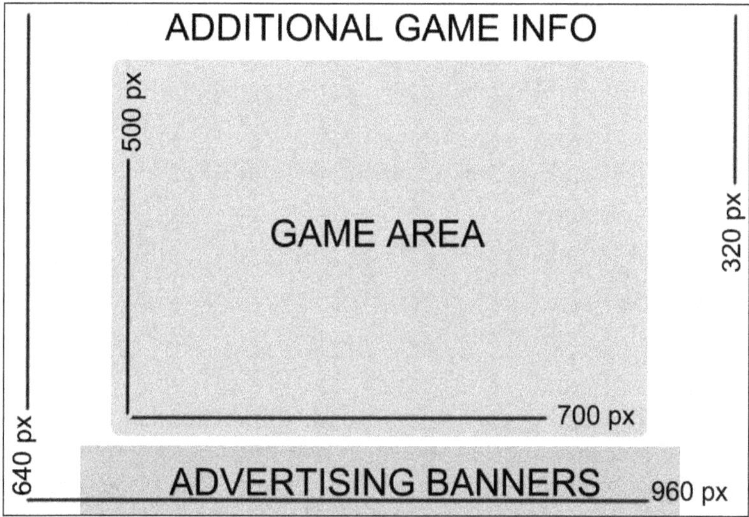

We ask you to detail this basic design and provide another one to be used for the Premium version of the game, which doesn't display advertising banners and thus frees the lower portion of the screen.

With a basic plan for the game interface, the next step is to declare the dimensions for the graphic assets: how large will Grof be? And which are the required dimensions for lilypads and insects?

The following figure represents the study for dimensions of the main game objects and text:

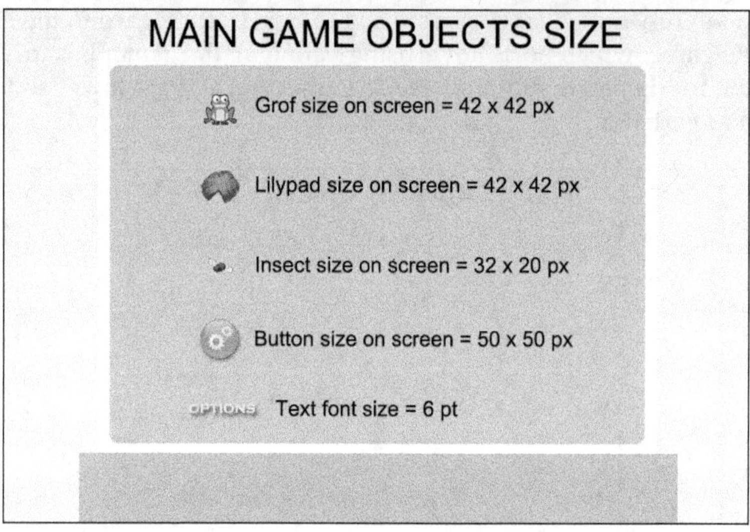

We also provide in the next figure a reference for dimensions of the ponds with regard to the game area size. This is an aspect that must be taken into consideration, especially for the design of the advanced levels, because the pond size affects the maximum number of lilypads that can be hosted to create each game level.

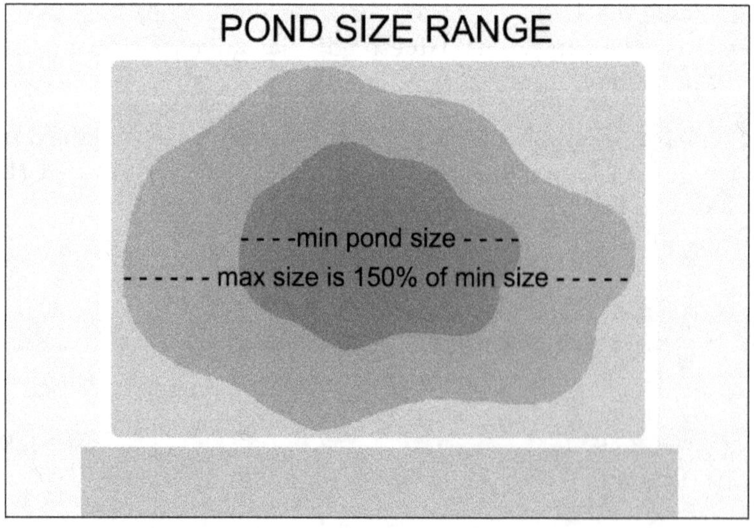

With that reference you can start planning the maximum number of lilypads that can be used to design the advanced levels of Lilypads and think of solutions to manage the limited resource of the pond size.

At this point you have gathered enough references to make a screenshot(s) of your game, which we strongly recommend you to provide, with any pitch document you create.

The next screenshot represent the main screen for Lilypads:

The next figure represents a screenshot from the game:

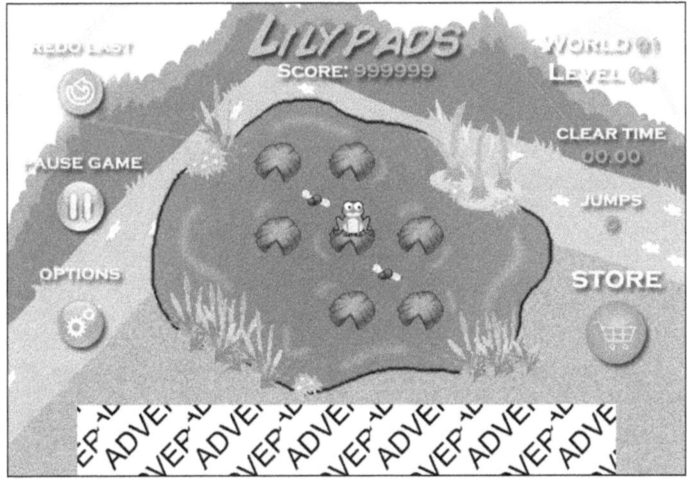

A list of assets

What follows here is a set of charts listing the number and type of the main graphic and audio assets required by what we designed for Lilypads so far. As this game requires more refinement and additional contents, we leave you the task of filling out this list with more items.

Graphics

This is the list of basic graphic assets needed for Lilypads:

GAME GRAPHICS			
2D			
	Backgrounds		
		World 1	
			Daylight
			Night time
		World 2	
			Daylight
			Night time
		World 3	
			Daylight
			Night time
	Sprites		
		Grof	
			Skin 1
			Skin 2
			Skin 3
		Lilypads	
			Type 1
			Type 2
			Type 3
		Insects	
			Type 1
			Type 2
	GUI		
		Buttons	
		Text	
		Animations	
	Animations		
		Grof	
			Jump 8 directions
			Eat 8 directions
			Idle
			Level complete good
			Level complete excellent
			Level failed
		Insects	
			Idle

Audio

This is the list of basic audio assets required for Lilypads:

GAME AUDIO				
Background musics				
	World 1			
		Day time		
		Night time		
	World 2			
		Day time		
		Night time		
	World 3			
		Day time		
		Night time		
Sound FX				
	Gameplay			
		Grof		
			Idle	
			Jump	
			Eat	
				Type 1
				Type 2
			Level complete	
			Level fail	
			Illegal move	
			Redo one move	
			Restart level	
		Player		
			Tap lilypad	
	User Interface			
		Make selection		
		Go back		
		Quit		

Software

In case you ask for support for buying the software licenses you need to develop a game, you can list at this point the number and costs of the licenses you need.

As an example, we represent here the cost for developing this game with Unity 4.

Unity and iOS license:

- Unity 4 Pro = $ 1500
- iOS Pro development plug-in = $ 1500
- iOS developer program fee = $ 99

We don't consider here the costs for other software such as image editors, as we have found out that you can save money on that field by using freeware tools!

Schedule and budget

We close this pitch document with two charts. The first chart represents the estimated development time for the list of assets provided:

Schedule					
Task Name	Duration	Start	Finish	Predecessors	Resource Names
Design Doc	14 days	Tue 7/2/13	Fri 7/19/13		Designer
Budget	2 days	Mon 7/22/13	Tue 7/23/13	1	Project Manager
Schedule	2 days	Wed 7/24/13	Thu 7/25/13	2	Project Manager
2D art	**11 days**	**Fri 7/26/13**	**Fri 8/2/13**		**2D Artist, Project Manager**
Main Screen	1 day	Fri 7/26/13	Fri 7/26/13	3	2D Artist
Options Screen	1 day	Mon 7/29/13	Mon 7/29/13	5	2D Artist
Game Play	1 day	Tue 7/30/13	Tue 7/30/13	6	2D Artist
Achievements	1 day	Wed 7/31/13	Wed 7/31/13	7	2D Artist
Shop	1 day	Thu 8/1/13	Thu 8/1/13	8	2D Artist
Credits	1 day	Fri 8/2/13	Fri 8/2/13	9	2D Artist
Grof	1 day	Fri 7/26/13	Fri 7/26/13	3	2D Artist
Lilypad	1 day	Mon 7/29/13	Mon 7/29/13	12	2D Artist
Insect	1 day	Tue 7/30/13	Tue 7/30/13	13	2D Artist
Small pond	1 day	Wed 7/31/13	Wed 7/31/13	14	2D Artist
Large pond	1 day	Thu 8/1/13	Thu 8/1/13	15	2D Artist
Sound	**10 days**	**Fri 7/26/13**	**Thu 8/8/13**	**3**	**Sound Engineer, Project Manager**
background musics:	1 day/day	Fri 7/26/13	Fri 7/26/13	3	Sound Engineer
Sound FXs	**9 days**	**Mon 7/29/13**	**Thu 8/8/13**	**18**	**Sound Engineer**
Grof jumps	1 day	Mon 7/29/13	Mon 7/29/13	18	Sound Engineer
Grof eats	1 day	Tue 7/30/13	Tue 7/30/13	20	Sound Engineer
Level complete	1 day	Wed 7/31/13	Wed 7/31/13	21	Sound Engineer
Level fail	1 day	Thu 8/1/13	Thu 8/1/13	22	Sound Engineer
Illegal move	1 day	Fri 8/2/13	Fri 8/2/13	23	Sound Engineer
back one move	1 day	Mon 8/5/13	Mon 8/5/13	24	Sound Engineer
restart level	1 day	Tue 8/6/13	Tue 8/6/13	25	Sound Engineer
make selection	1 day	Wed 8/7/13	Wed 8/7/13	26	Sound Engineer
back one screen	1 day	Thu 8/8/13	Thu 8/8/13	27	Sound Engineer
Programming	**36 days**	**Fri 7/26/13**	**Fri 9/13/13**	**3**	**Programmer, Project Manager**
Main Screen	5 days	Fri 7/26/13	Thu 8/1/13	3	Programmer
Options Screen	5 days	Fri 8/2/13	Thu 8/8/13	30	Programmer
Game Play	15 days	Fri 8/9/13	Thu 8/29/13	31	Programmer
Achievements	5 days	Fri 8/30/13	Thu 9/5/13	32	Programmer
Shop	5 days	Fri 9/6/13	Thu 9/12/13	33	Programmer
Credits	1 day	Fri 9/13/13	Fri 9/13/13	34	Programmer
Testing	5 days	Mon 9/16/13	Fri 9/20/13	29	Tester, Project Manager, Designer

The second chart details the costs for the development team, based on the estimated working hours:

Budget		
Resource Name	Work	Cost
Project Manager	**528 hrs**	**$13,200.00**
Designer	152 hrs	$3,800.00
Programmer	**576 hrs**	**$14,400.00**
2D Artist	**96 hrs**	**$2,400.00**
3D Artist	**80 hrs**	**$2,000.00**
Sound Engineer	**232 hrs**	**$5,800.00**
Tester	40 hrs	$1,000.00
Total		$42,600.00

We conclude that with a team of seven people each working for $25 per hour the project will take three months and cost about $42,000. These are very rough numbers using a quick mockup in MS Project. Your numbers may vary greatly! It is a good idea to have a project manager who is proficient with a project management program before constructing your own budget and schedule.

Summary

In this chapter, we discussed the characteristics and the importance of creating good pitch documents for mobile games.

We explained what a pitch document is, which sections it consists of and what content you are expected to put in each section.

Then we came up with a simple game mechanics idea for a puzzle game for the iPhone, and used that game to detail the actual pitch template for any mobile game.

Now that you have gotten to the end of this book, you possess the basics to start developing your first mobile game.

Still, there is much work to do ahead.

You need to build up the right team of people, who know the software and can productively work together.

You need to provide the money to fund your project throughout its development and carefully plan the development schedule, adopting an efficient working pipeline.

You need to come up with a nice gameplay idea, which relies on smart mechanics and a smooth interface to capture the hearts of the players.

You need to make the right strategic decisions with regard to your target audience and platform, the devices to be taken as reference models and the potential competitors of your game.

You also need to find excellent programmers who can code the game to run smoothly on the widest number of devices.

You need to plan an optimal marketing strategy and pick the best business model for your game, to let it spread among the community of players and make money.

Finally, you need all your determination, your patience, your enthusiasm, your rage, your hunger, and everything else you have and throw it to the winds.

If you complete these tasks and can stand the harsh, enthusiastic times of indie development, you eventually will make it.

Good luck!

Index

Symbols

2D game engine
about 172, 173
Cocos2D 173, 174
Corona SDK 174, 175
Torque 2D 173
2D graphic assets
about 45, 76
backgrounds 77
masking 78, 79
parallax motion 78
sprites 76
tiles 78
2D graphic assets, fields
backgrounds 45
concept art 45
interface 45
materials 45
sprites 45
terrains 45
textures 45
tilesets 45
3D environments 46
3D game engine
about 175
Shiva 3D 175, 176
Unity 3D 177, 178
3D graphic assets
3D model 80
3D models 81
about 46, 47, 80
animations 86, 87
baking 85
materials 82, 83
texturing 81, 82, 85
UV Mapping 84
3D graphic assets, fields
3D environments 46
animations 46
lighting 47
models 46
3D model
about 80, 81
importing 186-192
3D Studio Max 74
tuning, mobile game
strategies 233

A

Ableton Live
about 100
URL 100
abstraction 113
abstraction, programming language 109
academic formation, game designer 43
accelerometer 135
ActionScript 74, 120
ADT 14
adaptive audio 96
adaptive diegetic audio 96
adaptive non-diegetic audio 97
ADC 94
Adobe Flash Player 74, 120
Adobe Flash Professional 74
Ad supported 284
aesthetics, UI design 156
Agile software development
about 38
URL 38
alpha transparency 79

altered states 289
Amazon Appstore 13
analog sound recording
vs, digital sound recording 94
analog sticks 141
analog-to-digital convertor. *See* ADC
Android
about 11-13
Amazon Appstore 13
apps, developing 14
drawbacks 13
Eclipse 17
Google Play 13
Intellij 17
mobile game 15-17
Android developer
URL 279
Android Development Tools. *See* ADT
Android SDK 14
Android UI 13
Android Virtual Device (AVD) 15
animations 46, 86, 87
anti-aliasing
about 68
URL 68
Apple Developer
URL, for documentation 118
Apple Store 18, 19
apps
developing, for Android 14
App Store 19
AR
about 136
URL 136
arbitrate 58
AR Defender 137
Aron Granberg
URL 171
Artificial Intelligence 50
art schools, game artist 47
assets
software 319
Asset Store 178
Asus Transformer Pad Infinity TF700 75
Audacity
about 62, 100
URL 100
audio
adding, to game 171
designing, for mobile game 101
planning, for mobile game 101
roles, in mobile game 102, 103
audio assets 319
audio design
best practices 103
audio file compression 104
Audio Invaders 144
audio, mobile game
hardware limitation 102
audio output 278
audio personality 63
Augmented Reality (AR) 135
automatic memory allocation 112
Avid Pro Tools
about 98
URL 98
Axure
about 203
URL 203
Azure 272

B

backgrounds 45
backgrounds, 2D graphic assets 77
baking 85
balancing, mobile game
feedback loops 231
game director 231
randomization 231
statistics 231, 232
symmetry 230
BASIC Operating System 10
beta testing 54
BlackBerry
about 12, 32, 33
BlackBerry App World 33
game, developing for 33, 34
URL, for developing game 34
BlackBerry 10 33
BlackBerry App World 33
BlackBerry SDK 34
Blender
about 74

URL 74
blocks, Objective-C 118
BMP 71
Boehm-Demers-Weiser garbage collector
URL 112
Braid 40
brainwave readers
about 146
URL 146
brushes 44
budgeting 58
built-in devices
about 134
accelerometer 135
camera 136, 137
external controllers 139
GPS 134
microphone 138, 139
business model
about 283
Ad supported 284
Freemium 284
hybrid 285
premium 283
selecting 285, 286
button size, UI design 163
bytecode 110

C

C++
about 111, 112
complaints 113
memory management 112
objects 113
cabinets 143
camera 136
Canvace
URL 111
Canvas 44, 119, 120
cat herding 58
CGM 72
character design 306
character, mobile game
design process 87, 88
silhouette, creating 88
class extensions 117
CLDC 29
Cocoa 116
Cocoa Touch 116
Cocos2D
about 173, 174
advantages 174
disadvantages 174
coding department
about 49, 50
Artificial Intelligence 50
game engine 49
network 50
physics 49
physics programming 49
user interface 50
coding languages 48
cohesion 37
colors
using, for mobile game 89
commitment 37
communication 42
compatibility testing 53
competitors 297, 298
compliance testing 54
compression 95
compression, types
lossless 95
lossy 95
uncompressed 95
Computer Graphics Metafile. *See* **CGM**
concept art 45
conclusion, game program 124
Connected Limited Device Configuration. *See* **CLDC**
control scheme 298
control system 127
Corona SDK
about 174, 175
advantages 174, 175
disadvantages 175
Creator 184
Cubase 62
C++ Visual Studio 2012 Express
URL 112

D

DAC 95
DAE
Ableton Live 100
about 98
Audacity 100
Avid Pro Tools 98
Sound Forge 99
DeBabelizer
about 73
URL 73
designer resume, pitch document 301
designer tools
about 41
image editors 41
paper 41
pencils 41
software 41
text editors 41
desktop browser game 121
Diamond Dash 304
diegetic audio, types
adaptive 96
interactive 97
non-dynamic 97
diegetic UI 150, 151
difficulty settings, mobile game
global difficulty 234, 235
Digital Audio Editors. *See* **DAE**
digital audio workstation (DAW) 62
digital sound recording
vs, analog sound recording 94
digital sound technology
about 94
playback 95
sound recording 94
digital-to-analog converter. *See* **DAC**
discipline 38
disposable code 199
DOS Operating System 10
double tap 130
downloadable content packages (DLCs) 202
Draughts
about 303
URL 303
drawing 42
Drawing Exchange Formats. *See* **DXF**
dungeon
URL 200
DXF 72
dynamic audio 96
dynamic memory allocation 112
dynamic typing 108

E

easy fun 288
Eclipse
about 17
vs, Intellij 17
Eclipse IDE 14
educational engine
about 181
GameMaker 182, 183
GameSalad 183
encapsulation 113
enemy AI
programming 171
executable file
building 172
external controllers
about 139
analog sticks 141
cabinets 143
gamepads 139, 140
grip 142
headphones 143, 144
touch-enabled cases 141
eye tracking 145

F

Falcon Gunner 137
feedback loops 231
Filemaker 57
file size 279
finance 42
First Person Shooter (FPS) 230, 137
Flairbuilder
about 203
URL 203
Flash
vs, HTML5 120

flick 132
Freemind
URL 300
Freemium 284
Frog Bog 304
Full motion video (FMV) 72
full transparency 79
fun
about 287
types 287
functionality
defining, for UI design 162
testing 53
fun, types
altered states 289
easy fun 288
hard fun 287
people factor 289
future technology
brainwave readers 146

G

Gaikai 115
Gamasutra
URL 64, 105, 155
game
audio, adding 171
developing, HTML5 used 121
developing, XNA used 25-27
executable file, building 172
UI, creating 171
game artist
2D graphic assets 45
3D graphic assets 46, 47
about 44
art schools 47
brushes, used by 44
canvas, used by 44
creative types 47
reference link 47
Game Boy 235
game concept
about 295
competitors 297, 298
genre, defining 296
key features, describing 297
prototype 296
references 296
target audience 297
target platform 297, 298
game concept, Lilypads pitch document
character design 306
competitors 305
genre 303
key features 305
references 303, 304
target audience 305
target platform 305
game controls 277, 278
game depth 280
game design
donts 275
dos 275
game designer
about 40
academic formation 43
designer tools, used by 41
personality 43
reference link 44
skills 40, 42
game designer, skills
communication 42
drawing 42
finance 42
math 42
programming 42
psychology 42
scripting 42
scripting languages 42
technical writing 42
game design process 272-274
game development
transparency 79
game director 231
game engine
2D game engine 172, 173
3D game engine 175
about 49, 172
disadvantages 172
educational engine 181
functions 170-172
top quality engine 179

game environment
creating 171
game flow 300
game graphics
creating, software used 73, 74
game level
creating 171
game loop 123, 124
GameMaker
about 182, 183, 204
URL 76, 204
Game Maker Language 182
game master (GM) 200
game mechanics 294
about 298
achievements 299
control scheme 298
game flow 300
gameplay example 299
scoring system 299
screen flow 299
screens relationship 299
URL 201
game mechanics, Lilypads pitch document
achievements 311
additional game elements 311
game flow 313
In-App Purchase (IAP) 310, 311
leaderboards 311
scoring system 309
screen flow 312
virtual currency 310
gamepads 139, 140
gameplay example 299
game producer
about 56
key questions 57
role and tasks 59, 60
skills 58, 59
spread sheet, using 57
game producer, role
reference link 60
game producer, skills
arbitrate 58
budgeting 58
cat herding 58
negotiating 59
production management 58
quality assurance expert 59
scheduling 58
game program
conclusion 124
game loop 123, 124
initialization 123
structure 123
termination 124
game programming
about 110
conclusion 122
HTML5 119
Objective-C 116
Xcode 116
GameSalad 183
URL 184
game screen study 315-317
game sound, types
adaptive audio 96
diegetic audio 96
dynamic audio 96
interactive audio 96
non-diegetic audio 97
game tester
about 51
educational requirements 55, 56
game testing, aspects 53, 54
reference link 56
skills 54, 55
tools 52
game tester, tools
mobile interfaces 52
mobile phones 52
game testing, aspects
beta testing 54
compatibility testing 53
compliance testing 54
functionality testing 53
localization testing 53
stress testing 54
Garage Band 62
Garage Games
URL 173
garbage collection 20, 112
Garbage in, garbage out (GIGO) 110

genre
defining 296
Gestalt Principles
URL 159
GIF 70
GIMP
about 73
URL 73
GIT
about 49
URL 49
global difficulty 235
Global Positioning System. *See* **GPS**
GNU Image Manipulation Program. *See* **GIMP**
Google Docs 57
Google Play 13
GPS 134
Graphical User Interface (GUI) 203, 249
graphic assets
about 45, 318
importing 170
graphic file formats
about 70
raster graphics 70
URL 71
vector graphics 71
Graphic Processing Unit (GPU) 15, 67
Graphics Interchange Format. *See* **GIF**
grip 142
gyroscope 135

H

Half Video Graphics Array (HVGA) 15
hard fun 287
hardware limitation
about 276
audio output 278
file size 279
game controls 277, 278
processing power 279
screen size 277
Havoc Project Anarchy
about 204
URL 204
headphones 143, 144
Head's Up Display. *See* **HUD**
horizontal prototype 198
HTML5
about 119
Canvas 119, 120
issues 120
used, for developing game 121
vs, Flash 120
HUD 90, 91, 148
hybrid 285

I

iBBQ 138
iCade 143
iCade Jr 143
icons
designing 158, 159
IDE 14, 49, 204
image editors 41
ImpactJS
URL 111
implementation, programming language 109, 110
In-App Purchase (IAP) 284, 310, 311
inheritance 113
initialization, game program 123
input 128
input interfaces 134
input technology 128
Integrated Development Environment. *See* **IDE**
Intellij
about 17
vs, Eclipse 17
interactive audio 96
interactive diegetic audio 97
interactive non-diegetic audio 97
interactive prototype 201
interface 45
Interface Builder 21
iOS
about 12, 18
App Store 19
development 19, 20
Xcode 20

iOS SDK 19
iTunes 62

J

J2ME. *See* Java ME
Java
  about 114
  memory management 114
  syntax 115
Java Development Kit (JDK) 114
Java ME
  about 12, 27, 28, 115
  game, developing with 29
  NetBeans 30-32
Java Micro Edition. *See* Java ME
Java Runtime Environment (JRE) 114
JavaScript Flash language (JSFL) 74
Java Virtual Machine (JVM) 114
Joint Photographic Experts Group (JPEG) 70
JPEG File Interchange Format (JFIF) 70

K

key game features
  describing 297
keypads, configuration
  about 128, 129
  alphanumeric 129
  directional 129
  numeric 129
key questions, game producer 57
Key-Value Coding (KVC) 118
Key-Value Observing (KVO) 118
Kid Vector 157
kinetic gestural interaction 97
Kismet 180

L

Lazzaros theory 287
libraries, programming language 109
lighting 47
Lilypads
  pitch document 302
Lilypads Freemium version 303
Lilypads Gold version 303
Lilypads pitch document
  game concept 302, 303
  game mechanics 306-309
  tech 313
list of assets
  audio assets 319
  budget 320, 321
  graphic assets 318
  schedule 320, 321
  software 319
localization testing 53
Logic Pro 62
long press 131
looping background music 104
lossless compression 95
lossy compression 95

M

Magix 62
main screen, UI design 164
masking 78, 79
Massively Multiplayer Role Playing Games (MMORPGs) 135
materials 45, 82, 83
math 42
Maya 74
memory management, Java 114
memory management, types
  about 112
  automatic memory allocation 112
  dynamic memory allocation 112
  garbage collection 112
  static memory allocation 112
meta UI 154, 155
microphone 138, 139
Microsoft Excel 57
Microsoft Office 203
Microsoft Project 57
MIDI 94
Milkshape 3D 74
  URL 74
MIPD 29
MIPD 3.0 29
Mobile9
  URL 115

mobile audio designer
scripting skills 104
mobile decive
screen resolution 159, 160
mobile environment 280
mobile game
about 121
2D graphic assets 76
3D graphic assets 80
audio design, best practices 103
audio, designing 101
audio, hardware limitation 102
audio, planning 101
audio, roles 102, 103
balancing 230
character, designing 87
colors, using 89
control system 127
designing 276
difficulty settings 234, 235
fun 287
future technology 144
HUD 90, 91
input interfaces 133
listening conditions 103
resolution issues 75
tuning 232
UI 90, 91
UI design, approaching 148, 149
mobile game design, constraints
game depth 280
mobile environment 280
multiplayer 281
play time 279
single player 281
smartphones 280
mobile game, designing
hardware limitation 276
mobile game, future technology
brainwave readers 145
eye tracking 145
mobile gamers 282
mobile indie team
about 35
cohesion 37
commitment 37
discipline 38
game artist 44
game designer 40
game producer 56
game tester 51
key roles 36
passionate, for games 39
professional training 38
programmer 48
roles 39
software development methodology 38
sound designer 60, 61
team size 36
Mobile Information Device Profile. *See* **MIPD**
mobile market 281, 282
mobile operating system
about 11, 12
Android 11-13
BlackBerry 12, 32, 33
iOS 12, 18
Java ME 12, 27, 28
Windows Phone 12, 23
mobile web browser 121
models 46
Modern Style UI 23
monkey testing. *See* **stress testing**
MPEG-2 73
MS Skydrive 57
Mudbox 74, 80
multifinger scroll 133
multifinger tap 132
multiple save slots 165
multitouch operations 128
music
creating 61, 62
Musical Instrument Digital Interface. *See* **MIDI**
mutual capacitance 129

N

Native Development Kit (NDK) 14
negotiating 59
NetBeans
about 30-32
URL 32
network 50

NeuroSky
about 146
URL 146
non-diegetic audio, types
adaptive 97
interactive 97
non-diegetic UI 151, 152
non-dynamic diegetic audio 97
non-dynamic linear music 96
non-dynamic linear sounds 96
normal mapping
URL 83
NSArray class 117
NSDictionary class 117
NSError class 118
NSNumber class 117
NSSet class 117
NSString class 117
NSValue class 117

O

Objective-C
about 116
blocks 118
class extensions 117
Cocoa 116
Cocoa Touch 116
coding conventions 118
collections 117
getting started 118, 119
objects, working with 116, 117
protocol, using 117
values 117
objects 113
Ocarina 138
OpenGL
URL 111
OpenGL ES 2.0 15
Open Office 203
operating system (OS) 10, 11
OS X operating system 18

P

palettization 77
pan 132
Papa Sangre 143
paper 41
parallax motion 78
PC 10
Peg Solitaire
about 303
URL 303
Pencil project
about 203
URL 203
pencils 41
people factor 289
personal computers. *See* **PC**
personality, game designer 43
PhoneGap
URL 121
PhoneGap Build service 121
Photoshop 73
physics 49
physics programming 49
pinch 131
pitch document
about 294
designer resume 301
game concept 295
game mechanics 294, 298
importance 294
team resume 301
tech 294, 300
pitching 294
pixels 68
playback 95
PlayBook 34
Player Experience (PX) 287
play time 279
PNG 71
Polygon Cruncher 81
polymorphism 113
URL 113
Portable Network Graphics. *See* **PNG**
porting 109
PowerPoint 203
premium 283
primitives 108
processing power 279
production management 58
professional training 38

programmer
about 48
coding department 49, 50
knowledge 50
reference link 51
programmer, basic tools
coding languages 48
Integrated Development Environment 48
Version Control Systems 48
programming 42
programming language
abstraction 109
C++ 111, 112
features 107-109
implementation 109, 110
libraries 109
usage 110
Wiki URL 110
protocol, Objective-C
using 117
Pro Tools 62
prototype
about 296
building 198
defining 197, 198
fixing 198
testing 198
prototyping
about 197
benefits 202
dos and don'ts 202
styles 198
tools 203
types 199
prototyping process
prototype, building 198
prototype, defining 197, 198
prototype, fixing 198
prototype, testing 198
steps 197
prototyping, styles
horizontal prototype 198
vertical prototype 199
prototyping, types
disposable code 199
reusable code 201
psychology 42

Q

Qualcomm Snapdragon CPU 279
quality assurance expert 59
QuickTime 73
QWERTY keyboard 33

R

randomization 231
rapid prototyping
methods 200, 201
tools 204
rapid prototyping, methods
imagination 200
interactive prototype 201
pencil and paper 200
visual prototype 201
raster graphics
about 70, 156, 157
BMP 71
GIF 70
JPEG 70
PNG 71
RAW 70
TIFF 70
RAW 70
Real Time Strategy (RTS) game 149, 231
Reaper 62
references
about 296
searching, for UI design 160
reusable code 201
Rolando 136
rotate 133
rough concept document 272

S

sample rate 94
Scalable Vector Graphics. *See* **SVG**
scheduling 58
schools of sound production 63
scoring system 299
screen flow 299
screen flow, UI design 161
screen rotation 166
screenshot 301

screen size 277
screens relationship 299
script game event
programming 171
scripting 42
scripting languages 42, 122
scroll 131
self-capacitance 129
Senseye 145
sensors 128
Sensus 141
Shadow Cities
URL 135
Shiva 3D
about 175, 176
advantages 176
disadvantages 176
Sid Meyer
Wiki URL 232
silhouette 88
single tap 130
smartphones
about 281
built-in devices 134
touchscreen gestures 130
software 41
about 319
used, for creating game graphics 73, 74
software development kit (SDK) 204
software development methodology 38
Sonic Foundry. *See* **Sound Forge**
Sonic Lighter 138
sound designer
about 60, 61, 93
audio personality 63
audio skills 62
basic equipment 62
music, creating 61, 62
reference link 64
schools of sound production 63
sound fx, creating 61, 62
tasks 62
Wiki URL 93
sound designer, basic equipment
digital audio workstation (DAW) 62
hard disk recorder 62
software 62
sound libraries 62
two track audio editor 62
Sound Forge
about 62, 99
URL 99
sound fx
creating 61, 62
sound recording
analog 94
compression 95
digital 94
sample rate 94
word length 95
Space Invaders
3D model, importing 186-192
aliens, creating 211-220
audio effects, adding 261-266
barriers, creating 235-239
details, refining 240-249
firing, against aliens 220,-227
GUI, adding 249-260
particle system effects, adding 266, 267
players ship, implementing 205-210
players ship, reprising 239
scene, setting up 192-195
spatial UI 153, 154
spread 131
spread sheet
using 57
sprites 45, 76
spritesheet 76
Start() function 205
static memory allocation 112
static typing 108
statistics 231, 232
StoneTrip
URL 175
storyboarding 272
stress testing 54
SVG 72
Symmetry 230
syntax, Java 115

T

Tagged Image File Format. *See* **TIFF**
target audience 297

target platform 297, 298
team resume, pitch document 301
tech, Lilypads pitch document
game features 314
game screen study 315-317
iPhone 4 platform 314
list of assets 318
platform 314
technical writing 42
tech, pitch document
about 294, 300
screenshot 301
termination, game program 124
terrains 45
text editors 41
textures 45, 85
texturing 81, 82
theory of fun
reference book 290
TIFF 70
tiles, 2D graphic assets 78
tileset 45, 78
tools, prototyping
about 203
Axure 203
Flairbuilder 203
Microsoft Office 203
Open Office 203
Pencil project 203
PowerPoint 203
Visio 203
tools, rapid prototyping
Game Maker 204
Havoc Project Anarchy 204
Unity 3D 204
top quality engine
about 179
UDK 179-181
Unreal Engine 179-181
Torque 2D
about 173
features 173
touch, detecting
methods 129
mutual capacitance 129
self-capacitance 129
touch-enabled cases 141
touchscreen 128
touchscreen gestures
about 130
double tap 130
flick 132
long press 131
multifinger scroll 133
multifinger tap 132
pan 132
pinch 131
rotate 133
scroll 131
single tap 130
spread 131
transparency, game development
alpha transparency 79
full transparency 79
tuning, mobile game 232

U

UDK 179-181
UI
about 50, 90, 91, 147, 148
creating, for game 171
designing 155, 156
UI design
aesthetics 156
approach 233
approaching 148, 149
best practices 159, 160
button size 163
functionality, defining 162
icons, designing 158, 159
main screen 164
options 165
rasters graphics 156, 157
references, searching 160
screen flow 161
testing 164
vector graphics 156, 157
wireframe, creating 162
UI design, options
calibration 166
challenges 166
experiment 167
multiple save slots 165

reconfiguration 166
screen rotation 166
UI, videogame
diegetic 150, 151
meta 150, 154, 155
non-diegetic 150-152
spatial 150-154
uncompressed 95
Unity 3D
about 177, 178, 204
URL 204
Unity 3D tutorial
Space Invaders 184, 185, 204, 235
summary 268
Unreal Development Kit. *See* **UDK**
Unreal Engine 179-181
Update() function 205, 210
user interface. *See* **UI**
UV Mapping
about 84
URL 84

V

vector graphics
about 69, 71, 156, 157
CGM 72
DXF 72
SVG 72
vectors 68, 69
Version Control Systems 49
vertical prototype 199
videogame
UI 149-155
videos, creating 72
Visio 203
visual prototype 201

W

WesleyFG
URL 78
Wide Video Graphics Array (WVGA) 15
Windows Phone
about 12, 23
apps, developing with 24
game developing, with XNA 25-27
URL, for developing apps 27
Windows Phone Store 24
Windows Phone Emulator 8 25
Windows Phone Marketplace. *See* **Windows Phone Store**
Windows Phone SDK 25
Windows Phone SDK 8.0 25
Windows Phone Store 24
wireframe
creating, for UI design 162
word length 95

X

Xcode
about 20, 116
using 21, 22
XNA
about 24
used, for developing game 25-27

Z

ZBrush 74, 80
Zoom Zoom 138

About Packt Publishing

Packt, pronounced 'packed', published its first book "*Mastering phpMyAdmin for Effective MySQL Management*" in April 2004 and subsequently continued to specialize in publishing highly focused books on specific technologies and solutions.

Our books and publications share the experiences of your fellow IT professionals in adapting and customizing today's systems, applications, and frameworks. Our solution based books give you the knowledge and power to customize the software and technologies you're using to get the job done. Packt books are more specific and less general than the IT books you have seen in the past. Our unique business model allows us to bring you more focused information, giving you more of what you need to know, and less of what you don't.

Packt is a modern, yet unique publishing company, which focuses on producing quality, cutting-edge books for communities of developers, administrators, and newbies alike. For more information, please visit our website: `www.packtpub.com`.

Writing for Packt

We welcome all inquiries from people who are interested in authoring. Book proposals should be sent to `author@packtpub.com`. If your book idea is still at an early stage and you would like to discuss it first before writing a formal book proposal, contact us; one of our commissioning editors will get in touch with you.

We're not just looking for published authors; if you have strong technical skills but no writing experience, our experienced editors can help you develop a writing career, or simply get some additional reward for your expertise.

Unity 4.x Cookbook

ISBN: 978-1-84969-042-3 Paperback: 386 pages

Over 100 recipes to spice up your Unity skills

1. A wide range of topics are covered, ranging in complexity, offering something for every Unity 4 game developer
2. Every recipe provides step-by-step instructions, followed by an explanation of how it all works, and alternative approaches or refinements
3. Book developed with the latest version of Unity (4.x)

HTML5 Game Development with ImpactJS

ISBN: 978-1-84969-456-8 Paperback: 304 pages

A step-by-step guide to developing your own 2D games

1. A practical hands-on approach to teach you how to build your own game from scratch.
2. Learn to incorporate game physics.
3. How to monetize and deploy to the web and mobile platforms.

SFML Game Development

ISBN: 978-1-84969-684-5 Paperback: 296 pages

Learn how to use SFML 2.0 to develop your own feature-packed game

1. Develop a complete game throughout the book
2. Learn how to use modern C++11 style to create a full featured game and support for all major operating systems
3. Fully network your game for awesome multiplayer action
4. Step-by-step guide to developing your game using C++ and SFML

HTML5 Game Development with GameMaker

ISBN: 978-1-84969-410-0 Paperback: 364 pages

Experience a captivating journey that will take you from creating a full-on shoot 'em up to your first social web browser game

1. Build browser-based games and share them with the world
2. Master the GameMaker Language with easy to follow examples
3. Every game comes with original art and audio, including additional assets to build upon each lesson.

Please check **www.PacktPub.com** for information on our titles

www.ingramcontent.com/pod-product-compliance
Lightning Source LLC
LaVergne TN
LVHW062304060326
832902LV00013B/2035